The Forces Which Shaped Them

The Forces Which Shaped Them

A History of the Education of Minority Group Children in British Columbia

Mary Ashworth

With An Introduction By Rosemary Brown

New Star Books • Vancouver

New Star Books Ltd.
2504 York Avenue
Vancouver, B.C. V6K 1E3
Canada

Canadian Cataloguing in Publication Data

Ashworth, Mary, 1923-
The forces which shaped them

Bibliography:
ISBN 0-919888-92-5 bd.
ISBN 0-919888-91-7 pa.

1. Minorities - Education - British Columbia - History. I. Title.
LC3734.A84 371.9'7 C79-091174-4

Front Cover Photo by Mrs. Wyn Hutson.
Back Cover Photos (from top):
Baljinder Siddoo
Grace Tucker
Diane Waldron
Diane Waldron

The publisher gratefully acknowledges the financial assistance provided by the Canada Council.

This book was published with the support of the Multiculturalism Program, Government of Canada.

To

Patricia Wakefield, E.S.L. teacher, administrator and teacher-trainer, whose support and encouragement helped make this book possible.

Acknowledgements

I would like to thank the many people who assisted me in the preparation of this book: the Ministry of Education, the Vancouver School Board and the Victoria School Board, all of whom made their early records available to me; the staffs of the Provincial and Vancouver Archives and Special Collections, University of British Columbia, as well as a number of smaller museums and libraries in the province; all those who told me of their personal experiences either as minority group children or as teachers or administrators; and finally, those who took the time and trouble to read the manuscript and comment on it—they do not necessarily hold the views which are presented here, neither are they responsible for any errors of fact or interpretation.

Contents

It is the basic attitudes of our society towards its children which shape children's lives to a very significant degree and we fail all children when we let them go unexamined. Their consequences are too often detrimental, even for children protected by life in the mainstream of Canadian society. For those children living outside the mainstream—for the native child, for the immigrant child, and the handicapped child—the consequences are often severe.

Admittance Restricted: The Child as Citizen in Canada
CANADIAN COUNCIL ON CHILDREN AND YOUTH, 1978

Introduction

This book by Mary Ashworth records a culmination of systematic and objective research into the relationship between five minority groups in British Columbia and the province's educational system. The history of the education of these five groups of students betrays a fascinating picture of the accommodating and inconsistent ways of racism. The "assimilation" that governments and bureaucrats ruthlessly sought to impose on Doukhobor and Native Indian children was as vigorously withheld from Chinese, Japanese and East Indian children.

The Chinese, Japanese and East Indian immigrants were desperate in their desire to have their children learn English, attend public schools and become part of the Canadian community and work force as quietly and smoothly as possible; to them this was the only answer to the poverty and discrimination which was their lot in life. On the other hand, the Doukhobors and Native Indians were equally desperate in their desire to nurture and protect their language and their culture as the only answer to the attacks on their way of life and their dignity as human beings; so they chose to reject the Canadian educational ideology and system as well as the English language. The response of the British Columbia government to the first group was to disenfranchise them, to attempt to bar their children from school or to force them into segregated schools, and to deny them access to any but the most menial and lowest paying areas of the labour market. To the Doukhobors and Native Indians, the response of the British Columbia government was to hound and harass the parents, to compel the children to attend school, and to embark on a ruthless and calculated attempt to erode their language and destroy their culture. These policies may appear contradictory to us today but in every instance the government of the day was able to satisfy itself and the community at large that its decisions and actions were in the best interest of British Columbia—thus is the nature of racism.

Mary Ashworth has taken this opportunity to deal with the myth that racism is an accident of attitude. Her historical survey, however, exposes racism as a deliberate political policy legislated by elected representatives and implemented by bureaucrats. The law that deprived an entire race of people of the right to vote was a law, not an attitude. When the Victoria School Board tried to segregate students because of their racial difference, they were exercising their power to implement policy, not simply manifesting an attitude. It is good to get this reality into the open where it can be examined, and Mary Ashworth succeeds in doing this without emotion or bias.

This book is special in that it gives us the unique experience of viewing history through the eyes of our educational system. It heightens our realization that any act takes on an entirely different perspective when viewed in terms of the impact which it has on the lives of children. The relocation of the Japanese during the last war, now accepted as hasty and shameful, takes on an additional tragic dimension when experienced through the fears of parents, who, having struggled desperately to secure an education for their children, see this opportunity wrested away from them. There is much debate still as to whether the forcing of education on Doukhobor children had to be pursued with such relentless determination. Our increasing knowledge of the psychological impact of early childhood experiences on the development of adult lives must cause us increasing discomfort as we imagine the conflict of those children caught between the pacifist morals and principles of their home and the nationalistic, harsh philosophy and ideology imposed on them by public education.

Hannah Polowy, addressing an International Women's Day rally at the Pacific National Exhibition in 1975, raised the question of whether Canadians liked their children. She pointed out that the level of deprivation present among children across Canada could hardly be construed as an indication of a loving and caring concern for them, especially when this deprivation was maintained in most instances by the deliberate decisions of various levels of government to withhold much needed services and resources from their families. This book supports Ms. Polowy's position; it details the dislike of decision-makers and politicians for those children who are neither white nor English speaking. Few practising racists care or even stop to think of the impact of their prejudice on children—certainly the non-white children of this country carry as part of their life's burden and baggage memories of their traumatic journey through our school system, memories that fashion and shape their adult attitudes to themselves as well as to the world around them.

For some the scars go so deep that one despairs of their ever being erased; the Native Indians, for example, here long before white people came, suffered the gravest insult and humiliation to their language and their culture, and their pain can still be heard in the bitter words, recorded herein, of a citizenship judge speaking about her experiences as a pupil at a residential school. The severity of the problem can still be seen in the high drop out rate of native students in the schools today.

The miracle is that this is not a depressing book. It makes you angry, it makes you sad—but it is also filled with hope, because you cannot help comparing "now" with "then." You cannot help but see that the experiences of these five groups have resulted in the growth of a community determined not to allow the repetition of some of the the more gross injustices of the past. The children of "then" are the adults of "now" living among us, a trojan horse, a conscience. No government today could legislate successfully the disenfranchisement of an entire race of people in this province. It is true that racism has not fundamentally diminished, but racist acts no longer go unchallenged. British Columbia still convulses violently each time there is a new influx of immigrants, especially if they are non-white—but now there are no laws introduced to legitimize and enshrine these anti-human sentiments; now many voices join the voice of Harold Winch against attempts to legislate or rationalize racial injustice. There do remain school boards like

Surrey's which would still exercise their power to prevent the showing of a slide presentation on racism to the students of that district, but the British Columbia Teachers Federation task force on racism survives. Its survival is concrete proof that teachers are now aware of the political role of education, and that they are now ready to speak out against manipulation of the system by politicians and the community to enslave, exploit or deprive individuals or groups of the rights and opportunities which education can make available to them.

Racism as political policy is still manifest in immigration legislation; it is still manifest in the ongoing debate between federal and provincial governments as to who should be responsible for the cost of teaching English to the immigrant child. But surely there is hope to be gained from the fact that, unlike the politicians of yesteryear, politicians today operate in a climate that restrains their expressions of bigotry. Instead, they are increasingly forced to rely on one particular journalist to voice such sentiments.

In addition to educators, two groups of people must read this book. Minority group members and their detractors. They will learn from these pages that indigenous racism is part of the ongoing reality of British Columbia—that their experience today is history repeating itself. But as they look around they will witness that the Chinese, Japanese, Native Indians, East Indians, and Doukhobors are slowly but surely overcoming the hurdles in their path—"the forces which shaped them" retarded but could not stop their determined strides.

Rosemary Brown,
Vancouver,
August, 1979.

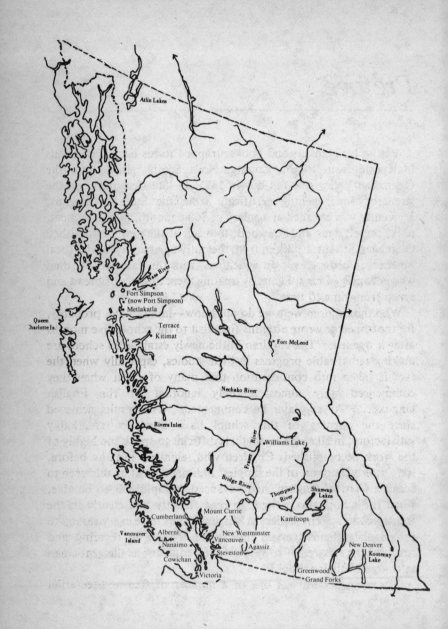

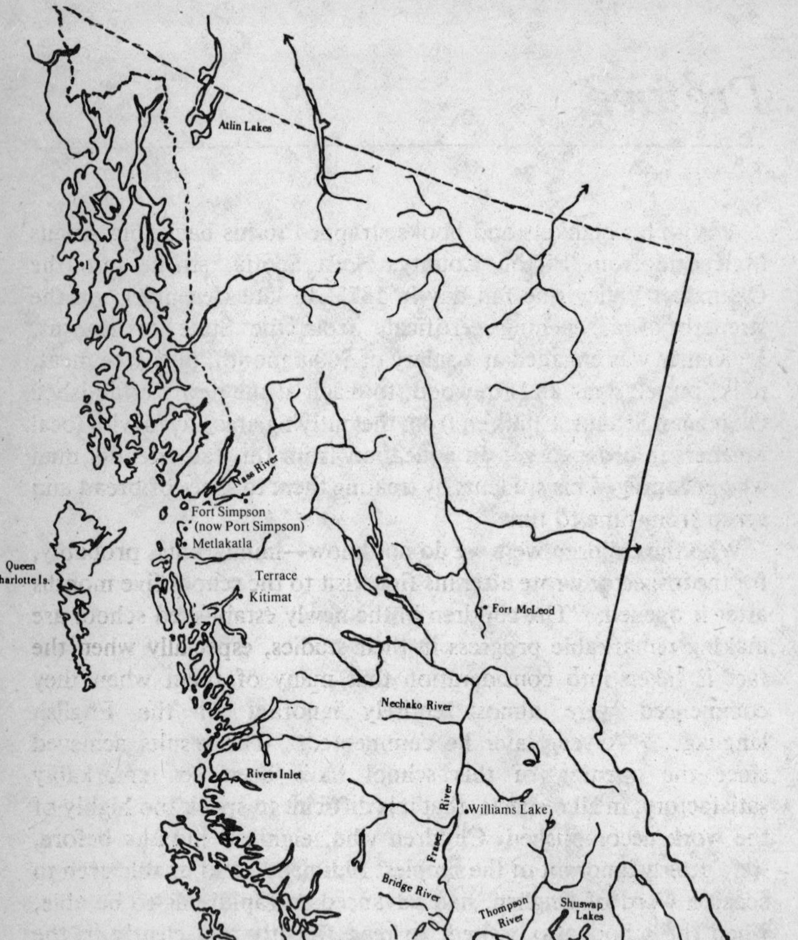
Atlin Lakes
Nass River
Fort Simpson
(now Port Simpson)
Metlakatla
Queen
harlotte Is.
Terrace
Kitimat
Fort McLeod
Nechako River
Rivers Inlet
Fraser River
Williams Lake
Bridge River
Thompson River
Shuswap Lakes
Kamloops
Mount Currie
Cumberland
Vancouver Island
Alberni
Nanaimo
New Westminster
Vancouver
Agassiz
Steveston
Cowichan
Victoria
Greenwood
Grand Forks
New Denver
Kootenay Lake

Preface

With his blankets and books strapped to his back, big Angus McKenzie from Pictou County, Nova Scotia, strode into the Okanagan Valley one fall day in 1875. In late December, on the strength of a teaching certificate from the State of Kansas, McKenzie was engaged at a salary of $60 a month, plus free meat, milk, butter, eggs and firewood, to teach at the newly established Okanagan School. Children from the outlying areas lived with local ranchers in order to get an education from this tall friendly man who encouraged his students by treating them to slices of bread and syrup from time to time.[1]

Who the children were we do not know—immigrants, probably, for the inspector wrote after his first visit to the school five months after it opened, "The children in the newly established school are making remarkable progress in their studies, especially when the fact is taken into consideration that many of them when they commenced were almost entirely ignorant of the English language."[2] A year later he commented: "The results achieved since the opening of this school have been so remarkably satisfactory, in all respects, that it is difficult to speak too highly of the work accomplished. Children who, eighteen months before, were utterly ignorant of the simplest rudiments, and unable even to speak a word of English, had advanced so rapidly as to be able, when the school was visited, to read fluently and clearly in the fourth reader . . . The settlers in Mission Valley have every reason to congratulate themselves on their good fortune in securing and retaining the services of so successful an educator as the gentleman in charge of their school."[3]

Okanagan School was one of a number of free non-sectarian

schools being established by the young colony of British Columbia. These schools were not for native Indian children—the churches had taken over the responsibility for their education—they were for the children of settlers. Schools had been established in Victoria and Craigflower in the early 1850s, and a free common school had been opened in Esquimault in 1865, but the real drive for public education began a few years after the two colonies of Vancouver Island and the mainland amalgamated in 1866 to form the colony of British Columbia.

Matthew Macfie, writing in 1865, expressed a common concern over the mixture of races on the north-west Pacific coast, and foresaw trouble to come. "It is to be feared that these varieties of humanity do not occupy our soil and multiply their kind, in every instance, without detriment to that type which we desire should preponderate...Does the presence, so largely of inferior races forbode the fatal tainting of the young nation's blood and signal its premature decay, or will the vitality of the governing race triumph over the contamination with which more primitive types threaten to impregnate it?"[4]

Macfie predicted that when the common school system was introduced there would be trouble if white and black children were forced to attend the same school; but it was not the blacks who were to be the focus of discrimination during the years to come for their numbers never grew sufficiently large to constitute a threat. The five groups who were to receive the harshest treatment were the native Indians, the Chinese, the Japanese, the Doukhobors, and the East Indians. What follows is the story of the education of their children. Although most of the children were Canadian-born, they were seldom given the status and rights due to them as Canadians; hence the chapter headings do not contain the prefix "Canadian." During the time their stories were taking place these children were in many ways treated as strangers in their own land.

Throughout the troubled days of the last century and this, a succession of children have sat in desks in schools all over the province wondering why an accident of birth, a skin colour or a belief should be sufficient to deny them a good education and a happy childhood. My hope is that by understanding the past we can do better for the children of the present and the future.

Chapter 1
The Native Indians

> ***Unless a child learns about the forces which shape him: the history of his people, their values and customs, their language, he will never really know himself or his potential as a human being.***
>
> Indian Control of Indian Education

The Early Missionaries

Fort Simpson, British Columbia, November 19, 1858

Through the mercy of God, I have begun school today. It has been a strange day to me, but the Lord helped me through. In the morning I plainly saw that a superstitious fear was spreading powerfully among the Indians: crowds wanted to come to school, but who were to be the first to venture? Here I reaped the fruit of my few weeks' labour in the chief's house during last summer. The little flock I had there eagerly enough rushed to the school when they saw me coming, and one even gladly mounted the platform and struck the steel for me, to call their more timid companions to the place. I had arranged to have the children in the morning, and the adults in the afternoon; but now I see reason to change that plan, and have all together, at least for a while. My first start was with only fifteen children; but, before we had finished, we mustered about seventy. In the afternoon came about fifty adults, and fifty children. I felt it very difficult to proceed with such a company, and should have found it much more so, but for the few children whom I had already had under training.

Both morning and afternoon I finished with an address, previously prepared, in their own tongue; in which I endeavoured to show them my intention, their need and condition, and also the glorious message which I had come to make known, namely, salvation through Jesus Christ, the Son of God. They were very attentive, and I hope and pray the Lord will now begin His work amongst them, to the glory of His great name.

From the journals of William Duncan[1]

Young William Duncan, a recent convert to evangelical Christianity and the mission field, reached Fort Simpson from England on October 1, 1857. Three years earlier he had begun his training as a missionary at Highbury Training College for Schoolmasters in London run by the Church Missionary Society. In early 1857 a captain of the Royal Navy wrote to the C.M.S. describing the awful state of life of the west coast Indians, and Duncan was chosen to go and work among them. His arrival in Fort Simpson, a small settlement on the northern British Columbia coastline, coincided with the period of Indian winter ceremonies and dancing, customs which contrasted strongly with those of Victorian England and which confirmed for him that "the dark mantle of degrading superstition enveloped them all." He was appalled at the conditions under which the Indian people lived, and within a very short time set himself the task of showing them "my intention" and "their need and condition."

The conditions of those tribes which had had contact with white people was, in many aspects, deplorable. It had not always been that way: the old Indian societies were organized and integrated, each had a strong value system, each had come to terms with its environment. But during the one hundred years preceding Duncan's arrival, Indian contact with whites had accelerated steadily. First came the maritime explorers: Bering, Hernandez, Cook, Meares, and Vancouver; then the land explorers: Mackenzie, Fraser, and Thompson. They were followed by the traders who brought goods to barter for furs, but who also brought measles, smallpox, tuberculosis, syphilis, and alcohol. The old way of life was destroyed not only by disease and alcohol but also by the changing pattern of life brought on by the new economic system based first on the fur trade but expanding into lumbering, farming and mining industries which required land—Indian land. Many of the coastal tribes were quickly decimated and degraded by the new developments against which they had no defence. This adverse influence of the white man was acknowledged in 1862 by Richard Charles Mayne who wrote, "The Indians of the interior are, both physically and morally, vastly superior to the tribes of the coast. This is no doubt owing in great part to their comparatively slight intercourse with white men, as the northern and least known coast tribes of both the island and mainland are much finer men than those found in the neighbourhood of the settlements."[2]

Duncan's solution to what ailed the Indians was to Christianize them, but this meant more than bringing them the gospel, it meant Europeanizing them. "Civilizing" was the word to be used most frequently by the missionaries and government officials during the years ahead. Duncan began his task by learning Tsimshian, the language of the tribe he was to live and work among for many years. He then addressed himself to the task of acculturating the Indians and one of his major instruments was to be the school. The first school he started was inside Fort Simpson with five half-breed boys, but in the summer of 1858, less than a year after he had arrived, he built a larger school outside the fort, and on November 19, he opened the doors to a hundred children and adults. His experiment in schooling the Indians was to become a model to be followed by other religious groups within a very short time.

Schooling, that is the separating of children from adults for set periods each day in order that they may be formally instructed, was unknown amongst the Indians, but education was not; all the tribes educated their children. It is somewhat dangerous to draw too many generalizations about the manner of education of Indian children in British Columbia prior to the coming of white people for the area which now constitutes the province was extremely rich in a linguistically and culturally diverse population. Probably somewhere close to thirty or more mutually unintelligible languages were spoken by people as different as the sea-going Haida, the

Nishga in their lovely Nass Valley, the Shuswap of the interior plateau, and the Kootenay people of the eastern mountain region, to name but a few of the many different tribes which inhabited the land. But there appear to have been some relatively common child-rearing practices.

Education was the responsibility of all and it was a continuous process. Parents, grandparents, and other relatives naturally played a major role, but other members of the tribe, particularly the elders, helped to shape the young people. The children learned the practical tasks common to their sex. The girls learned to weave, to design and make clothes, to prepare and cook food, to keep house, to care for the sick, and to master all the other duties of a wife and mother. The boys learned to make tools, to build houses, to hunt and fish, and to survive in the wilderness. They learned by observing their elders, by testing their knowledge in play, by working alongside adults, and by taking their place in the society. They also came to understand the structure of their society and their role within it, and the relationship of the individual to the group and vice versa. Much of this they learned through attendance at the various ceremonies, by hearing over and over again the songs and stories passed down from generation to generation, by listening to the speeches of the elders whose years had brought wisdom, and by participating in games which have always been the great teachers of the head, the heart, and the body.

Spiritual and moral values were absorbed through myths which illustrated vividly for the children those actions which would bring honour and those which would bring dishonour. Children who misbehaved were not disciplined by corporal punishment for it was felt that doing violence to children did not help them to learn self-control; rather, a look, a gesture or a word were used to indicate displeasure. Puberty rites differed from tribe to tribe, but generally their purpose was to give the young people the opportunity to show that they had achieved both knowledge and self-control and were worthy to be counted as adults; and in some tribes this was the occasion when the young people heightened their degree of spirituality by undergoing a particular experience.

The children's days were busy. From an early age they would have light chores to do. Later the boys would accompany their fathers on hunting or fishing trips while the girls assisted their mothers in the collection of roots and berries and the preparation of food, both for immediate consumption and for the winter months. There was time for play with their peers as well as the chance to attend adult gatherings. Children were a part of the total group, not an appendage to it, and the concept of schooling with its separation of children from adults and with its emphasis on time and attendance was foreign to them.

Harold Cardinal, writing of the days before contact, said, "In the old days the Indian peoples had their own system of education. Although the system was entirely informal and varied from tribe to tribe or location to location, it had one great factor going for it—it worked. The Indian method, entirely pragmatic, was designed to prepare the child for whatever way of life he was to lead—hunter, fisherman, warrior, chief, medicine man or wife and mother.

"Children of each sex were trained to perform the various functions that would be expected of them once they assumed their eventual place in the social strata. Generally the band elders or wisemen, in conjunction with the parents, were responsible for the value orientation of the child. This education-to-a-purpose enabled the child gradually to become a functioning, contributing part of his society. Since all of the social institutions of his society were intact, he was able to become part of and relate to a stable social system. His identity was never a problem. His education had fitted him to his society; he knew who he was and how he related to the world and the people about him."[3]

But the coming of white people had destroyed that stable society, and it was William Duncan's intention to replace that old society with a new one, a Christian society founded on the beliefs, attitudes and customs of Victorian England and the church. It seemed to him, as it did to others later, that the fastest way to do this was through the school. However, after some years at Fort Simpson Duncan decided that if he was going to make any real progress with his flock he must move them away from those influences which worked against him, away from the fort to a more isolated situation where he would have more direct control over the Indians not just during school time but throughout twenty-four hours of the day. So in 1862 he and a group of followers moved to

Metlakatla, the site of an old Tsimshian village up the coast, and here he established a little piece of Victorian England: the streets were laid out as in an English village, the people were required to pay a village tax, to rest on Sundays, to attend religious instruction, to be clean, industrious, and peaceful, and to send their children to school. Discipline was strict. A band of constables kept order, and all authority, religious and secular, stemmed from Duncan. As the years progressed, he became the expert on the education and civilization of Indians. Other missionaries tried to emulate him; the government consulted him.

Year by year new schools were established in various parts of the two young colonies still known as Vancouver Island and the mainland colony of British Columbia until they united in 1866. In 1859 Father Charles Pandosy, an Oblate, established a mission in the Okanagan. He encountered some of the same difficulties as William Duncan when he tried to set up his school. First he had to persuade the parents that learning to read and write would be beneficial; then he had to get and keep the children in school. But these were difficulties which would face the missionaries for many years. During 1860, the Rev. A.C. Garrett took charge of the school on the Indian reservation across the harbour from Victoria. It appears that in the early days, as there was no suitable building, Mr. Garrett held school in a bell tent. One day he arrived to find only the ribs of the tent left standing, the canvas having been used to make sails for the canoes. On December 22, 1860, his pupils were subjected to a public examination observed by the Governor, the Bishop, the Colonial Secretary, the Chief Justice of British Columbia and other dignitaries. "We began by singing," writes Mr. Garrett. "Then Mr. Mallandaine, the catechist, examined them in reading the diagrams, and showed that they knew the English names for the various objects, and could spell and pronounce them. This, for three months' work, was considered very excellent by the Governor and all the visitors. After this the most advanced class, who have been somewhat longer at school, read in their books, and satisfied the suspicions of the Chief Justice of British Columbia by reading *backwards*, thus showing they were not crammed like parrots, but that they thoroughly understood what they had learned."[4]

Thomas Crosby was sent by the Methodists to Nanaimo in 1863

to teach in the Indian mission school there. In 1907, looking back on his experiences, he recalled: "My pupils were a wild-looking lot of little folk, with painted and dirt-begrimed faces and long, uncombed hair. Some of them were clothed in little print shirts, others had a small piece of blanket pinned around them, while some had no clothing at all. One of the first difficulties was my ignorance of their language. Hence I had to use the language of signs. Beckoning and pointing to the school-house, I sought to persuade them to come into school. They would look at me, laugh at my efforts, and make a bolt for the bushes near by. Sometimes I made an attempt to capture them, but they would run like wild hares, and I could not get near them.

"I had always a love for children, and prided myself on my ability to win them; but these, I was afraid, were going to outdo me. Finally I took an Indian with me to the woods and secured two stout poles or posts, with which we fixed up a swing at the back of the school-house. Then I started again with my sign language, and at last succeeded in getting one of them into the swing. As I swung the little fellow to and fro I noticed the others peeping out curiously from among the bushes. Pointing to the swing and then to the school-house, I beckoned to them, as much as to say, 'If you come here and have a swing you will have to go to school.' By this means I got acquainted with them and won their confidence."

Mr. Crosby had great difficulty learning the local language. Day by day he worked on pronunciation and vocabulary. Finally one day he walked through the village shouting, "Muck-stow-ay wilth May-tla-ta school" meaning "All children come to school." That had an effect. "The old people ran out of their houses to see what old Indian was passing. Putting their hands to their ears they said, 'Listen to him! He speaks it just like an Indian,' and then they laughed."[5]

Further north in 1864 in the Nass Valley, the Rev. A. Doolan founded a mission along the lines of Metlakatla at Kincolith, and almost twenty years later the Rev. J.B. McCullagh opened his school at Aiyansh. McCullagh succeeded in producing a written system for the Nishga language which he used in teaching the people to read and write. Moeran in his book *McCullagh of Aiyansh* wrote: "The success of this system of educating people in their own language before teaching them anything more than conversational English was very marked." From time to time McCullagh circulated among the people a small cyclostyled newspaper written in the Nishga language called *Hagaga*. "Our little boys," he wrote, "meeting with some hunters from a distant tribe, taught them the rudiments of spelling in the vernacular, and gave them a few copies of our little *Hagaga*. These young men were very much taken with the idea of learning to read and write in their own language, and perservered with the lessons the winter through in their own village, using pieces of split wood for slates and burnt sticks for pencils. About a year after this, not knowing what had been going on meanwhile, I was much astonished to receive letters from men of this tribe in rapid succession, stating their intention of coming to live at the Mission, that they had already 'repented to God', and wanted to be further instructed and baptized. And so they came and had their desire fulfilled."[6]

Residential Schools

Out of the experiences of the early missionaries grew a pattern of education which was followed by each of the three major denominations: Roman Catholic, Anglican, and Methodist or Weslyan, later known as the United Church. The preferred model was the residential or boarding school, with the day school a distant second. Those residential schools which included some trade training became known as industrial schools.

In 1871, the colony of British Columbia, which by this time comprised the two colonies of Vancouver Island and the mainland, joined Confederation and thereafter matters pertaining to the Indians came under the jurisdiction of the federal Department of the Interior and later the Department of Indian Affairs. The new province was not interested in taking over control of the education of Indian children; and as the British North America Act (section 93) stated that "Nothing in any law shall prejudicially affect the right or privilege with respect to denominational schools which any class of persons have by law in the province at union," the province saw no reason to change the status quo and so it left Indian education in the control of the churches. Under the new regime some schools were able to get small government grants to aid in their operations.

The federal government set up a network of Indian agents throughout the province, and it is through their reports and the reports of residential school principals that the policies and procedures of both the government and church officials in regard to the education of Indian children take on substance. In 1878, I.W. Powell, Indian Commissioner in Victoria, wrote to his superiors in part as follows. His comments regarding day schools, attendance, industrial schools, and funding were to be echoed by himself and others many times in the years to come; his belief that he was dealing with savages and barbarians was common, as was his faith in the beneficial effects of education and Christianity.

> This process of Christianizing Indians scattered over such an extensive coast line is, however, exceedingly difficult, mainly from the baneful influence of White men, whose principles are not at all in accord with such designs, and who live among and freely mingle with them chiefly for the gratification of evil desires. It is no doubt greatly due to the many untoward effects arising from this circumstance, that the present race of Coast Indians is fast disappearing, and at the rate with which they are now being swept from light and life, it will not be long hence ere they exist only in memory. Even in such a field of labor, instances of failure either from the want of funds or fitness for the position, are not wanting among the Missionaries, who have from time to time tried their hand at redeeming the savage in various parts of the Province.
>
> Day schools requiring no excessive outlay have been tried in a few localities, for it is manifest that barbarism can only be cured by education, but in several instances they have been given up as failures.
>
> In such examples, however, Indians have not been isolated from the corrupting influences of bad associations, nor is it possible under such circumstances to interfere materially with irregular habits and customs incident to life in the wigwam, the

destruction of which is so necessary ere the much desired higher life can be obtained.

During the year just passed, three of the Mission Schools in this Superintendency participating in the grant allowed by the Government, have ceased, from the impossibility of keeping the average attendance required, and it is doubtful whether in these instances the efforts put forth, or the money already expended, will result in any permanent benefit.

The Indian who has been subject to such teaching, if indeed he has experienced any interruption at all to his listless habits and nomadic ways, soon resumes them, and the impressions made upon the child or youth are quickly lost in the greater attraction of his later associations.

The establishment of Industrial Schools, though necessitating a much greater outlay, is I think more prudent and economical; and I do not believe that any Mission will ever achieve very important or permanent results without such a valuable adjunct to their religious teaching.

A large expenditure in a few of the most popular centres for this purpose, and in a proper direction, would go much farther in my opinion in civilizing and christianizing the Indian, than the smaller outlay, which is often frittered away in vain attempts of day schools to confer the benefits of education upon the untutored Indian, or give him instruction in the rudimentary lessons of civilization, which, after all, must have a well ordered home for their nurture and encouragement. The importance to the country, of rendering the native young useful and industrious citizens is itself of the greatest importance, while the increased revenue which would accrue to the country, would justify a sufficient expenditure of its funds in the manner best calculated to bring such a desideratum about.[7]

Mr. Powell then reported that grants had been given to three Weslyan schools at Fort Simpson, Nanaimo and Victoria; one Roman Catholic school, St. Mary's near Mission; and two Anglican schools, Metlakatla and Kincolith. The total sum expended was $1,712.50 of which Metlakatla received the largest grant of $500. Two years later Mr. Powell reported with favour on

Metlakatla.

> Among the schools worthy of special remark, I may refer particularly to that at Metlakahtla, which being of an industrial character, has been attended with the most gratifying and satisfactory results.
>
> There is a prolific field in the Province, inhabited as it is by such a large Indian population, for the establishment of other schools upon the plan of that at Metlakahtla, and as to the real and permanent good which would thus be conferred upon neighboring and distant Tribes there cannot be a doubt.
>
> I am not aware of the annual cost to the Church Missionary Society of the Metlakahtla School, but the grant allowed by the Government is small compared with its effective worth as a most valuable civilizing and christianizing centre.
>
> Mr. Duncan's plan in the first place, of isolating the Indians, founding a sort of municipal government among themselves, and then, being empowered to prevent contamination with evil disposed Whites was, I think, more the result of good judgement than pecuniary expenditure.[8]

—but Mr. Duncan's grant was reduced to $350!

Indian agents from time to time reported on the one hand that Indian people in their agency had requested a day school, and on the other complained about the difficulty of achieving anything approaching regular attendance at the day schools. In 1883 Mr. Powell reported:

> I much regret my inability to report in very favorable terms of the general results afforded by missionary day schools as at present conducted, the frequent changes of teachers and the want of experience and qualification in many of them for such a position, are the chief drawbacks to success.
>
> The migratory habits of the Indians and the questionable utility of endeavoring to educate in this way children who attend most irregularly, and who spend much greater intervals amid the opposing but more attractive scenes of camp life, tend to frustrate the object in view.[9]

And again Mr. Powell recommended the establishment of industrial schools. The following year he repeated once more, "The influence of the camp and the inherent attractions of nomadic life, are much greater than that of the teacher."[10] The agent at Cowichan was similarly concerned: "...when the Indians leave for the canneries or hop fields the children leave also, and in a few months of idleness, forget much of the knowledge they have acquired. This can never be prevented until orphanages or industrial schools are established where a number of Indian children would be constantly under a course of education and where any well-to-do Indian could place his children when leaving his reserve on the payment of a fixed amount for their board."[11] Over the years a number of industrial schools were established and most remained in operation until very recently. Some of the best known ones were Alert Bay, Alberni, Christie School at Clayoquot, St. Joseph's at Williams Lake, Kamloops, Kootenay, St. Mary's near Mission, Coqualeetza near Chilliwack, and Squamish. Fundamental to these schools was the teaching of religion. The Superintendent-General of Indian Affairs wrote in his report of 1887: "...one has but to visit one of these institutions, and enquire into the system followed, and observe for himself the intelligence shown, and the proficiency displayed by the pupils, in order to be convinced that the emancipation of the Indian from his inherent superstition and gross ignorance is being wrought out thereat, as the light which a knowledge of the Christian religion invariably imparts dispels the illusions in which his benighted though infantile mind have been nurtured from the cradle, and as his intellect expands and develops under the influence of the instruction imparted by those who have taken upon them the laudable but responsible task of helping these poor children of the forest or of the prairie upward and onward."[12]

It is not surprising therefore that moral and religious training was of prime importance in the curriculum in the industrial schools. Father Carion, O.M.I., principal of Kamloops Industrial School wrote in his report for 1896 that "The moral and religious training of the Indian children is the most important of all: without it, all other instruction would be of little use to them.... We keep constantly before their mind the object which the Government has in view in carrying on the industrial schools, which is to civilize the Indians, to make them good, useful and law-abiding members of society."[13] And again, two years later he wrote: "The pupils are constantly reminded of their duties toward God, their neighbour and themselves, and of the necessity and advantages of cleanliness, purity of body and mind, honesty, industry and self-control. To make our teaching effective, a continuous supervision is exercised over them and no infraction of the rules of morality is left without due correction."[14] The same year the principal of the Kootenay Industrial School said: "The children, with slow but steady steps, are acquiring habits of civilization which daily take deeper root, and are becoming more and more familiar with the ways of politeness and delicacy, which practices, though still feeble, lead to hopes of culminating at a point not much inferior to that attained in ordinary white schools."[15]

The constant supervision and the emphasis placed on good behaviour resulted in a docility in some of the children which would hardly prepare them adequately to face the competitive white world; but not all conformed. In 1899 Father Carion ran into trouble. "The conduct of the pupils does not correspond always with the efforts of the teachers; at times, the wild nature of the Indian reasserts itself. Six boys deserted one evening last March, and were brought back only three days after. In such cases, severe measures have to be resorted to."[16]

Father Carion did not state what severe punishment he meted out, but corporal punishment, a method of correction which had not been generally used by Indian parents but which had always been a foremost disciplinary measure in English boarding schools, was common in most industrial schools, the whipping sometimes taking place in view of the other students. Father Chirouse, principal of St. Mary's Mission, seems to have recognized this difference in child-rearing practices and tried to keep corporal punishment to a minimum, but not all principals were that considerate. Father Chirouse had other methods, however. "As regards punishment," he wrote, "I must confess that our methods seem rather strange to those who have only had dealings with white children. The Indian thinks it an awful disgrace to be struck, and to avoid the bad effect which would more than counterbalance any good arising from such treatment, we usually punish the boys by giving them lines to write, depriving them of play, or by giving them a meal on their knees in the refectory, though occasionally they receive a slap on the hand with a light cane. The girls are so docile and gentle that punishment even of the mildest kind is altogether unnecessary."[17]

The curriculum in the industrial schools consisted of the usual reading, writing, and arithmetic along with industrial subjects such as shoe-making, carpentry and farm work for the boys, and house-work, needlework and dressmaking for the girls. There were two reasons for the inclusion of the industrial subjects. One was to give the students a grounding in matters which the authorities saw as practical, those which would help the students to raise the standard of living on the reserve when they returned or which would give them skills they could use in employment. The other reason was simply economic: funding for the schools was very limited; the greater part of the money was found by the respective church, with in some cases, a small grant from the federal government. It was necessary therefore for the schools to be, at least to some degree, self-supporting. The children spent about four hours a day at their academic studies and the remainder of the time working on the farm, mending or making clothes, or in other practical activities. The schools covered grades one to six, but as many of the children were well over six years old before they arrived at the school some were well on in their teens before they left; indeed, a number of the older girls left grade six to get married. Taking into account the limited time spent on academic work, the age at which the children began school, and their poor comprehension of English on entry, it is not surprising that it was many years before Indian children made their way into high school.

Accommodation for the students was simple and limited. "The dormitories are supplied with iron bedsteads and each bed has a tick filled with hay, two white sheets, two pairs of blankets, a quilt, a woollen pillow with white cotton slip. The girls' dormitories are fitted up with washstands, pitchers and basins. Each boy has his own hair-brush, comb, towel and basin in the lavatory," reported one school principal in 1898.[18]

Each school provided some form of recreation for the children. Naturally, in true British tradition, "walks are taken daily by the pupils in suitable weather."[19] Football, running games, skating, swinging, and other activities were outdoor favourites; activities indoors were naturally a little less boisterous—the phonograph provided a lot of pleasure for some of the older pupils. The health of the children often gave cause for much alarm; many of them had been exposed to tuberculosis, and infectious diseases such as measles or an influenza epidemic from time to time resulted in deaths.

As the century ran out, the authorities in Ottawa still could not understand why all Indian parents were not eager to have their children entered in school—but somehow the British school system did not appear quite so admirable to the Indians as it did to those who tried to export it from middle-class Victorian England to the coast, interior plateaux and mountains of British Columbia. "Speaking generally, it is disheartening to find the wide-spread indifference manifested by Indian parents with regard to regularity of, or indeed any, attendance by their children at the day schools," wrote the Deputy Superintendent-General of Indian Affairs in 1895. "No doubt this may to some extent be attributable to the fact that the fondness for their offspring, which is so admirable a characteristic of Indian parents, prevents the exercise of firmness, which, of course, is necessary even to compel children more or less prepared by hereditary to undergo the confinement and discipline of school."[20]

Eight years later the Deputy Superintendent-General was still frustrated; the Indians did not seem to appreciate what was being offered. "The pagans outside the sphere of civilization," he commented, "are disposed to regard education as an attempt to erect a barrier between themselves and their children. Contact with Christian civilization tends to rapidly modify these views, and the necessity for protection in dealing with the superior race awakens an appreciation of education which increases in proportion to the extent and complexity of such dealings."[21]

In the fall of 1916, Margaret Butcher, an Englishwoman, went to Kitimat to help to look after the children in the residential home and to teach sewing. During the three years she was there, she wrote many letters commenting on her life and that of the children, and describing the village and the nearby surroundings. A few excerpts present an interesting first hand account of life in a small, fairly isolated residential school run by the Women's Missionary Society on the British Columbia coast. In Margaret Butcher's day, Kit-a-maat consisted of one street parallel to the water's edge. The church was in the centre of the village; near it stood the mission House, the Home, and the school.

September 17, 1916

The Kit-a-maat are one tribe of Indians (so far as I can learn) and have no connection with any other place. They speak a language of their own which is understood nowhere else. Now at Port Simpson they speak a language that is spoken and understood widely, so that is worth learning. This is not. Also the children are forbidden to speak it in the Home so that I shall not learn Kit-a-maat.

September 22, 1916

[Tuberculosis is] a rampant enemy in the village. They say there is not one family with a clean record. Let a child cough a few times and he or she is mustard poulticed at night, painted with iodine in the morning and a cough mixture given.

Margaret Butcher then goes on to outline her day's work.

6:15—Rising bell.

6:45—Prayer bell when each teacher goes to a Dormitory and the children say prayers at their bedside altogether.

7:00—I watch the girls wash in the washroom. The big girls do the little girls hair.

7:15—First bell rings and the children not on duties come to Sewing Room and learn the Catechism.

7:30—Prayers. I take Morning prayers every day. Then we troop into breakfast. The children sit 8 at a table. Miss Clarke stands guard. After breakfast we go to Sewing Room. (Teachers breakfast at same time as children but in the

Teachers Room) and there we sew until the first school bell rings.

9:50—First school bell when little children put work away and go outside.

10:00—Second school bell. The older girls and I sew until 11:30. What do we sew? Just everything that they wear. The stocking and general mending occupies nearly all the time and the stock of new clothes has to be kept up. Every garment of every child has to be marked. I know most of their names but not their numbers yet.

The afternoons for Margaret Butcher were fairly quiet—she remarks, "I still get my daily rest."

4:00—Walk. I have been every day so far although I'm only in charge 3 days per week I think. Our village path takes exactly 12 min. to perambulate and there is no where else we can go, at any rate for a walk. I keep them out for an hour if I can. Then they play until

5:30—When supper bell goes. I stay with them at supper. After supper they are free [until]

6:30—When prayer bell goes. Then one teacher takes little girls to bed; another the boys.

8:00—Big girls go to bed and our day is done.

September 29, 1916

Matron says the young folk who have been educated in this school and at Coqualeetza will have more chance when some half dozen of the old folks of the village, who still hold fast to their ancient customs, are dead, and one hopes that it is so. In all our bunch of 37 children there are only two who appear cunning and they are half-breeds. The others are all quite manageable and some of the little ones, the offspring of Christianized parents are lively and merry and quite smart at their work so that if they can be shielded from tuberculosis they will be an advance upon the present inhabitants.

Margaret Butcher describes the arrival of six new girls from Bella Coola.

November 6, 1916

The children ranged from 7-13 years. Three being sisters, 3 single individuals. Poor little souls it was an immense ordeal for them. Leaving their parents and all home surroundings to take a 3 days journey with white men to a strange place like this Home! They understood neither English nor Kitimaat so it was fortunate they were six and could speak to each other but they were almost too scared to do so.

After describing the Christmas concert put on by the school, she continues:

January 22, 1917

There is no interest to the old folk in recitations for of course it is all in English. I suppose that in a few years time Kitimaat speech will be extinct for the young folks learn to speak English in the schools and one of our Senior girls told me they cannot understand all the Kitimaat of the old folks.

April 17, 1917

When they [the children's relatives] are in the village the children are allowed down to their own Homes on Saturday afternoons provided they are "called for" and brought back. That proceeding always seems so comical to me in this wee village with its one pathway but the Matron is Guardian of the children and she delivers them to their relatives and receives them formally thus giving no room for complaint that they mix with the wrong people.

Margaret Butcher describes the deaths of three sisters, Maud in August the preceding year, Amy in January, and Maggie in June. She goes on:

> *July 1, 1917*
>
> Nora has just married, Hazel and Sarah are still in the Home—which one will die next? Do you wonder that we fuss when a child gets a cough? I asked Miss Clarke whether the Civilization had anything to do with the T.B. She said, "Compare the physique of the Home and the village children: more children die in the village than in the Home. We pull them through many illnesses and they live longer for being civilized."
>
> *November 20, 1917*
>
> In the history of the school English has never before been the ordinary language of the children as it is now. I hope they will continue to speak it. Their language is correct too for of course they only hear correctly formed sentences.
>
> *June 9, 1918*
>
> Oh, Nell, it is a grand work we are engaged in. There is a delight in it that is beyond anything I know: the children are so amenable to our control and so devoted to us.[22]

A few months later the village was hit by the "Spanish flu." Many of the children were very sick with vomiting, dysentry, nose bleeds, and halucinations. Margaret Butcher put mustard plasters on each child. A number of people in the village died and one of the little girls from Bella Coola.

George Manuel, co-author of *The Fourth World*, paints a black picture of life in a residential school in British Columbia as he experienced it much later. "Hunger is both the first and last thing I can remember about that school. I was hungry from the day I went into the school until they took me to the hospital two and a half years later. Not just me. Every Indian student smelled of hunger."[23] Naturally the boys soon learned to steal in order to assuage their hunger. Manuel describes the afternoons spent doing manual labour on the farm and carrying fifty pounds of green cord wood one and a half miles from the river to the buildings watched by brothers who had whips to keep the boys moving.[24] The kind of education the boys received did not, in Manuel's opinion, fit them to live in either the European or the Indian world.

> Our values were as confused and warped as our skills. The priests had taught us to respect them by whipping us until we did what we were told. Now we would not move unless we were threatened with a whip. We came home to relatives who had never struck a child in their lives. These people, our mothers and fathers, aunts and uncles and grandparents, failed to represent themselves as a threat, when that was the only thing we had been taught to understand. Worse than that, they spoke an uncivilized and savage language and were filled with superstitions. After a year spent learning to see and hear only what the priests and brothers wanted you to see and hear, even the people we loved came to look ugly.[25]

Another account of life in a residential school was given in an interview by Marjorie Cantryn, presently a judge of the Citizenship Court. When Judge Cantryn was six years old her mother took her to the Alberni Residential School and tried to enter her, as the opportunities for education in their village on the west coast of Vancouver Island were limited. The school refused to accept the child; had she come from a broken home, she would have been admitted at once, but because her home life was stable it was two years before Judge Cantryn was admitted. She recalls that because she was bilingual she spent a large part of her first year acting as translator between students who spoke her dialect of the Nootka language and their English-speaking teachers. Alberni took students from grades one to eight so that by the time Judge Cantryn had reached the upper grades she had been joined by her other brothers and sisters until at one time there were six of them in residence. Alberni was, of course, modelled on the British system which divided girls from boys and kept them apart. It was difficult, therefore, for Judge Cantryn to talk to her brothers, much less to embrace them, and coming from a culture in which families were traditionally very close she found this hard to bear. Looking back, she feels that it should have been possible for the school to have permitted greater communication between children of the same family.

Having completed grade eight in the residential school, she and some other Indian students enrolled in the local white high school. The next four years were difficult: those on the academic program found it very hard to keep up with their white peers; those on the commercial program survived a little better, but four dropped out at the end of the first year, and some others left in the years that followed. Judge Cantryn thinks there were probably a number of reasons behind the difficulties the students encountered: poor counselling, a different curriculum, the unfamiliar constant race with time as classes moved from room to room, different teaching styles, and the difficulty of building warm relationships with teachers whom they met only in class. Judge Cantryn had a personal disadvantage in that she was two years older than the students in her grade. She wonders whether the white students and teachers understood the problems some Indian students faced in just getting admitted to school—or did they think these over-age students were simply slow and dumb? It is not surprising that the Indian students were self-conscious but Judge Cantryn said they tried to make the best of it, and they soon found that students who took part in school sports or dances were better accepted than those who did not. However, active participation in school life was difficult. The Indian students lived in the residential school and were taken to and from the white school by bus. There was little opportunity to get to know the other students on a social basis: it was difficult to strike up a real friendship during busy school hours, and the girls were not allowed outside the residential school gates except to go to school; the boys were allowed to go to a show in town on Saturday afternoon but had to be back for supper. There was, therefore, no opportunity for dating or mixing with white peers, and this made the transition from residential school life to the world of further education or the world of work a difficult one for many of the students. Judge Cantryn said that after leaving Alberni she worked as a maid in the Nanaimo Indian

Hospital prior to taking training as a practical nurse, and that she and five other girls from the residential school went out every week-end for the first two months to savour their new freedom—and then realized that all their allowance had gone on entertainment. In comparing her experiences with those of Indian girls who had attended residential schools across Canada, Judge Cantryn notes two commonalities: all were forbidden to practise their native culture; all were forbidden to speak their own tongue. She feels that the repression of the native languages was wrong, and she also wonders why, if the authorities had good reasons for banning the use of the mother tongue, they could not have explained their reasons to the children instead of strapping them. Judge Cantryn's experiences, far from making her bitter, have made her sensitive to the needs of today's Indian students and an active worker in eductional projects.[26]

For most students thoughts of home were never far away:

Thoughts on Silence

What am I doing here
Among these strange people
Sitting in these funny desks
Staring at this paper?
Oh yes, I am in school.
These people are my classmates.
Though they chatter all the time
They are silent now.
Now I can think.
I see a bird flying high in the air.
Maybe it is flying south.
My heart leaps with the bird
Taking a message to my mother.
My mind is heavy, thinking something sad has
Happened at home.
But the birds are singing
Everything is all right.
The breeze has whispered something in my ear.
I hope it whispers the same joyous words to my people.

I get lonely for my family and I especially miss my mother
But I shall see them all soon.

When we meet we won't even touch hands
But our hearts will leap with joy
And in our minds we will be glad.[27]

Mary Jane Sterling,
A member of the Thompson River
(Nteakyapamuk) Indian Band

Language Suppression

When the early missionaries set up their schools, they had no way of learning an Indian language before they arrived. Some of them, Duncan and McCullagh for example, immediately set to work to master the local language, but there were no written systems for these languages. In the view of the missionaries it became imperative for the Indians to learn English if they were ever to read and understand the gospel, or to learn the catechism or the church rituals and liturgy. School readers and text books were likewise all in English. The schools therefore quickly adopted an "English only" policy so that in 1892 Father Coccola, O.M.I., principal of Kootenay Industrial School wrote: "Thus about one year after the opening of the school we had the pleasure of seeing them giving up their own dialect to adopt the English language, which alone has been spoken since."[28] While a year later Father Donckle, principal of Kuper Island Industrial School commented: "The fact that many do not yet perfectly understand the English language has, however, been a serious drawback to their general advancement. The use of the Indian language is prohibited, but it will take some time before we can have this rule complied with."[29] At Williams Lake the use of English was increasing: "Amongst the boys, the Indian language is a thing of the past; English is the order of the day, but I must confess that their pronunciation is not yet perfect, although improving slowly at all times. Amongst the girls, the English language does not take as well as amongst the boys. The girls take no pride in being able to speak English."[30] Mary Augusta Tappage was one of those girls. She was put in St. Joseph's Mission School at Williams Lake in 1892 at the age of four and many years later, recalling her school days, she said, "What I could never understand, we weren't allowed to speak our language. If we were heard speaking Shuswap, we were punished. We were made to write on the board one hundred times, 'I will not speak Indian any more.' " She went on, "And now we are supposed to remember our language and our skills because they are almost lost. Well, they're going to be hard to get back because the new generations are not that interested."[31]

In 1893 the Superintendent of Indian Affairs made it abundantly clear that it was the intention of the federal government to destroy the Indian culture over the years by denying Indian children access to it:

> Experience has proved that industrial and boarding schools are productive of the best results in Indian education. At the ordinary day school the children are under the influence of their teacher for only a short time each day and after school hours they merge again with the life of the reserve. . . .
>
> But in the boarding or industrial schools the pupils are removed for a long period from the leading of this uncivilized life and receive constant care and attention. It is therefore in the interests of the Indians that these institutions should be kept in an efficient state as it is in their success that the solution of the Indian problem lies.[32]

Two years later the Superintendent gave his official blessing to the "English only" policy in the residential schools virtually ensuring the demise of the Indian languages:

> To a certain stage in an Indian's advancement there exists but little doubt that he should be kept in communities; but as soon as that stage is reached, and it should be at an early period, he should be brought to compete with his fellow whites; but in order that this may be done effectually he must be taught the English language. So long as he keeps his native tongue, so long will he remain a community apart.

If the Indian has not had, with his white neighbours, the same chance to acquire industrial knowledge, he cannot be blamed for not having these qualities equally with us, and for all we do for him we must from the first consider the English language quality, for without it he is permanently disabled, and from what Indians have said to me and from requests made by them, it is evident that they are beginning to recognize the force of this themselves. With this end in view the children in all the industrial and boarding schools are taught in the English language exclusively.

. . . If it were possible to gather in all the Indian children and retain them for a certain period, there would be produced a generation of English-speaking Indians, accustomed to the ways of civilized life, which might then be the dominant body among themselves, capable of holding its own with its white neighbours; and thus would be brought about a rapidly decreasing expenditure until the same should forever cease, and the Indian problem would have been solved.[33]

In his annual reports for the three years following the Deputy Superintendent-General's statement, Father Carion, principal of Kamloops Industrial School, made his policy on the use of English very clear:

1896

For two months after their admission the new pupils were allowed to speak their mother tongue; but after that time, they were obliged to use English at all times like the older pupils.[34]

1897

It is hardly necessary to state that the use of the Indian language is never tolerated, but it is gratifying to say that the pupils never attempt to speak Indian.[35]

1898

English is the only language used at all times by all the pupils.[36]

Sr. Mary Placide, reporting on Christie School at Clayoquot in 1902, said: "All pupils without exception have made gratifying progress in the past year. Their mother tongue has been entirely eradicated and English is spoken by all the children in the school."[37] In 1905 Sr. Mary Amy of the Squamish Boarding School commented that "...the Indian language has been eradicated and English is spoken by all the children in the school."[38]

The First World War came and went, but the policy of suppressing the Indian languages continued. "In my first meeting with the brother," wrote George Manuel, describing his first day at a Catholic residential school, "he showed me a long black leather strap and told me, through my interpreter, 'If you are ever caught speaking Indian this is what you will get across your hands.' "[39]

Fr. E.C. Bellot, O.M.I., of the Squamish Mission School is quoted by Levine and Cooper as writing in the *St. Paul's Annual and Reference Book* for 1937 as follows:

> Only a generation has elapsed and from an ignorant and wild tribe, we find one educated and speaking English better than they speak their own language. Not forty years ago, when first their school was opened, not a child spoke a word of English; today the only language you hear among them (exception made for the old people) is English. Many among the rising generation do not even know their own language. This great change has been wrought through the Squamish Indian School. All honour and praise to its able and devoted teachers.[40]

The Provincial Archives in Victoria has over the last few years taped interviews with British Columbia Indians to prevent unwritten history from being lost. The following is part of an interview contained in the Orchard Collection:

Mr. Levine: Bernice, what was the name of the boarding school you attended?

Ms. Touchie: I attended the Alberni Residential School.

Mr. Levine: Was this school run by any particular religious order or was it non-denominational?

Ms. Touchie: It was the United Church which operated the school.

Mr. Levine: Were you allowed to use your language or were you forbidden to?

Ms. Touchie: For the most part we were forbidden to, although a lot of the students used it while at play, but I clearly remember that they were immediately stopped.

Mr. Levine: Do you recall ever being punished yourself or seeing anyone else punished for using the language?

Ms. Touchie: Oh yes, more so by the supervisors [than] the teachers—the supervisors of the children, who ran into more Indian-speaking, like out of classes, were usually the more strict staff.

Mr. Levine: What were the punishments you saw; how severe were they?

Ms. Touchie: Well, depending on the member of the staff and depending probably on what the punishments were at the time—sometimes the worst punishment was to scrub I don't know how many flights of stairs, or do a large amount of work, where you're working all day—or else most of the punishment was done by straps on the hand.

Mr. Levine: Your language is Nitinat?

Ms. Touchie: Yes, I speak a Nitinat dialect.

Mr. Levine: Were the other people at this boarding school all Nitinat, or were there people from other groups also?

Ms. Touchie: Oh, no, this was why it was such a real novelty for the students to speak, because they all spoke languages right from the Queen Charlotte Islands right down the coast and even the Interior of B.C., so there were several languages there.

Mr. Levine: And all of them were forbidden to use the language; there wasn't one Indian language that was OK to use but the rest couldn't be?

Ms. Touchie: Oh no, not that I know of.

Mr. Levine: When you came to the school, did you find that as a result of these punishments you stopped using your language?

Ms. Touchie: Yes—because of the punishments—because you sort of wanted to have a good reputation in the school, and besides, there was no program in our classes which encouraged speaking. Besides, being [away] from our own people for so long, you're just all English-oriented; you're bound to let it slip by.

Mr. Levine: When you would be alone with other people from your school who spoke your language, were you tempted to speak to them in Nitinat, or did they try to speak to you in Nitinat?

Ms. Touchie: Oh yeah, we thought it was [a] challenge to us, and we enjoyed sort of teaching each other what we didn't know.

Mr. Levine: But you knew that if you were found out, you'd be punished?

Ms. Touchie: Oh yeah, as I say, depending on which staff member found you.

Mr. Levine: When you got out of boarding school, did you find that you had difficulty communicating with other people, those who hadn't been to boarding school, when you tried to talk with them in your own language?

Ms. Touchie: Oh yeah. I had a real difficulty, mostly in pronouncing the words, thinking in Indian again, that sort of thing....

Mr. Levine: How old were you when you went to that boarding school?

Ms. Touchie: The maximum required age at that time was 7 years old, so I went when I was 7.

Mr. Levine: What language was it that your parents spoke to you at home?

Ms. Touchie: My parents spoke a lot of Nitinat, but more so continually [it was used] by my grandparents. My parents, who went to school, were even more forbidden, or more severely punished for speaking—

my mother entered school in Coqualeetza, not knowing any English, and it seemed to be the main objective, to teach English right away.

Mr. Levine: Do you remember her ever telling you about things that happened to her, punishment for being found speaking Nitinat?

Ms. Touchie: I'm quite sure she did, but I'm not quite sure what the punishments she said were—largely hard work —they worked hard anyway, because they worked shifts and made their own food and vegetables; but I'm pretty sure she had a strap, too.

Mr. Levine: She was strictly forbidden to use Nitinat at Coqualeetza?

Ms. Touchie: Yeah.

. . .

Mr. Levine: When you had just started going to the school, and before you went, did you just think in your Nitinat dialect?

Ms. Touchie: I think by then I was thinking more in English.

Mr. Levine: By the time you started going to school?

Ms. Touchie: Yeah, my mother spoke English quite a bit, but it wasn't forced upon me to speak to her, so. . . I was still able to sort of make conversation with my grandparents, but I remember clearly that my grandparents were becoming very disappointed in me going to school and would rather that we stop going to school so that we didn't lose our language. She was very disappointed every year we came back and were getting worse and worse, not remembering our language.

Mr. Levine: Your grandparents felt strongly that one of the reasons you were not speaking Nitinat so much as you were speaking English was because of the influence of the school on you?

Ms. Touchie: Oh yes, definitely, one of my sisters was kept out of school till she was 9 years old and then I was always encouraged right from secondary school to drop out. It was more favourable to my parents and more so to my grandparents that I stayed home, rather than sort of uneducating myself in their culture.

Mr. Levine: The one who did not go to school until she was 9, did she retain the use of Nitinat longer?

Ms. Touchie: I suppose she would've, but she also became ill, so it's hard to tell in her case. She was hospitalized for a while in the school.

Mr. Levine: None of the teachers in this school were particularly interested in your language or the languages of the other people who were going to the school?

Ms. Touchie: Not that I can recall, although some supervisors, a few became very close to the students and would ask them how do you say this in your language? and how do you say that? But I also noticed that the staff that became too closely involved with the children were somehow discharged, or they weren't allowed to remain. They weren't allowed to mix too personally with the students.

Mr. Levine: So that the element of the staff that stayed from year to year were people who were unsympathetic to your language and culture?

Ms. Touchie: Oh yes, some of them were there just for the job.

Mr. Levine: When your parents speak to your grandparents, is English used or is Nitinat used?

Ms. Touchie: Most likely Nitinat.

Mr. Levine: So your parents would speak primarily to your grandparents in Nitinat and primarily to you in English?

Ms. Touchie: Yes.

Mr. Levine: Had both your parents been to boarding school?

Ms. Touchie: No, only my mother. My father—my grandparents were so strict with him that they just wouldn't let him go. He only went for three years.

Mr. Levine: Would you say that your father speaks or uses his language more than your mother does?

Ms. Touchie: No, about the same, because they remained on the reserve. But my father is more knowledgeable concerning different dialects. He can speak three different dialects, whereas my mother would have sort of a problem.

Mr. Levine: When your parents speak to other people of their generation, what language do they speak?

Ms. Touchie: A lot of the time it would be Indian, quite a bit Indian.[41]

The policy of language suppression continued during and after the Second World War. Judge Marjorie Cantryn recalls that her mother took pains to make her bilingual before she went to Alberni Residential School, but when she left she was no longer able to speak her language fluently, and today has difficulty conversing with the older members of her band.[42]

Residential Schools in Retrospect

There are many different views on residential schools. "Few other topics evoke such an extraordinary range of opinions of all intensities. Old pupils talking about residential schools range in their utterances from blame and anger to earnest requests for aid in securing the entry of their own children. . . . The intense opinions of the Indians are fully understandable. In many ways these schools symbolize the whole ethnic conflict," wrote Hawthorn.[43]

In discussing the early missionaries Harold Cardinal commented: "The unvarnished truth is that the missionaries of all Christian sects regarded the Indians as savages, heathens or something even worse. They made no attempt to understand Indian religious beliefs, virtually no attempt to appreciate Indian cultural values and paid little heed to Indian ways. The true purpose of the schools they established was to process good little Christian boys and girls—but only Christians of the sect operating the school. In those early church schools, academic knowledge occupied one of the back seats. Since the Indian was expected to live in isolation from the rest of society, obviously all the education he needed was a bit of reading and writing, figures and some notion of hygiene."[44] But an administrator who has been connected with Indian education since 1954, pointed out in an interview that it is easy to condemn the past today, but a hundred years ago when the Oblates first came over things were very different: the Indians were not going to school, they were living in ghettoes called reservations, the whites did not want them in their schools, and the government did not want to be bothered with them.[45] It is interesting to note that during the last hundred years the provincial government has not permitted the teaching of religion in its public schools beyond the recitation of the Lord's Prayer and the reading of a selected passage from the Bible. Taxpayers' money was, however, used throughout this period through grants made to the residential schools to ensure that Indian children were brought up as either Roman Catholic, Anglican or United—there was virtually no other choice.

Chief Dan George expresses another point of view. In his well-known piece "My Very Good Dear Friends," after talking about the breakdown that occurred in the Indians' social and cultural environment in the past, he goes on, "What did we see in the new surroundings you brought us? Laughing faces, pitying faces, sneering faces, conniving faces. Faces that ridiculed, faces that stole from us. It is no wonder we turned to the only people who did not steal and who did not sneer, who came with love. They were the missionaries and they came with love and I for one will ever return that love."[46]

The early missionaries were unfortunately not aware of the close bond that exists between language, culture and personal dignity. McCullagh of Aiyansh was one of the few who attempted to use the native language in the early weeks of instruction; other missionaries did, however, take on the task of providing a writing system for the local Indian language, even though they did not recommend the use of the vernacular in school. Some of the missionaries, while they had the zeal and dedication, simply did not have the necessary training; as far back as 1899 the Deputy Superintendent General of Indian Affairs was saying that "... so far from an inferior class of teachers being, as is commonly supposed, quite good enough for

Indian schools a decidedly superior class is required, not only for the direct instruction of the pupils, but to exert an influence upon and arouse interest in the parents."[47]

The authors of a report entitled *The Indians of British Columbia* (1958) looking back over a hundred years of Indian education felt that while parents saw the schools as both helping their children to enter the white economy and at the same time removing them from sub-standard living conditions, the students saw themselves as dominated by white people in a system which refused to recognize either their native language or culture. The residential schools caused a conflict for the children between what they learned at home and what they learned at school, which made it difficult for them to be reintegrated into their bands after years away from home. The report also pointed out that it was not easy for residential schools to match the quality of teaching found in provincial schools particularly in the upper grades, and that most principals of residential schools were not adequately trained for the job and were often inexperienced. The report recommended that the residential schools do everything in their power to humanize the living conditions of the children so as to provide a stimulating atmosphere for their growth and development; but more importantly it said, "We consider that the joint education of residential school children with white children in the upper grades and extending downward is a step in the right direction."[48]

Two Decades of Reports

Early in 1954 the University of British Columbia was asked by the Department of Citizenship and Immigration, under whose jurisdiction Indian Affairs now lay, to undertake a thorough study of the Indians of British Columbia. The study, directed by Dr. Harry B. Hawthorn, Dr. Cyril S. Belshaw and Dr. Stuart Jamieson and published in 1958 under the title *The Indians of British Columbia*, covered a wide range of topics beginning with the cultural and historical background of the people, going on to examine the role of Indians in various industries, and looking at their living conditions and their education.

The report found that out of a total of over 31,000 Indians in the province, 7,665 were in school in March 1955, or approximately one-quarter, double the number in attendance in 1945. Of this figure, 5,805 were in schools supported by Indian Affairs and 1,860 were in provincial or private schools. There were thirteen Indian residential schools with an enrolment of 2,521 and sixty-seven day schools on reserves with 3,118 children; 118 students lived in residential schools and attended a provincial high school; 166 were in hospital schools; fifty-four were attending some institution of higher learning, most likely a vocational school. There were about three times as many children in Roman Catholic schools as in Protestant schools. But what was concerning was the high rate of age-grade retardation among Indian children as compared to white children, and the high drop-out rate. Two-thirds of the teachers in responding to a questionnaire spoke negatively about much of their work in Indian schools, emphasizing failure rather than success.

The compilers of the report were sufficiently concerned about some of the comments made by teachers that they set out certain principles they felt "should govern the teachers' outlook and the general aims of the Indian school system." They believed that teachers and administrators "should be convinced that differences in group biology imply no inequality in non-physical attributes;" that they should be conversant with the local Indian cultures and respect them and the way of life in which they are embedded; that they should help each child to develop as an individual and not try to "remake the child beyond the recognition and acceptance of his community;" and they should not "try to detach children from their present home and village bonds in the expectation that the next generation will produce a home and village life dearer to the teachers' own hearts."

The report pointed out that the Indian child has to learn in school some things which the white child learned at home, such as standard English, a different concept of time, different social relationships, and it related these to the need for improved teacher training. All teachers accepting jobs in Indian schools should, the authors felt, have a knowledge of elementary linguistics, anthropology, sociology and psychology; all should know something about contemporary Indian life; all should be prepared for the physical, social and emotional adjustments they might have to make in an Indian community.[49] Their recommendations fell largely on deaf ears; it was to be almost fifteen years before the teacher training institutions were to respond in any direct and positive way.

In 1960 the Joint Committee of the Senate and the House of Commons on Indian Affairs heard briefs from Indian bands across Canada; a variety of concerns were expressed by spokespeople for a number of British Columbia groups. The Similkameen Indian band said: "The Superintendent has been sending our children to the Kootenay Residential School. We believe that if we had a school built in Penticton it would be near our homes and more children could attend school and take up vocational training."[50] The Anahim Indian Band asked that a junior high school be built at Anahim.[51] A number of bands asked for improved opportunities for vocational training for their young people. The chief and councillors of the Sechelt Indian Band were deeply concerned that their children had increasingly been getting into trouble with the law, and they asked for the right of parents to have considerably more say in the education of their children. They pointed up the problem: "We the Sechelt Band people have two places to send our children for their education. If the children are waifs they can be registered in the residential school at Sechelt with all others attending day school at Sechelt. Most of the fathers of the Sechelt Band children are fishermen and loggers and must leave home for long periods of time so that there is no systematic paternal control over their children during these periods. It is the day school children who break the laws of Canada, while residential school children do not get in trouble with law enforcement." As the original builders of the Sechelt Residential School in the early part of this century, the Sechelt Band asked to be allowed to send to the school those children whose parents wished to do so in order to keep them out of trouble. Currently the school was accepting Indian children from other areas of British Columbia and places were in short supply.[52]

The Aboriginal Native Rights Regional Committee of the Interior Tribes of British Columbia expressed its concern at the overcrowding in the interior residential schools and the long waiting lists for places. During a discussion period George Manuel explained the problem facing Indian people in isolated areas who move from place to place at different seasons of the year seeking employment, and he re-emphasized the need to increase the number of places in residential schools.[53] The committee also asked that higher wages be paid to teachers in order to attract the best teachers.[54]

The British Columbia Department of Social Welfare reported that since 1955 10 to 20 per cent of the school population of Brannan Lake Industrial School for Boys had been Indian boys. "While the Indians do not, as a group, present any particular problem while in our School," stated the Superintendent, "we do feel that in many instances they have been sent to the School for rather minor offences. Many of the older Indian boys are committed here for violations of the Liquor Act." The Superintendent of Willingdon School for Girls also reported an increase in the number of Indian girls committed and indicated that most of them were sent for "being in a state of intoxication off the reserve."[55]

In 1967 Dr. Hawthorn produced another report, *A Survey of the Contemporary Indians of Canada*, in which he outlined some of the essential environmental differences encountered by the Indian child and the middle-class white child. He discussed housing, clothing, food, playthings; he pointed out the differences in learning styles, use of language, methods of disciplining, and opportunities for decision-making. He described the dilemma of the teacher who would like to do more for the children but who is prevented from doing so by administrative pressure to cover the set curriculum. He noted the conflict set up by the school's emphasis on competition in a community where co-operation is valued, and concluded that the result of these major differences in life styles was too often failure. Once again Hawthorn emphasized the need for better trained teachers, better programs, and more parental involvement, and he endorsed the trend begun in the fifties of integrated education. He found that, "On the whole, Indian adults were more in favor of public education than of reserve education or residential schooling. However, the majority of parents were opposed to having the very young children off the reserve. They felt that an ideal schooling plan would include kindergarten and primary school on the reserve and all other education in public schools. At the same time, parents recognized that it is harder for the older children to transfer into the public schools than it is for the beginning students to start in the public system."[56]

On March 15, 1967, the Minister of Indian Affairs and Northern Development, the Hon. Arthur Laing, spelled out the government's seven point policy with respect to Indian education in Canada:

1. A complete education for every Indian child for whom the government has responsibility, according to his needs and ability.
2. Close collaboration with the provinces to provide education for Indian children in provincial schools, colleges and universities; the transfer of federal schools in reserve communities to public school boards where the Indian community agrees to this transfer; provincial inspection of Indian schools which remain as federal schools.
3. Fuller participation by Indian parents in school affairs through consultation between parents, band councils and reserve community school committees; the participation of Indian people on the established school boards where Indian children are a significant part of the school population in provincial established school districts.
4. School curriculum in federal schools is to be that of the province in which the Indian schools are situated. Curricula will be modified only where this is necessary to meet the special needs of the pupils.
5. Residential schools will be used only for those primary school pupils for whom they are an absolute necessity. They will operate under the full control of the Department under regulations established in close consultation with the churches who operate them.

6. All federal schools will operate at the provincial standards applicable in their locality.
7. The educational program will be closely co-ordinated with the Development Directorate of the Branch to ensure that the needs of the rapidly developing community are adequately met.

The aim of the policy was to provide effective education to:

1. All Indian children of school age.
2. All Indian children of kindergarten age.
3. All Indians who wish to continue their schooling beyond high school as far as their talents, ability and willpower will take them.
4. All adult Indians who wish to improve their educational status.[57]

In 1971 the results of a longitudinal study entitled *5,000 Little Indians Went to School* was published by the Education Branch of the Department of Indian Affairs and Northern Development. The study followed for four years the progress of 5,000 children who began their education in federal schools in 1964. Three major conclusions were "...that the earlier the child leaves the federal school to enter a provincial school the better are the chances of successful progress in the early grades;" "...that ability in the language of instruction, which means mastery of a second language for most Indian pupils, is a key factor in success in school;" and "...that unless the schools encourage Indian children to study their own language as a curriculum subject children who reach the high school level and continue their education in various secondary programs might give up their Indian language entirely."[58] With respect to the last conclusion, the report had noted earlier the high degree of acculturation in British Columbia "where English appears to be displacing the use of an Indian language in the home."[59]

Legislation passed in 1951 had enabled the federal government to enter into contracts with the provinces or with local authorities to provide integrated education for Indian pupils. Earlier attempts at integration by individuals had often met with failure. In 1929 three Indian children were refused admittance to West Saanich School even though the municipal authorities were prepared to allow them to enter because some white parents protested their presence. The Minister of Education pointed out that the responsibility for the education of Indian children rested with the federal government but that in a few cases Indians were allowed to attend public schools provided no objections were raised by parents of other children.[60] In 1950, twelve Songhee children, all Roman Catholics, were barred from Craigflower School because the Indian Act stated that Indian children must attend schools of their own faith. The parents felt that the facilities at the Roman Catholic school on the reserve were sub-standard and they wanted their children to have an education equal to that of the local white children.[61] When the parents decided to keep their children out of the reserve school in protest, their Family Allowance cheques were cut off.[62]

The new legislation on integration produced its crop of difficulties which had to be overcome such as the distance of some reserves from the public schools—naturally the Indian children were expected to go to the white school. Some Indian parents objected to the lack of religious instruction in the public schools, but as more and more children entered the public schools integration was generally accepted as beneficial and the movement gained momentum throughout the sixties. It was easy to sit back and look with satisfaction at the rising statistics, but Chief Dan George looked at the children and said:

> You talk big words of integration in the schools. Does it really exist? Can we talk of integration until there is social integration? Unless there is integration of hearts and minds you have only a physical presence. . . and the walls are as high as the mountain range.
>
> Come with me to the playgrounds of an integrated high school. . . see how level and flat and ugly the black top is. . . but look. . . now it is recess time. . . the students pour through the doors. . . soon over here is a group of white students. . . and see. . . over there near the fence. . . a group of native students . . . and look again. . . the black is no longer level. . . mountain

> ranges rising...valleys falling...and a great chasm seems to be opening up between the groups...yours and mine...and no one seems capable of crossing over. But wait...soon the bell will ring and the students will leavc the play yard. Integration has moved indoors. There isn't much room in a classroom to dig chasms so there are only little ones there...only little ones...for we won't allow big ones...at least, not right under our noses...so we will cover it all over with black top...cold...black...flat...and full of ugliness in its sameness.
>
> I know you must be saying...tell us what *do* you want. What do we want? We want first of all to be respected and to feel we are people of worth. We want an equal opportunity to succeed in life...but we cannot succeed on your terms...we cannot raise ourselves on your norms. We need specialized help in education...specialized help in the formative years...special courses in English. We need guidance counselling...we need equal job opportunities for graduates, otherwise our students will lose courage and ask what is the use of it all.[63]

But decisions as to what was good for Indian children were still being made almost exclusively by white civil servants and politicians, and then, at last, came a statement from the Indian people in their historic document *Indian Control of Indian Education*, published in 1972 by the National Indian Brotherhood and accepted in 1973 by Jean Chretien, then Minister of Indian Affairs and Northern Development, as the basis for change in Indian education:

> We want education to give our children the knowledge to understand and be proud of themselves and the knowledge to understand the world around them.
>
> We want education to provide the setting in which our children can develop the fundamental attitudes and values which have an honoured place in Indian tradition and culture....
>
> We want the behaviour of our children to be shaped by those values which are most esteemed in our culture....[64]

> What we want for our children can be summarized very briefly: to reinforce their Indian identity; [and] to provide a good living in modern society.
>
> We are the best judges of the kind of school programs which can contribute to these goals without causing damage to the child.
>
> We must, therefore, reclaim our right to direct the education of our children.[65]

The paper called for Indians to have the right to form their own school districts, to have their own Band Education Authorities, to have representation on school boards, to develop curriculum, and, for Indians of all ages to have access to a wider variety of educational opportunities. While specially trained non-Indian teachers and counsellors were seen as necessary, the report also made the point that "the need for native teachers and counsellors is critical and urgent. It is evident that the Federal Government must take the initiative in providing opportunities for Indian people to train as teachers and counsellors." The authors of the report also sought an end to unsafe and obsolete school buildings and their replacement by modern, functional units.

The paper acknowledged that there is no single type of educational institution which will meet all the needs of Indian children. The residential school will continue to play a role, though a considerably diminished one; day schools, group homes or hostels, and denominational schools will also continue to exist alongside the provincial schools. The paper had this to say on integration:

> Integration in the past twenty years has simply meant the closing down of Indian schools and transferring Indian students to schools away from their Reserves, often against the wishes of the Indian parents. The acceleration with which this program has developed has not taken into account the fact that neither Indian parents and children, nor the white community: parents, children, and schools, were prepared for integration, or able to cope with the many problems which were created.

Integration is a broad concept of human development which provides for growth through mingling the best elements of a wide range of human differences. Integrated educational programs must respect the reality of racial and cultural differences by providing a curriculum which blends the best from the Indian and the non-Indian traditions.

Integration viewed as a one-way process is not integration, and will fail. In the past, it has been the Indian student who was asked to integrate: to give up his identity, to adopt new values and a new way of life. This restricted interpretation of integration must be radically altered if future education programs are to benefit Indian children.

...Indian children will continue to be strangers in Canadian classrooms until the curriculum recognizes Indian customs and values, Indian languages, and the contributions which the Indian people have made to Canadian history.

...The success of integration is not the responsibility of Indians alone. Non-Indians must be ready to recognize the value of another way of life; to learn about Indian history, customs, and language; and to modify, if necessary, some of their ideas and practices.[66]

Two years later George Manuel and Michael Posluns wrote:

The Canadian school systems serve the urban middle-class community extremely well. They should. It is the urban middle class who have designed them for the use and benefit of their children. The experience of the school is continuous with the experience of the home for many of those children. It is true that more and more children from the middle class are expressing dissatisfaction at the failure of the school to meet their needs. The danger, from our point of view, is that the schools will change in a direction that meets their needs without diversifying to give equal consideration to the needs that we have. So long as the schools are run by boards on which we have only token representation, if any, that is not so much a danger as an inevitability.[67]

Later they reminded their readers that

> Education is the first key to the Fourth World. Without the knowledge and understanding, skills and training, both traditional and modern, we will continue to find ourselves hobbled in any attempt to move forward.[68]

Hope and Hopelessness

In 1969 at a conference in Kamloops on integration in Indian education, the B.C. Native Indian Teachers' Association, an organization of Indian teachers, aides and other educational workers was formed, with leadership for the group coming from George Wilson, Alvin McKay, Bert McKay, George Clutesi, Robert Sterling and Joe Michel. The association quickly identified as one of its priorities the establishment of a native Indian teacher education program, and in the fall of 1972, George Wilson, president of B.C. NITA, presented a proposal for such a program to an official of the B.C. Department of Education who, it is alleged, refused to consider it on the grounds that it was discriminatory on the basis of race.[69] In the summer of 1973, Dr. John Andrews, newly appointed Dean of the Faculty of Education at the University of British Columbia, invited members of the faculty to submit proposals for alternative teacher education programs. Early in the fall he met with members of the B.C. NITA Centre Council and as a result of his encouragement, along with the co-operation of B.C. NITA and the efforts of Dr. Art More, a member of the U.B.C. Faculty of Education, NITEP (Native Indian Teacher Education Program) enrolled its first group of approximately sixty students in September, 1974.

One of the aims of the program was to increase the number of certified native Indian teachers in British Columbia. At the inception of NITEP, there were about twenty-five Indian teachers in the province; had they been represented in the teaching force in accordance with the proportion of native Indians to others in the total population, there should have been more than twenty times that number. Another aim was to give the students an opportunity to study their Indian heritage and to look at the particular needs of Indian pupils. It was not, however, to be a program which prepared the student-teachers to teach only in Indian schools, neither was it to be a watered-down version of the regular teacher education program. At the completion of the program, students would be properly certified to teach in any school in British Columbia and those who satisfied the necessary requirements would receive degrees. Three years after it began, NITEP was described as "a program in which the clear emphasis is on helping Indian students to become teachers, rather than on providing Indian teachers for Indian schools. Said another way, the emphasis is on facilitating the aspirations of individuals rather than on meeting community needs. Not necessarily is there any incompatibility between these two emphases but they are different, and can lead to different educational strategies."[70]

In order to offset the shock of coming directly from a small community to the University of British Columbia and to make it easier for the students to keep in close contact with their families, the first two years of the program were to take place in four centres: Williams Lake, Kamloops, Terrace, and North Vancouver. Students who successfully completed years one and two at an off-campus centre would move on campus for the remaining two years of the Bachelor of Education (Elementary) degree. Facilities at the Williams Lake centre were rather cramped but it had the smallest enrolment; most of the students were Chilcotin or Shuswap with one or two Carrier or Bella Coola people. The Kamloops centre was located in one of the buildings on the grounds of the old residential school and drew its student body largely from the Interior Salish people, that is, from the Thompson, Okanagan, Lillooet, Nicola and Southern Shushwap bands. Further north, the Terrace centre was well housed in the Northwest Community College and drew its students from the Haida, Nishga, Tsimshian and Gitksan; while the North Vancouver centre was set up in Norgate Elementary School to serve the Indian people in the metropolitan Vancouver area, a rather more heterogeneous group.

Each centre had its co-ordinator who planned the local program and counselled the students. Instructors from the University travelled out to the centres to give some of the courses while other courses were staffed by local people. The students took the same courses as students on the regular university program, though sometimes in a different order, but, in addition, they took Indian Studies, a course developed locally in each centre which focussed on the surrounding cultures. Schools near to the centres provided classrooms for the practice teaching component of the program.

By the time the first class of NITEP students had completed the first two years of the program and were ready to continue their studies at the university, there had been a heavy loss in numbers so that of the original sixty only fourteen began their third year in 1976. The reasons for the high drop-out rate were varied: for some with less than grade twelve on entry the educational expectations were too high, for others family responsibilities kept them home, some felt that a teaching career was not what they wanted, others decided to postpone their final two years and to take teaching assistant jobs or other employment for the interim. Since the program's beginning the average age of the students has decreased, the average educational level on entry has increased and the drop-out rate has declined.

A survey of the students enrolled in the NITEP program in 1976-77 showed that seventy per cent were status Indians and thirty per cent non-status; forty-four per cent had one or more people dependent upon them for support; seventy-seven per cent were female; eighty-eight per cent were under thirty years of age; seventy-one per cent had completed grade twelve compared to eleven per cent of their parents; forty per cent had spent a year or more in an Indian residential school; forty-nine per cent had gone to an integrated school while living away from home.

Two major difficulties faced the students. One was personal—inadequate financial support; the other educational—organizing their time and coping with the written assignments. As a result of these and other difficulties fifty-eight per cent indicated that they had, at some time, seriously considered dropping out of NITEP. But in their overall assessment sixty-one per cent described the program as good and thirty-five per cent as excellent, an envious rating for a teacher-training program.[71] The first NITEP graduates are already working in schools in British Columbia, some in schools which have a large number of native students and some in schools which have few or none.

NITEP continues to change: the Williams Lake centre closed down after three years having, for the moment, apparently drawn out of the area most of the potential students, and Terrace is presently low in enrolment. On the other hand, a new centre at Coqualeetza near Chilliwack has opened up and other areas in British Columbia are being considered as potential centres.

NITEP was not the only teacher training program in the province directed specifically towards native Indians. In August, 1973, a locally-elected all-Indian school board took over control of the Mount Currie Community School near Pemberton which had formerly been run by the federal Department of Indian Affairs. The new board wasted no time in inviting the Faculty of Education at Simon Fraser University to join it in setting up a native teacher education program on the reserve, and in July, 1974, credit courses were offered at Mount Currie for the first time and a year later eight experienced teacher aides enrolled in a teacher preparation program sponsored jointly by the Mount Currie School Board and Simon Fraser University.[72] The courses were given on the reserve and practice teaching was completed in the Community School. One of the strong points of the program was the attention given to the native culture and the local situation. It was possible for the students to complete all the work for the basic teaching licence at Mount Currie, and it is likely that further work towards a higher certificate may also be completed there, but the amount of financial support available to the program will determine its future. The first group of eight students all obtained their teaching licences in December, 1976, and a second slightly larger group admitted in July, 1976, obtained theirs in December, 1977.[73]

In his two reports, Hawthorn had underlined the need for better training of white teachers who intended to work with native Indian children, but the recommendations met with little action. The Native Indian Brotherhood added its recommendations:

> Federal and provincial authorities are urged to use the strongest measures necessary to improve the qualifications of

> teachers and counsellors of Indian children. During initial training programs there should be compulsory courses in intercultural education, native languages (oral facility and comparative analysis), and teaching English as a second language. Orientation courses and in-service training are needed in all regions. Assistance should be available for teachers in adapting curriculum and teaching techniques to the needs of local children. Teachers and counsellors should be given the opportunity to improve themselves through specialized summer courses in acculturation problems, anthropology, Indian history, language and culture.[74]

Slowly, one by one, the universities and colleges added Indian Studies or Cross-Cultural Education courses to their programs, but these remain today largely electives. The Brotherhood also recommended that Indian teacher-aides be put in classrooms where there are significant numbers of native children. A limited number are now employed in this capacity.

The Mount Currie band had obtained a considerable degree of control over the education of its children and its example was followed by others. In January, 1975, by an order-in-council the Nishga School District was set up in the Nass Valley incorporating the three villages of New Aiyansh, Greenville, and Kincolith, where native Indians made up approximately ninety-five per cent of the population. The school at New Aiyansh was quickly enlarged so as to take in kindergarten to grade twelve making it unnecessary for children to be sent out of the valley for any of their education. The Greenville children attend their own school until the end of grade seven after which they are sent daily to New Aiyansh by bus. The older children from Kincolith have to board in New Aiyansh as the distance is too great for them to commute every day, but they are able to get home some weekends.

The new Nishga school board inherited a number of teenagers who had dropped out of school after suffering repeated failure, and while the board has developed a program to try and salvage these lost students it is hoping, by working on three different fronts, to prevent other children from being similarly disenchanted with school. First, through a program of Indian studies incorporating both the Nishga language and culture, the board is hoping to build pride and confidence in its young people; second, it is working with parents to help them understand the educational system and the opportunities open to their children, and it is encouraging parents to make their own decisions regarding their children's future instead of leaving these decisions to the school authorities; third, it is extremely careful who it hires on its teaching staff, and as applications considerably outnumber positions, it does not have to compromise on quality. The result after only four years is that there has been a sharp decline in the number of drop-outs among the children who have taken all their education in the Nass Valley.

A growing phenomenon throughout the interior of the province during the last few years has been the birth and growth of a number of Indian language programs for children. Every child in the Nishga school district from kindergarten to grade twelve is receiving some instruction in Nishga. This has meant the preparation of teaching materials for the students and teachers. Similar courses involving such languages as Haida, Shushwap, Chilcotin, and Halkomelem are being introduced in schools in other parts of the province. One of the most advanced programs is that produced by the Central Carrier Indians which consists of two teachers' manuals, a Carrier-English dictionary, a number of readers, flashcards, and a record. Most of the language programs are accompanied by units of work dealing with different aspects of the local culture.

Other events occurred during the late sixties and early seventies which, though not related to each other in any direct way, were significant in the total picture of Indian education in British Columbia. In 1968 Mrs. Arnold Pearson, a resident of the Queen Charlotte Islands, was the first Indian to be elected to a local school board;[75] later, others were to follow suit. In the same year Premier W.A.C. Bennett announced that a bill would be introduced at the next session of the legislature which would establish a $25 million fund called The First Citizens' Fund which would provide $1.2 million in interest annually for scholarships for Indian students born in British Columbia. The money could be applied to any area of education—public school, technical, vocational, or university education—and the fund would be administered by government representatives.[76] Two years later, with the help of federal funding, the Indian Resource Centre was established at the University of British Columbia. It was operated almost entirely by Indian people who, in addition to other activities, developed materials to meet the needs of Indian pupils and their teachers. In 1973 an Indian, George Wilson, was appointed to a post within the Department of Education, and in 1974, Mrs. E. Dailly, then Minister of Education, set up an Indian Education Committee which included representatives of the Union of B.C. Indian Chiefs, the Indian Homemakers Association, the B.C. Native Indian Teachers' Association, and the B.C. Association of Non-Status Indians. According to a newspaper report, Mrs. Dailly promised the Indians that the Department would not make educational changes affecting Indians without consulting them.[77]

Today more and more bands employ under their direct control home-school liaison workers and have set up Parents' Committees with direct input into both the philosophy and the daily operation of the schools their children attend; but for some teenagers the changes are too little and too late, and although there are programs both on the reserves and in the urban areas whose aim is to salvage the badly-damaged youth, the drop-outs, the delinquents—those who learned to believe in failure from an early age and who never tasted success—the mental and emotional injuries inflicted on them may be beyond the skill of men and women to cure. On November 27, 1978, the *Vancouver Express* published the following news item:

Despairing Young Indians on Suicide Slide

Unemployment, alcoholism, overcrowding, a lost cultural heritage and general feelings of despair are the mileposts to death.

In the last two months six young Indians in the Cowichan Valley looked at those depressing conditions affecting their lives and decided there was only one way out—suicide.

There is no simple explanation for the suicides, according to Cowichan band chief Dennis Alphonse. In addition to trying to determine what has happened to his band members and what preventive steps can be taken, Alphonse has his own private torment—last month his 16-year-old son Joe took his own life.

"It's hard to pinpoint what it is, a general depression. It's mainly with the young people," Alphonse said in a telephone interview.

"I think our kids are mixed up because they don't know which way to go—there's a modern way and there's the old way," he said.

Alphonse said the band is initiating programs which will try to build up young members' pride in their past and form stronger ties between all band members.

"My own concept is that we have to try and get our elders communicating with our young people and build up their confidence and discipline, build up our cultural heritage.

"We have to think seriously of how to cope with it and bring in some preventive programs," he said. Alphonse says a number of problems have combined to leave young band members with the feeling that they have no brighter future.

High unemployment and reliance on welfare have undermined self-confidence and alcohol contributes to the depression, he says.

And the school system has failed to provide young Indians with the incentive to complete their education, Alphonse said. "There's a problem in the education system—there's still a high dropout rate. They (young band members) seem to get to grade 8 or 9 and then drop out."[78]

In 1972, the same year that the Native Indian Brotherhood published *Indian Control of Indian Education*, UNESCO put out its report on world education entitled *Learning To Be*. One of its recommendations was that "Teaching, contrary to traditional ideas and practice, should adapt itself to the learner; the learner should not have to bow to pre-established rules for teaching,"[79] yet with few exceptions, Indian children are still expected to adapt to white people's style of learning in white people's schools. The results over the last 120 years in British Columbia have not been good. "For most Canadian children, compulsory education has meant in some measure the acquisition of skills needed in a modern industrial society. For native children, it has too often resulted in a period of cruel isolation from their home communities, the acquisition of skills and attitudes irrelevant to those communities and, upon graduation or dropping out, a profound sense of alienation from their parents and the values and traditions of their home communities."[80]

What is the alternative? The National Indian Brotherhood says: "Let Indian people control Indian education."[81]

Chapter 2
The Chinese

The lives of these people centre around their children
JUDGE HELEN G. MACGILL

Segregation, 1901-1923

Victoria, B.C. February 13, 1901

"Ladies and Gentlemen, you have heard the petition from residents of the Rock Bay district requesting that we either withdraw permission from Chinese children to attend Rock Bay school, or that we place them in a separate room in the building. What is your pleasure?" The chairman of the Board of School Trustees for Victoria, B.C. did not have to wait long before the arguments began.

"Put them in a separate school," called out Trustee Grant. But the chairman quickly pointed out that in his opinion the board had no legal right to initiate such action.

"Then change the law," counterattacked Trustee Grant. In an attempt to cut off further debate, Trustee Brown moved that the petition be referred to the legislative committee and Trustee Huggett quickly seconded the motion.

But Trustee Belyea was not going to be denied his right to voice his opinion. "I would like to point out, Mr. Chairman, that Chinese children, under our existing law, have the same right to free education as children of any other race, and we, as the elected trustees, have no power and no right to take action on this petition. I would consider it very unfortunate if we should establish a precedent by attempting to interfere with the law, and much as I would like to meet the views of the petitioners, this board cannot grant their request." He paused and looked around. "I believe, Mr. Chairman, that we must educate these Chinese children and teach them English. If our Anglo-Saxon civilization cannot stand before the effects of educating a hundred or so Chinese, then, Mr. Chairman, it is time this school board were abolished. If these petitioners seek redress, they must apply to the legislature. I should add, Mr. Chairman, that if there are enough Chinese children in the city to warrant the establishment of a separate school and if the law permitted it, I would certainly advocate that such a school should be opened. Under the circumstances, however, I must oppose the motion." Trustee Belyea sat down, while Mr. Huggett muttered that he still could not see any harm in referring the matter to the legislative committee.

In answer to a question from Mrs. Grant, the Superintendent informed the trustees that there were at present about sixteen Chinese children attending the public schools in Victoria.

"And another 108 of school age in the city," broke in Mr. Belyea. "I repeat," he went on, "I would like to see all these Chinese children educated in a separate school, but under the present School Act we do not have the power to do this. I will move an amendment: that the petitioners be informed that this board has no power to separate the Chinese from the other children." Mrs. Grant seconded the amendment but Messrs. Brown and Huggett pressed the chairman to uphold the original motion.

Mr. Belyea pleaded with his fellow trustees to stand by those basic principles of fair play on which the Empire had been founded, "If we take action on this petition," he argued, "we shall establish a precedent which will strike at the vital principle of our common schools in which children of all races and creeds have equal rights. While on the one hand, I believe there is merit in the petition, on the other hand, it is quite

> clear that so long as the law remains as it is we have no power to deal with this question." So close was the vote on the amendment that it was not declared carried until the chairman cast his deciding vote in favor and the petitioners had to leave with their grievance not satisfied.[1]

The rising antipathy towards the Chinese children in the public schools manifested in this scene—a scene to be replayed many times in the next three decades—had its roots in the past.

The Chinese first entered the province during the late 1850s working first in the gold fields, but as the years passed they dug coal, built railroads, and became merchants and house servants. By the mid-1870s anti-Chinese groups were forming, and pressure was put on both the provincial and dominion governments to curtail Oriental immigration and to restrict the activities of Orientals already in British Columbia. Strong words were used such as these contained in a petition to the Provincial House of Parliament by the Anti-Chinese Association in 1880.

> We being still determined to oppose the terrible evil of Mongolian usurpation, monopoly of all our industries, and, with cheap labour, the future deprivation of our lands, thus dispossessing our own flesh and blood and congenial races, and to guard against a miscarriage, wrong presentation, misapprehension, and to avoid the possibility of failure in any shape of our obtaining the happy result of British Columbia and the Dominion of Canada for the white man;
>
> We respectfully ask your Honourable Body to pass such a measure, Resolution, or Bill as you in your wisdom shall decide, in order to abate the evil complained of and stop the future immigration of Chinese to this country, and to use such necessary means as will make your Act effectual and successful.[2]

Or these words from a report of a Committee of the Executive Council, approved by His Honour the Lieutenant-Governor on the 19th of August, 1882, which presented certain "facts" amongst which was the following:

> That Chinese, as a class, are injurious to a young community, as they trade almost exclusively among their own people, send all their earnings to Asia, introduce loathsome diseases and demoralizing habits, put the authorities to constant expense in endeavouring to suppress crime among them, and in granting charitable aid to their sick and infirm.[3]

Over the years the provincial government passed various pieces of anti-Chinese legislation, only to have many of them disallowed by the dominion government. Successful legislation sometimes had unfortunate repercussions as reported here by the principal of the Nanaimo Boys' Public School in 1888:

> Owing to the exclusion of Chinese from the mines a great many of our boys left school to fill their places, and consequently deprived us of some of our best material; and you will notice by the annual report that most of the boys are between ten and fourteen years of age.[4]

Individual acts of violence along with strikes and riots punctuated the last few years of the nineteenth century in British Columbia as hostility against Orientals grew, resulting finally in discriminatory legislation being passed by both the provincial and federal governments. In 1885 the dominion government imposed a head tax of $50 on all Chinese entering Canada. This was increased to $100 in 1901 and to $500 in 1904. The right to vote in any election including that for school boards was taken away, and Chinese parents were discouraged from sending their children to the public schools, not that there were very many Chinese children, but they were not welcome. The Chinese were seen as a caste apart, an unassimilable group:

> In spite of the fact that thousands of these Chinese have been in British Columbia for upward of twenty years, they still remain Chinese in every respect. They live together in their Chinese districts, in their own Oriental way, wearing their native dress, and import their own food, supplied from their own stores, they save their money and send it to China and

usually return there for their old age.[5]

But whereas it was possible for the adults to practice apartheid, each year a few more Chinese children managed to enrol in the public schools, so that in early 1902 the writer of a section in the *Victoria Colonist* called "The World of Labour" drew the attention of the readers to what had already became a serious political issue:

> The intermingling of Chinese children with children of Occidental parentage in the classrooms and playgrounds of the public schools is being called into question. The objection is raised not against Chinese as Chinese, but against the mode of life, customs and characteristics of these Asiatic younglings, which, it is held, tends to lower the surrounding influences of school life. Such being the case the remedy must be sought in hiving—undesirable as it may appear. It is regrettable indeed that it should be found necessary to separate at the public schools the children of one portion of the inhabitants from the other for the preservation of the Anglo-Saxon standard of moral and ethical culture. But it is only carrying into the schools what already exists in every other institution of society—the branding of Chinese as Ishmaelites.[6]

On March 12, 1902, Mr. Kelly, President of the Trades and Labour Council in Victoria, presented another petition to the Victoria School Board. In his preamble he pointed out that the object of his coming was to protest the presence of Chinese children in the public schools. "It is," he said, "our belief that separate buildings and playgrounds should be provided for these children, the unsanitary and other conditions of their homes being such as to afford quite sufficient reason for their being kept to themselves."

The brief which Mr. Kelly presented on behalf of the deputation had been widely discussed throughout the city and had received a fair amount of support. The Trades and Labour Council represented 25 trade unions, a sizable group, and certainly not one which public servants could ignore, particularly as many of the trade unionists had children in the public schools. One member of the deputation pointed out that children in the public schools were often moved from one school to another for various reasons and setting apart a room for the Chinese children did not seem to go against the present school laws; indeed, as the schools were overcrowded this move would help to relieve the pressure. Mr. Kelly interjected that the small school at Rock Bay could well be set aside exclusively for the use of the Chinese children and the Japanese children.

Trustee Drury agreed that these children should be kept by themselves and that the white children should not be obliged to associate with them. He felt that the Chinese children were not at home either in school or on the playground and were subjected to various "little discomforts" at the hands of the other children. A motion was then made that the request be complied with.

Trustee Jay reminded the board that only a year ago they had turned down a similar request from Rock Bay residents because they felt they had no power to discriminate between pupils. He was still of the opinion that setting up a separate school would contravene the existing regulations, but Superintendent Eaton, who spoke next, said that he did not think that the establishment of a separate room for Chinese boys and girls would conflict with the regulations. He informed the meeting that there were currently 20 Chinese children scattered in five schools in different classes and that one boy was preparing for the high school examination. Classes in the Victoria schools were very large, averaging around 67 per teacher, twice what the Superintendent felt there should be, resulting in a lack of individual attention by the teachers. For this reason placing the Chinese children in a separate room might benefit them. The Superintendent described the Chinese children as obedient, attentive, studious, and often setting a good example to the other children.

Trustee Huggett suggested that the board should confer with the Department of Education in order to avoid any possible friction from arising, and Trustee Hall agreed that if after consulting with the Department it was found that the board had no power to deal with the matter, legislation giving the board such power could perhaps be introduced during the current session. A committee consisting of members of the board and members of the Trades and

Labour Council was set up to look into the matter.[7]

Meanwhile the issue was kept alive in the press. In the April 20 edition of the *Victoria Colonist* the call for the segregation of Chinese children was justified as follows: "The lack of cleanliness is one reason; another reason is the aptness of Chinese to use words without knowing their meaning, and disregard for decency in giving expression in English to their lascivious thoughts, and the latter is a very serious aspect of the question, and one parents of children will not care to be long continued."[8]

Some months later the matter had still not been resolved, and the Trades and Labour Council, adamant that Chinese children must be separated from white children, called a public meeting on November 3 to debate the issue. Miss Cameron, principal of South Park school, stated it as her opinion that the school board did have the power to establish a separate school in Victoria's Chinatown. Mr. T.H. Twigg, of the Trades and Labour Council, told the meeting that a committee representing his organization and a committee representing the school board had jointly prepared a memorial urging the government to take steps towards arranging for the segregation of the Chinese children, but in the meantime the school board would not commit itself one way or the other. The chairman of the board of school trustees, however, denied that the board was responsible for the memorial, and reiterated his views that the board had no power to segregate the Chinese children. Trustee Belyea agreed with him.

At this point, the chairman of the meeting, Ed Bragg, sharply reminded the trustees present that the Trades and Labour Council meant business and would find a way to settle the matter to their liking. Another trustee, after trying to get the meeting to recognize the limits placed on the power of the board to initiate the desired action, asked for fair treatment for the Chinese. He did not feel that the Chinese children should be ostracized on the grounds of immoral conduct, a charge which he felt had not been established.

Another speaker suggested that the best way out of the impasse was to test the matter in the Supreme Court. If the legislature had not said the school boards could not establish separate schools under special conditions, then he did not think the Department of Education had any right to forbid it. He pointed out that all thinking men agreed that the line had to be drawn somewhere in the matter of social relations between whites and Chinese. His comments "The Mongolianization of British Columbia must be prevented at all hazards" and "We cannot have them in equal citizenship" were received with applause. Arguments continued on the advisability of seeking a supreme court decision, and points previously made were given a second airing. The meeting finally closed by passing a motion urging the school trustees to take the necessary action to remedy the current unsatisfactory situation.[9]

While the public meeting called by the Trades and Labour Council was going on, the City Council was also in session and had on its agenda an item pertaining to the public schools. To get discussion going Alderman McCandless moved that a new school district be created in Chinatown, which would result in de facto segregation. He said his object in making the motion was to get an expression of opinion from the Council for the school trustees, who had the power to act in the matter but who would be obviously strengthened if they knew that the Council would support them in any expenses that might be involved.

The mayor then spoke at length: "I suppose that while the school law exists as it is, and taxes are collected from Chinamen, it is the duty of the trustees to provide their children with school accommodation and tuition. But there is nothing in the school regulations, so far as I know, to prevent the trustees deciding as to who, and what, children shall attend the several schools. As a matter of fact, a rule to this effect is in operation today, and has been recognized for years." The mayor felt, however, that the trustees might take offence at the motion as made and suggested that it be amended to read: "That this Council is impressed with the necessity which exists for establishing a separate school for the accommodation of Chinese pupils, but inasmuch as it is the duty of the Board of School Trustees to deal with the matter, it is not desirable that the council should appear to interfere with the prerogatives of that board. The Council, however, desires to intimate that they are prepared to at once favorably entertain a reasonable request from the school trustees to provide the funds required for such a school."

Alderman Yates suggested that the school trustees could take a teacher from the primary school in the afternoon and send him to Chinatown to teach in the Chinese school, but Alderman Barnard did not agree. They had to be fair, he said, pointing out that the Chinese paid the school tax and it would not be right to give their children a half day's tuition when they paid the full amount of the taxes. They should either be given a proper school or their taxes should be abolished. In time, after further expressions of opinion, the amended motion passed.[10]

A few days later the superintendent of schools for Victoria held his regular monthly meeting with principals and teachers. One of the topics covered the presence of Chinese children in the Victoria schools. The previous year the teaching staff had been asked whether they felt it was desirable to have Chinese children in the same classes as white children. Superintendent Eaton put the identical question to the staff at the meeting and received the same answer as a year ago: the presence of Chinese boys in the classes produced no discord whatsoever. After the meeting Mr. Eaton stated that there was absolutely no truth to the suggestions that order in classrooms had been subverted due to the inability of the Chinese pupils to understand English. He described such reports as pure fabrication.[11]

The motion passed by the City Council at their November 3 meeting placed such pressure on the school trustees that they were forced to take action, unpalatable though it might be to some, and the matter came to a head at their November 12 meeting. Trustee Boggs opened the discussion by criticizing the action of the City Council in taking the initiative. He felt, however, that something must be done at once. After reminding the board that they had been informed that they had no jurisdiction in the matter, he moved a resolution to the effect that a special room be set aside for the tuition of Chinese children in Chinatown. Mrs. Jenkins opposed the idea saying that in the light of the communication received from the Council of Public Instruction, school boards should not discriminate between children in regard to colour, creed or race, and the amendment was then watered down to say merely that a suitable room should be found in the Chinese quarter. But Trustee Jay saw problems arising in that if a school was established in Chinatown "a host of Chinese waifs would attend whereas now there are only 20 or 30." He suggested setting aside a room for Chinese boys in North Ward school and limiting the attendance, but his amendment was not seconded.

Arguments continued back and forth. The Superintendent was asked point blank if he would comply with the board's wishes if they decided to set aside a room for Chinese boys at North Ward school and he said he would, but he took the opportunity to review for the board the history of the controversy.

"Allegations have been made," he pointed out, "perhaps in good faith, regarding the Chinese children which were erroneous. It is the duty of this board to investigate the truth of those allegations. It has been said that the presence of Chinese in the schools is demoralizing and dangerous to the white children owing to their coming from unsanitary conditions. I submit, however, that the case of the petitioners has not been proven; it has, in fact, fallen to the ground. Therefore I do not see how the board can justify the expenditure of $860 or more dollars for the establishment of a separate school. Personally I have no objection in dealing with the Chinese in the manner suggested; my objection lies with the question of expense."

In reply to a question as to whether he anticipated any trouble from the Council of Public Instruction if the suggested action were taken, Superintendent Eaton said that he understood that the government was prepared to allow the city the fullest latitude in all questions of management. "I have no objections," he continued "to putting 15 junior Chinese scholars in a separate room but I would object to any attempts to degrade them." After further discussion during which it was pointed out that to educate the Chinese to compete with the whites would be a very dangerous action, two resolutions were passed: one set aside a small room in North Ward school for Chinese pupils; the other required the board to meet with the Council of Public Instruction with the object of securing an amendment to the Public Schools Act which would give the board the power to deal with such questions in the future with a free hand.[12]

But the matter was by no means resolved. During the next few weeks Mr. Twigg, Labour Candidate in the upcoming elections for the school board, declared publicly that the trustees had been insincere and inconsistent in dealing with the question of the Chinese pupils and that what they did at one meeting they undid at the next.[13] The chairman of the school board, Dr. Hall, had certainly run into trouble over the issue and at the final meeting before the new board took over he made it clear that while the board favored segregating the Chinese, the government had informed them that they did not have the power to do so.[14]

A year later in the local paper the writer of "In the World of Labour" announced that the trustees had decided to rent special classrooms for Chinese children, and he thoroughly chastized the trustees for taking so long to do what, in the opinion of Labour, they had always had the power to do.[15]

The lull which followed was short.

On August 24, 1907, the *Victoria Colonist* ran an interesting headline: "Victoria Now Has a Chinese Question," as if the last few years had not seen a surfeit of articles dealing with various aspects of the "Chinese Question." What the writer meant was that Victoria had a new Chinese question, one which centered on recently arrived older Chinese boys who sought admission to the public schools.

In 1904 the head tax for Chinese new arrivals had been raised from $100 to $500. Certain classes of people such as diplomats or merchants, could gain exemptions from the head tax; others could at a later date obtain a refund of the head tax. Students were included in this latter classification. The act stated:

> Persons of Chinese origin claiming on their arrival to be students but who are unable to produce the requisite certificate as hereinbefore provided for shall be entitled to the refund of the tax exacted from them on the production within eighteen months from the date of their arrival in Canada of certificates from teachers in any school or college in Canada showing that they are and have been bona fide students in attendance at such school or college.

The chairman of the Victoria Board of School Trustees felt that the number of older Chinese students seeking admission to the public schools was so high that the situation was critical. He therefore instructed the superintendent of schools to refuse admission to any more Chinese students and on August 23 called a special meeting of the board. He described what he saw as an inequity: the city and province were compelled to bear the cost of educating Chinese students who twelve months later entered the labour market receiving a refund of their head tax, but neither the city nor the province were recouped for their expenses.

In an interview with the customs authorities who collected the head tax, Chairman Jay had learned that between April and August, twenty-six Chinese boys had paid the $500 head tax and declared themselves students. During the final year of the $100 head tax, thirty to thirty-five Chinese boys had applied for permission to enter the schools. The chairman reminded his audience that in order to combat the language problem, the board had at that time engaged a special teacher and set aside a room for them.

"The matter is a serious one," Mr. Jay continued. "We have these twenty-six applications and I am informed that others are expected. Whether the Dominion government is in the right or in the wrong in refunding the head tax under these conditions is not for us to say, that is a question between the Dominion government and its own conscience, but I will say that I believe that it was never the intention of the government that this provision of the act should apply to boys attending primary grades. It was only to apply, I am convinced, to those taking advanced science or arts courses.

"If we are to admit these boys to ordinary graded schools and put them in the ordinary classes it will impede our own pupils. Ignorant of the language, the Chinese students will require special attention. If we engage a special teacher we are taxed the cost of that teacher's salary and the cost of a room in order that they may get back their $12,000 or $13,000."

Mr. Jay advocated that the matter should be brought to the attention of the Department of Education and the provincial government in the hope that they might pass some legislation which would take care of the problem. Under the present statute Mr. Jay did not feel that the Chinese students could be excluded from the schools, though he admitted that it was a debatable point, and for the moment he advised that the superintendent should be instructed to withhold permits. The meeting finally approved a motion calling on the Chairman to interview the provincial educational authorities, and instructing the superintendent to refuse permits to any Chinese youths seeking to attend school.[16] Six days later at another special meeting, the board passed a motion that no pupils be admitted to the schools until "they can so understand the English language as to be amenable to the ordinary regulations and school discipline."[17]

Meanwhile, over in Vancouver the same debate was taking place with headlines such as "How Chinese Evade the $500 Head Tax—Enter as Students and Money is Returned to Them—Regulations in Need of Amendment" appearing in the local press.[18] On September 7, 1907, the latent hostility of the whites to the Orientals erupted into savage violence in Vancouver when a public meeting called by the Asiatic Exclusion League got out of hand and hoodlums and others poured into Chinatown and the Japanese quarter smashing every window they could find. A somewhat chastened newspaper a few days later under the headline "Orientals in City Schools Do Not Exceed 150" reported, "The question of Oriental attendance at the public schools of Vancouver is not much of a factor save at the Central School." It gave as the opinion of the school authorities that the Oriental children "are model pupils and exceedingly apt," and that they "are well dressed and cleanly, and give practically no trouble to the teaching staff."[19]

But back in Victoria the school board's decision not to admit Chinese boys who were unable to speak English was challenged by the Hon. Fred Peters, K.C. on behalf of some Chinese clients. Mr. Peters stood by while the following letter submitted by him to the board was read at its September 11 meeting:

> Dear Sirs:
>
> I am instructed in the interest of several Chinese boys who have lately arrived in Victoria to write to you pressing for their admission in the public schools in Victoria.
>
> As I understand the position of affairs is as follows: There are, I believe, about fifteen children lately arrived from China who have made application for permits to attend the primary

schools. These permits have been refused, and an order of the board passed, I believe last Friday, to the effect that no child shall be permitted to attend the primary school who does not know enough English to be able to understand the proceedings in the school, and to be amenable to school discipline.

I understand from you personally that if these children choose to attend private schools, and thus acquire a knowledge of English, there would perhaps be no difficulty in their getting permits to attend the public schools, say, at the beginning of next year.

You will remember that on the 27th August last, I had an interview with you, at which it was arranged that before the board passed finally on the matter I should be allowed an opportunity of presenting the views of my clients to them. You will also remember that owing to the meeting at which the resolution was passed being called hurriedly I was not afforded the opportunity promised.

I also understand from you that permits have been granted to all Chinese applicants who were in Victoria before the 1st of April last, and if this is correct, which I do not doubt, the question immediately at issue will be confined entirely to the children who have arrived here since the 1st April.

The question raised is one of principle, and my clients now wish to present their case with a view if necessary of taking legal steps to enforce what they believe to be their rights.

1. We contend that under our school law all children of school age resident in British Columbia have an absolute right to be educated at the public schools.
2. That this right is the same whether the children are English, French, German, Chinese or any other nationality.
3. That the fact that the Chinese children cannot speak English is no reason for their exclusion. Many such children have heretofore been admitted and experience has shown that in a very short time they become well able to follow the class work.
4. If there are too many children unable to speak English to be conveniently admitted to the general primary class, the school board is bound to supply such children with a

separate room and teacher. This course has in the past been followed by the board.

5. The Chinese in Victoria pay a large amount of school tax and it is submitted on every principle of fair play they are entitled to receive the same benefits as other tax payers.
6. If a similar number of French Canadian children unable to speak English, and there are many such in Canada, should apply for admission on the ground that they cannot speak English, we venture to say no such question would ever be raised. Why should it be different with the Chinese?
7. In the newspapers it has been suggested that these Chinese children only attend school so that they may be enabled to receive back the $500 tax paid on landing in Canada, and that in some way this question was before the school board. I understand from you that the board have not acted on any such proposition, and have taken the same view that I submitted to you verbally, viz: That the return of the $500 is a matter absolutely between the individual child and the government, to be decided when the application is made, if it ever should be made, and that right to be educated is precisely the same whether the student intends in the future to be a laborer or a professional man, or a merchant. The question simply is not within the jurisdiction of this school board.

I sincerely hope some solution of this question may be arrived at, but I am bound to inform you that my instructions are positive to take legal steps to enforce our clients' rights, and that quickly as the term is slipping away quickly.

Our contention is that the board should at once appoint a teacher to teach the primary Chinese class, or failing that admit them to the general class.

Fred Peters

Mr. Peters was allowed to address the board and he reiterated and expanded on a number of the points in his letter. Several trustees questioned him before he retired from the meeting and left them to their deliberations.

Trustee Lewis then quickly gave his opinion that the Oriental influx was growing more serious and must be tackled. "We must keep them out," he concluded. But Trustee Huggett believed that the board might have exceeded its powers and wanted to see a special class for Chinese boys organized until the end of the year by which time they would probably know enough English to enter regular classes. Trustee Lewis was adamant, however, that the board should stick to its guns. "Let the matter go to the courts," he said, "then we shall all know where we stand. If the Chinese have rights let them go and get them." The board stuck to its guns and voted to maintain its present policy.[20]

A few days later another meeting of the trustees was held at which time Chairman Jay read into the records two letters dealing with the education of Chinese children. The first dated August 20, 1907, was from the Acting Minister of Education, R.G. Tatlow, to the Deputy Minister of Trade and Commerce and Chief Controller of Chinese Immigration, Ottawa. The letter set out the current serious situation whereby a large number of Chinese boys aged nine to fourteen had sought entry to the public schools in Victoria. The final paragraph asked for an interpretation of the term "student" as used in the act governing the head tax, and sought from the department a ruling as to whether or not such "students" should be admitted as their purpose in calling themselves "students" seemed to be to evade the head tax.

The reply of E.T.C. O'Hara, Acting Chief Controller for the Department of Trade and Commerce in Ottawa dated September 4, 1907, made it plain that the federal government saw nothing wrong in the Chinese boys paying the head tax and later obtaining a refund—the act specifically provided for this. The letter continued:

> As for any inconvenience that may be caused by the arrival of so many Chinese children who desire to attend school, I may observe that of course it is expected that British Columbia will have more of such arrivals than any other province, and at the same time British Columbia's share of the capitation tax is very much larger than that of any of the other provinces. Recently this department paid over to British Columbia $18,000, and this was very much less than the amount paid in former

> years when the capitation tax was only $100. For the year ended 30th June, 1903, it amounted to $258,000. It might be held, and I think with some reason, that in view of such a large payment to a province, such province would be called upon to provide any additional accommodation or other requirements necessary.

The *Victoria Times* which printed the letters in full, noted that they were received and filed without comment.[21]

The Minutes of the meeting of the Victoria School Trustees for September 23, 1907, record the next shot in the battle when the superintendent reported that legal action had been entered against himself and the board to compel them to admit Chinese students to the public schools.[22] But while Mr. Peters was preparing to go to the courts, white youths were taking the law into their own hands:

> Complaints have been made that white boys have made an organized attempt to prevent Chinese pupils from attending the Rock Bay and Central schools. It seems that gangs of enthusiastic youthful exclusion league sympathizers have been congregating at the corner of Herald and Douglas streets and also at some point between Chinatown and Rock Bay school and not allowing Chinese pupils to pass them on their way to school. On several occasions the lads have been assaulted and in some cases prevented from going to school at all.[23]

In January, 1908, the board softened its position a little by issuing permits to native-born Chinese children,[24] but as the weeks passed requests for permits for other Chinese children were frequently tabled and decisions deferred.

Over in Vancouver a report to the school board on the Oriental question resulted in some fairly prompt action. The report indicated that the main problem lay in Central School situated close to Chinatown. Here 117 Oriental pupils sat in junior classes already overcrowded. The *Vancouver Province* described "the strange spectacle of Chinese boys nineteen or twenty years old seated at desks alongside little white and Oriental children under twelve years of age." The report recommended removing all Orientals over the legal school limit of sixteen and giving them independent instruction in a separate room. The newspaper fed one tit-bit to its readers:

> Incidentally Vancouver can lay claim to a unique distinction, one that is unparalleled even in the province of Quebec. Twenty-seven pupils, all the children of one Chinese father, are in attendance at the Central School. The fond parent has three wives living, and has buried several other spouses. His offspring were gifts from all of them.

The article went on to speak well of the scholastic ability of the Chinese, and pointed out that the older children with their maturer minds would progress more rapidly if they were separated from the younger children. The separation of the younger children by race had never been contemplated as this would involve duplication of services and a considerable increase in the teaching staff.

The article ended with a forward-looking statement:

> Members of the school board have recently been urged to establish a class in one of the local high schools for teaching the Chinese and Japanese languages in view of the growing commercial relations between Canada and the Orient. Leading educators hold that the acquirement of these Asiatic languages by young white men who intend to engage in a business career would be a potent factor in stimulating trade between Vancouver and the transpacific countries.
>
> Germany's success in developing trade in all quarters of the world and crowding out fossilized competitors is ascribed to attention devoted by Germans to the study of foreign languages. A Canadian able to speak Chinese or Japanese would, it is claimed, be in a position to visit China and Japan and duplicate the success of the Germans in securing orders for Canadian business houses. The possibilities of trade with the Orient are regarded as almost illimitable.[25]

The representations to the dominion government by the Vancouver and Victoria school boards and the Department of

Education brought some results. In his annual report for 1908 the chairman of the Board of School Trustees for Vancouver said:

> This Board has also to its credit a change in the Immigration Act, by which the Chinese will no longer be able to obtain a rebate of their $500 head tax by taking a nominal course for twelve months in the elementary schools. There is no doubt that this change is both in the interests of education, as well as in the best interests of our City School expenditure.[26]

A separate class was, however, established in Vancouver with apparently satisfactory results:

> The separation of Orientals from white children, which commenced two years ago, has been continued, and I am glad to say all friction has ceased. This separation more particularly applies to the segregation of those desiring to enter the junior classes and who are older than the average pupil of that class.[27]

But back in Victoria the arguments continued with the firm of Peters and Wilson pressing for permits for Chinese boys to attend school and the board continuing to refuse admission or to defer decision.

At the end of March, 1908, there was an unfortunate incident at Rock Bay school when it was discovered that a sixteen year old Chinese boy had been drawing obscene pictures in the exercise books of younger white children. The board suspended the student, but the propriety of allowing over-age Chinese boys to sit in classes with younger white children was raised again and covered in some detail by the press. At the board meeting of March 27 there seemed to be strong support growing again for the establishment of a separate school for Chinese pupils.[28] At a further meeting some days later a committee was set up to consider such a move, and in August the minutes of the board recorded a suggestion that Rock Bay school be made a separate school for Chinese and Japanese. The superintendent pointed out that as there were fifty-seven Chinese and four Japanese students, two teachers would be required, but he did not feel it necessary to include the Japanese children as they were few in number and of the better class. Mr. Christie, however, reminded the board that it was the future they had to look to and they should make both groups attend the one school.[29] A newspaper article covering the meeting printed in full a letter from Mr. Fred Peters in which he presented in detail the history of the negotiations to date, and gave it as his opinion that the best solution would be the appointment of a separate teacher for the Chinese children.[30]

A headline in the *Victoria Colonist* for September 19 read "Chinese Problem Is Still Unsettled—School Board Considers Report But Takes No Definite Action,"[31] but by October 15 the headlines had changed to "Secures Quarters for Chinese Pupils—School Board Rents Room For Orientals of the Lower Grades."[32] The committee's recommendation that rooms be rented at the Chinese Methodist Mission for junior classes of Chinese children had been accepted.

The tide seemed to have turned against the Chinese. The Hon. Fred Peters, K.C., who had taken legal action against the Victoria School Board to force it to admit Chinese children to the public schools, lost his case. The writ was declined on the grounds that the statute expressly designated the Council of Public Instruction as the court to which appeals of this nature should be taken.[33]

For the next few years the segregation of Oriental students from white students continued to be raised spasmodically as a public issue. One of its strongest proponents was J.H. Hawthornthwaite, M.L.A. for Nanaimo. On February 18, 1910, he proposed an addition to the Public Schools Act which would read as follows:

> School boards shall have the power to exclude any child if, owing to racial or other difference, it is deemed inadvisable to admit them.

He trotted out the old arguments regarding the danger and inadvisability of allowing Oriental children to associate with Anglo-Saxon children in the public schools. Not that he was attacking the Orientals in any way of course; they were here and had as much right to live as any other race, etc., etc., but when it came to allowing their children to associate with white children that was something that should not and could not be permitted. He described it as an evil, as an affliction which in time would bother every town. Men were generally able to avoid associating with Orientals during their work or daily life, but children were forced to associate with them during one of the most important and formative periods of their life—and on and on he went. Later, he agreed to cut out the words "or other" in his amendment which, it was pointed out, could be used to refer to denominational differences.[34] But the Legislative Assembly did not see eye to eye with Mr. Hawthornthwaite and a few days later when the vote was taken the members overwhelmingly rejected the amendment.

Separate classes for Chinese children continued in Victoria for some years, opening and closing according to numbers, but this was merely a period of uneasy truce which culminated in an even more bitter struggle in the early 1920s.

The first sign of trouble resulted from the school board's decision in 1921 to hire a Chinese woman as a teacher at Rock Bay school which was attended only by Chinese pupils. The Asiatic Exclusion League immediately objected and in its letter of protest to the board pointed out that the number of Orientals in the province would become a "political issue of no inconsiderable magnitude," and therefore Orientals "must be under the guidance and supervision of one whose heart is centred in the British Empire," that is, a white teacher.[35] A year later she was fired. While the board had believed that her knowledge of the children's ways and their language would be valuable, her discipline had been weak, and, Inspector George Deane added, "As a result of investigations, I am convinced that both the Chinese students and their parents would rather have white teachers in the Chinese classes, and probably the general public will prefer it too."[36]

Municipal Inspector George H. Deane of the Victoria City Schools was to be referred to part way through the upcoming controversy, which took on international proportions, as a man who let his personal animosity against the Chinese influence his reports to the school board.[37] In early January, 1922, Mr. Deane informed the board that there were 216 Chinese students in four schools. In his opinion it would be better to have all the Chinese students in a central location. It was not fair to expect teachers to teach fifteen and sixteen year old boys who could hardly speak English. "There is a danger in these Chinese boys," he said, "many of whom cannot speak English, coming from their insanitary living quarters downtown and mixing with other children with no attempt at segregation." He went on, "We know there is not only a tendency with the Chinese to live in insanitary quarters, but a practice."[38] A trustee remarked that as the school population was increasing, more space would be needed and if accommodation for the Chinese pupils was found at Rock Bay school, this might relieve the congestion, whereupon the chairman, George Jay, suggested that it might be advisable to fall back on the regulation passed sixteen years ago whereby no Chinese were admitted unless they knew enough English to make them amenable to discipline.[39]

During the following weeks the school board decided on a policy of segregation and agreed to place the Chinese children in three schools, Rock Bay, King's Road, and at a new location on Railway Street where temporary classrooms were to be erected. The Railway Street site, while close to Chinatown, was in a white area, and the inhabitants were quick to protest the establishment of a school for Chinese. They approved the policy of segregation, they told the board, but if it meant putting in a school at Railway Street they preferred the old system of accepting Chinese at all the schools and they threatened to take out an injunction.[40]

Meanwhile the Chinese challenged the board to prove that they lived in insanitary quarters. The board did not take up the challenge, but refrained thereafter from using it as reason for segregating the Chinese children, concentrating solely on the issue of language, maintaining that the presence of illiterate Chinese pupils retarded the progress of white pupils.

When school opened in early September, 1922, the principals endeavored to implement the policy of segregation. They called their Chinese children out of their classes, lined them up and marched them down to King's Road school where, to the discomfort of the principals, the students disbanded and vanished. For the remainder of the school year, the Chinese parents and their children boycotted the separate schools. The drama of the ensuing months was reported extensively in the press as accusations, suggestions, compromises, refusals, questions, answers, and rebuttals—indeed, expressions from the whole range of human interaction—followed one after another.

The Chinese citizens, usually fairly passive, were furious. Much as the school board might like to justify the action later as educationally sound, to the Chinese it was blatant discrimination. "This is the first time that a complete segregation of the Oriental pupils from others in attendance at the schools has been made," said the *Victoria Colonist*, "although segregation to a limited extent was in force in some schools."[42] Josephine Wong was excluded from the public schools in spite of the fact that her father, Joseph Wong, had been born in Victoria in 1891, had attended the local schools and had never been away from Victoria; and his father had been a naturalized British subject in Canada since 1892. Josephine was therefore a third generation British subject.[43] Chinese ratepayers said they could readily accept "a mild form of separation, such as forbidding children of sixteen years and over from the junior grades, but to take steps to debar Chinese students of British birthright, irrespective of age, location of residence and class grade from the public schools cannot be tolerated" and they threatened to take legal steps.[44]

The board quickly backed off and at its September 13th meeting passed a resolution which did not mention any specific race, but simply stated that pupils who could not pass a satisfactory test in the English language would not be admitted to the ordinary graded schools. By extending the regulation to cover all non-English speaking children regardless of race, the board felt it had removed any hint of discrimination. The schools to which the children were to be sent, however, all lay in or close to Chinatown, but the board remained confident that the Chinese, once they understood the new policy, would send their children back to school. But the Chinese did not—they continued to boycott the schools.

In early October a delegation representing the Chinese community met with the school trustees and presented their views and made some suggestions on which they felt a compromise could be worked out. The Chinese parents were opposed to the total segregation of Chinese children who lacked facility in English from English-speaking children. For the past eight years older Chinese students arriving from China had been put onto a four year program at Rock Bay school, and had emerged with a very limited reading and writing expertise, and even less facility in the spoken language. The parents pointed out that the students in Rock Bay school heard no English except from the teacher and had no one on whom to practice their English. As the program at Rock Bay had proved to be a failure they saw no reason for expanding it. They suggested instead that what they called kindergartens should be established for children between the ages of six and ten and younger if possible; that the recent practice of sending young children to Rock Bay school should stop and that only children over the age of ten who could not speak English should attend; that children who were backward in school should have an extra hour of classes every day; and that Chinese children and all other foreign born children should have an opportunity to engage in sports.[45] Their suggestions were turned down and the boycott continued.

The school board issued an ultimatum on October 5 to the parents that unless the Chinese children registered at the separate schools immediately the schools would be closed until the new term in January. The Chinese ignored the ultimatum and the separate schools closed. Further ultimatums were issued in January and April, but the children did not appear, the parents preferring to keep their children at home rather than have them segregated.

As the weeks wore on the board made further concessions which allowed some children to receive permits to return to their former schools, but these concessions were not enough to assuage the anger of the Chinese, who made plans to set up a school in Chinatown in which the children would be taught in Chinese. If the board was going to try and force them to remain Chinese, then they would assist the board, and they began renting rooms and hiring teachers. The Chinese were naturally feeling frustrated at their political impotence. Although they paid taxes, they were not allowed to vote in municipal, provincial, or federal elections and so were left with no public voice except what was raised for them by white citizens.

The daily press contained a plethora of articles and letters, some cool and calm, some hot-headed and decidedly bigoted. The editorial in the *Victoria Colonist* for October 14 did not feel that the issue was one which could be solved by the isolated action of a single school board, but was, in fact, a matter for decision by the provincial government.[46] But the controversy raced swiftly beyond the provincial boundaries when the Chinese Ambassador to Washington, Dr. Sze, passed through Victoria on November 11 and expressed surprise that Chinese students who could speak English had been segregated from white pupils. The press quoted him as saying that he would take the question up with the Chinese government on his return to Peking.[47]

Local church ministers attempted to mediate an end to the dispute but without success. Their intervention was not entirely gratuitous—their missionary work amongst the Chinese had suffered severe setbacks as a result of the controversy.

The boycott of the schools continued after Christmas, and the Chinese Consul-General in Canada, Dr. Tsur, talked of a possible boycott of Canadian-made goods in China. "It will be a blemish on the fair name of Canada," he said, "if this city by its segregated school policy shows a lack of fairness to the people of a friendly nation like China which is anxious to do business with this country."[48] The trustees tried to demonstrate that Dr. Tsur had a mistaken impression of the situation: all senior Chinese students were now allowed to go to the white schools without interference of any kind; all students who reached the junior fourth grade were permitted to join the white classes and continue in them until the end of their school days; in the classes below the fourth grade any Chinese student able to speak good English could receive a special permit to attend the white school; teachers in the segregated schools had been instructed to give special permits to students who would profit by going to a white school.[49]

In March parents and trustees met again. The trustees made a further concession reducing the level at which segregation would end from the fourth year reader to the third year reader, but the Chinese reiterated their earlier argument that segregation would never cure the English deficiency the board complained of, and that in their view the deficit was confined to one or two dozen students at the most. They also contended that the board had not extended its policy to Hindu, Negro, or Japanese students and therefore all Chinese children should be sent back to their regular schools.[50]

In early April the board agreed to allow an additional forty which followed its passage were quiet years for the Chinese. Clearly their numbers could no longer increase at the former rate now that immigration had ended, and there was no loophole in the law, as there was under the "Gentlemen's Agreement" for the Japanese, whereby the Chinese could bring in wives for the many single men. The number of Chinese children in school grew very slowly. Anti-Oriental hostility was, from this time on, directed largely towards the Japanese.

But the Chinese were hedged around with many restrictions: they could not vote, access to jobs and entry into the professions were very limited, and there was naturally frustration which forced some to take ship to China. One young Chinese wrote:

> Even for the most highly educated Chinese there is little desire in many cases to study hard, because if a person intends to stay in this country, the amount of education received will not decide the type of work one will get. There is no choice for the young people here as to what they will do, it's just a matter of taking whatever turns up, or remaining idle. No matter what high ambitions are held by the young people, unless they leave for China to realize them they will never be realized. After many repeated setbacks here they feel disgusted and give up hope. The situation as it stands, where young people live in a state of shattered hopes and ambitions, is deplorable, because instead of an aggressive, quick thinking bunch of Chinese Canadian youths, one finds a submissive fatalistic group of young people. A few do save and go to China in search of better things. The opportunity for university students is no greater. Because they expect more than the average person, they all see a time when they will be in China, using the best of their ability to help both themselves and China. If they remain too long after graduation in this country, they also begin to resign themselves to their fate and lose their ambition. University graduates are granted a prestige in China which they do not receive here.[55]

There continued to be segregated classes in Vancouver and Victoria and in other parts of the province for those who lacked facility in English. The Chinese children in these classes were all Canadian-born but came from homes where their ancestral language was spoken. After spending the day in school, many would go to Chinese school in the late afternoon or on Saturday mornings.

One of the earliest Chinese schools had started in Victoria in 1899. The opening day announcement in the newspaper gave out that while the Chinese fully appreciated the advantages of free English education they had come to the conclusion that more was needed to equip their children for life in British Columbia: it was necessary for them to have an education in Chinese as well as in English. But for some it was not simply a case of adding Chinese education to English education, there were a number of children in Victoria at that time who for different reasons were not attending the public schools and for whom a Chinese education would be the only education. In 1907 the school moved to a new site and continued to flourish so that in 1947 when it celebrated its fortieth anniversary on Fisgard Street the *News Herald* said it was rated as one of the most efficient Chinese language schools in North America.[56] The Chinese Public School in Vancouver also became well known, and along with smaller schools all over the province carried on the work of teaching the Chinese language and culture to second, third and fourth generation children. Judge Helen MacGill of the Juvenile Court in Vancouver saw this attendance at Chinese school as one of the contributing factors to the low delinquency rate amongst Oriental children.

Writing on juvenile deinquency in 1938, Judge MacGill began by saying:

> The dissimilarity of the family attitude of the Oriental and that of the white immigrant is very marked. The ugly hostility between parents and children which, in the case of white nationalities, breaks out in Court in bitter reproaches and fierce recriminations is unknown in Oriental cases here. The Oriental family sits in Court, restrained, deeply anxious, alert, and eager to help. A child gone wrong is a sore anxiety, but never "cast off." Every relative to the remotest degree feels responsibility for the welfare of the younger members. The lives

had been permitted to enter the country as immigrants.

The repeal of the Chinese Immigration Act did not, however, mean that the Chinese could enter unrestricted on the same terms as Europeans. Canada was not, according to Prime Minister W.L. MacKenzie King, ready for that:

> There will, I am sure, be general agreement with the view that the people of Canada do not wish as a result of mass immigration to make a fundamental alteration in the character of the Canadian population. Any considerable oriental immigration would, moreover, be certain to give rise to social and economic problems of a character that might lead to serious difficulties in the field of international relations. The government, therefore, has no thought of making any change in immigrant regulations which would have consequences of this kind.[62]

On the repeal of the old act the Chinese were placed in the same category as other Asians whose admission was controlled by Order-in-Council 2115 which restricted entry to the wives and unmarried children under eighteen of Canadian citizens. There were various delays before the first group of immigrants landed in British Columbia but by late 1949 reunification of families was underway.

A new immigration act passed in 1952 did not do much to increase Chinese immigration as it gave the Governor-in-Council almost unlimited powers to exclude or limit the admission of a wide range of people based on their nationality or ethnic group, or on their probable inability to assimilate. In 1962 there was some easing of certain aspects of racial discrimination contained in the immigration regulations, but non-Europeans were still not permitted to sponsor the same wide range of relatives as Europeans. But in 1967 the regulations were changed so as to remove at last the discriminatory restrictions and to place all applicants on an equal footing under a point system. After forty-four years of exclusion the Chinese were now as free to come to Canada as those of other races and nationalities. Finally, in 1976 the House of Commons passed a new immigration bill which had as its stated fundamental objectives: family reunification; non-discrimination; concern for refugees; and the promotion of Canada's economic, social, demographic and cultural goals.

In 1949 the Chinese won the vote and as the years passed barriers which had kept them out of various professions and occupations tumbled. The effect of this easing of restrictions was felt by the Chinese language school teachers who noticed a decline in attendance as the young people realized that they no longer had to speak Chinese in order to get a job—English alone was sufficient.[63]

The relaxing of the immigration regulations coupled with the general world situation, political and economic, resulted in a considerable rise in the number of people entering British Columbia during 1973-1975, but no other group recorded such a high increase as the Chinese. Anxiety regarding the future caused many Hong Kong residents to seek security in Canada; others came from Taiwan and Singapore; and a few, sometimes Spanish-speaking Chinese, moved north from South America. Whereas in 1964 only 810 Chinese gave British Columbia as their destination in Canada, ten years later the figure was 4,558.[64] There was a corresponding increase in the number of Chinese and other foreign-born children enrolling in the public schools which now faced once again many of the problems they had encountered in the early part of the century, not the least of which was the inability of the provincial and federal governments to come to some amicable arrangement regarding the financial burden which devolved on urban school districts like Vancouver where the bulk of the new immigrants settled.

The federal government in 1971 in its response to the recommendations contained in book IV of the *Report of the Royal Commission on Bilingualism and Biculturalism* said: "The federal government approves in principle aid towards the teaching of official languages to children of immigrants and will be discussing it with the provinces,"[65] but nothing happened. It was left largely up to the metropolitan school districts to make their own applications for federal funds to assist them in the education of immigrant children, but funding was of course refused on the grounds that education is a provincial responsibility. The British Columbia Ministry of Education did provide some additional money to assist in the setting up of special ESL (English as a

Second Language) classes, but this was insufficient to meet the needs of the urban school districts and many immigrant children did not receive help when and for as long as they needed it. An editorial in the *Vancouver Province* in May, 1977, began by saying:

> It is all very well for B.C. Education Minister Pat McGeer to say funding for extra English language training for the children of immigrants is a federal problem because immigration is under its jurisdiction. But if these children are having difficulty in handling other subjects because of language, then it is a provincial problem that should be dealt with.[66]

The question of funding was raised in the House of Commons on May 12, 1977, by Mr. Benno-Friesen (Surrey-White Rock) who quoted from a brief submitted by the Vancouver School Board which pointed out that forty per cent of its elementary school population came from homes where English was the second rather than the primary language. The brief stated that previous presentations made to the federal government had been turned down. The brief continued:

> We find the negative responses from the federal government difficult to understand when we consider that:
>
> a) the Joint Parliamentary Committee has recommended to the government that direct funding be made available to school boards to assist in the education of immigrant youngsters;
>
> b) the problems regarding ESL students are a direct result of federal government policies;
>
> c) although we have been told that constitutionally the responsibility for education lies with the provincial government, the federal government provides substantial grants for French language instruction and in the past has entered

into agreements with provinces to upgrade vocational-technical facilities in secondary schools throughout the country and to provide funds for post-secondary education;

d) both the former and present B.C. ministers of education have assured us that there would be no problem in accepting federal funds for distribution to school districts for the education of ESL students.

Mr. Benno-Friesen then put his question: "Is it [the government] going to implement a policy which works hardship on people and simply forgets them? Is it going to neglect them? Is it going to provide the $2.9 million that is necessary for just the Vancouver School Board, let alone the outlying regions of Vancouver, to provide the kind of education that is necessary if these youngsters in school and their parents at home are to become properly adjusted in our way of life and be able to make it on their own once they have been invited here? The people of Vancouver deserve an answer."

After a short preamble, Mr. Fernand Leblanc, Parliamentary Secretary to the Secretary of State for External Affairs, gave the answer: "I am informed that the Secretary of State is considering raising this matter with the Council of Ministers of Education, Canada; and no doubt the school boards in the major immigrant reception areas—Toronto, Montreal, Vancouver and Winnipeg—will wish to convey their views on this to their respective departments of education."[67]

The B.C. Ministry of Education was well aware of the problems facing Vancouver. In mid-1974 the school board had established a Task Force on English to look into the reading and writing programs in the Vancouver schools from kindergarten to grade twelve. As one of its projects in its search for information, the Task Force initiated a survey to determine the number of ESL students in its schools. When completed in the spring of 1975, the survey showed that almost 34 per cent of the elementary students and 21 per cent of the secondary students spoke English as a second language. By 1977, when the survey was repeated, these figures had increased to 40 per cent and 28 per cent respectively. The number of Chinese-speaking students in the Vancouver schools in 1974 was 8,042 out of a total school population of 66,667 or 12.1 per cent: by 1977 the number of Chinese-speaking students had increased to 9,454 while the school population had declined to 63,299, raising the Chinese to 14.9 per cent of the total enrolment.[68]

In 1975 with the figures it had obtained from its first survey the Vancouver School Board approached the provincial government and received a grant of some $800,000 which enabled it to expand and improve its program to some degree. The 1975 report of the Task Force also recommended that teachers with special training be assigned to ESL classes, that ESL classes be limited to twelve students, and that an ESL consultant be appointed.[69] The school board complied with these and other recommendations.

While this was going on Doug Collins was resurrecting the old cries and the old fears under headlines which read, "Clamp Down, Immigration, Before Things Get Worse"[70] and producing the old argument: "A side effect of this matter is that progress in English is being retarded even for pupils who were born here."[71]

History also repeated itself elsewhere, for once again a large number of older Chinese students aged approximately fifteen to nineteen sought admission to the secondary schools and once again no one really seemed to have the answer as to what to do with them. The new students quickly learned that graduation from high school depended upon collecting credits, and as no credits were given for attendance at an ESL class there was little motivation to take the program; it was better to sign up for a full load of academic courses and gamble on passing sufficient of them to go on to college or university. High school teachers faced two problems: the first was the pedagogical one of trying to teach a subject area and English as a second language simultaneously, a not impossible task for those who had a knowledge of linguistics and ESL methodology along with expertise in their own subject area, but very few regular teachers had received any training in ESL; the second lay in the decision teachers must make at the end of each school year whether to pass or fail a student whose knowledge of English was below average but whose potential looked good. Many were passed who would not have been had they been native speakers of English, and the problem in time moved into the colleges and universities who had to set up special sections of first year English courses for students who, in describing their school experiences, wrote sentences like these:

> Certain people needs certain help. My weaknesses may not be the other one's cases. In the high school I attended I would say that the teaching methods were quite well.
>
> To learn English, first thing is the actual contact with Canadian. To socialized means to know well, but I only know how to say but I cannot work it out.[72]

The problem, first acknowledged in 1907, of what to do with the teenage ESL student remains still largely unresolved.

After 1975 rising inflation and high unemployment in Canada put the brake on the number of immigrants entering the country and the pressure on the schools eased. But by 1978 it was obvious that the heavy wave of immigrants between 1973 and 1975 was producing a second wave as their young children, brought up in homes where English was not spoken and where frequently both parents worked, were being entered in day care centres and kindergartens. Sadly, the opportunity to create bilingual-bicultural adults out of these small children is being missed, the lessons of the past and the knowledge of the present not yet having joined forces.

Chapter 3
The Japanese

Home was the uprooting;
The shiver of separation,
Despair for our children
Fear for our future.
DOROTHY LIVESAY
Call My People Home

Hostility Builds, 1877-1920

New Westminster in the mid-1870s was endeavoring to shrug off its past and prepare for its future. In 1866 it had been rejected as the capital of the new colony, formed by the union of British Columbia and Vancouver Island, in favour of Victoria. The Canadian Pacific Railway had not yet reached the coast to link New Westminster with the rest of Canada; only a corduroy road joined it to the nearby town of Granville, later to become Vancouver. But the 500 or so inhabitants were far from idle. Confederation in 1871 had given new life to the industries of logging, fishing, and farming, and many ships arrived at this little port on the Fraser River to carry exports to distant places.

It was at New Westminster in 1877 that a young Japanese sailor, a boat builder by trade called Manzo Nagano, decided to leave his ship and try his luck in British Columbia, the first of his race to do so. He fished for salmon on the Fraser and worked as a longshoreman before taking ship back to the Orient. In 1884 he returned but by this time about a dozen Japanese had settled along the coast and were busy fishing. Nagano moved to Seattle and returned once more to Japan before finally opening a store in Victoria in 1892. He brought his wife over from Japan, and for the next thirty years engaged in various profitable activities until he went back to his native country for good in 1923. Manzo Nagano was the first of many Japanese who were to come to the young Dominion and to suffer many indignities and hardships before they were accepted as citizens and equals in the rich but intolerant province of British Columbia.

As the years passed, small settlements of Japanese were established in different parts of the province wherever jobs might be found in fishing, mining, lumbering or farming. In 1887 Gihei Kuno, a carpenter from Mio in southern Japan, got word back from his village that the prospects for fishing along the coast off Steveston were good, and a community was born which, in spite of the tumultuous events of the 1940s, has managed to keep a little of the flavour of those early Japanese pioneers. Labourers were brought in during the late 1880s to work in the mines at Cumberland where they established the "Japtowns" as they were called; others followed to dig coal at Wellington. The lumber camps and sawmills along the Fraser were glad to employ the cheap labour of the Japanese, while, as the years passed, other Japanese were attracted to the market gardens of the lower mainland or the orchards of the interior. By the close of the century Japanese could be found working on railroad construction or holding jobs as cooks and domestic servants or operating small stores.

The settlers who came were largely single men; it is thought that the first Japanese woman came to Canada in 1887, and that the first Nisei, or second-generation Japanese-Canadian, was born the following year, but reliable records of the number of Japanese arriving in British Columbia were not kept before 1900. It has been estimated that between 1896 and 1900 nearly 13,000 landed at ports in the province, but these people were by no means all immigrants: some were destined for the United States, while others stayed a short time and returned to Japan. The 1901 census gave the number of Japanese in British Columbia as 4,597 with only 141 in all the other provinces, and of these 84 were in the Yukon, caught probably by the lure of gold or the opportunities the gold rush towns offered. Ten years later the census showed 8,587 Japanese in the province and by 1921 the figure had risen to just over 15,000.[1]

The number of Japanese children resident in British Columbia in the years immediately following the turn of the century were few, but nonetheless attention was paid to their education. In 1901 the Reverend Goro Kaburagi working through the Vancouver Japanese Mission of the Methodist Church established an elementary school for Japanese children where teaching was carried on in both English and Japanese so that the newly arrived children could continue their education begun in Japan while they made the necessary adjustment to the Canadian culture and to the educational system.[2] In 1903 Tzeuzo Tanaka, a student at Cumberland School, successfully passed his midsummer examination which would allow him to proceed to high school: he was probably the first of his race to have his name recorded in one of the annual reports of the public schools of British Columbia.[3] By 1906 there was a Japanese Language School operating on Alexander Street in Vancouver and others were opening up elsewhere in the province wherever communities of Japanese were forming. For the adults there were night schools in Victoria, New Westminster, Sapperton, Steveston, Cumberland and other places to help them learn English, usually conducted by volunteers at the various church missions.

But the fear of the "yellow peril" grew over the years resulting in some strong anti-Japanese feeling in the last decade of the nineteenth century. Attempts were made to exclude the Japanese from working in the mines and on certain public projects, for while the employers were glad to use the cheap labour of the Japanese, who were often paid only a little over half what a white person received, the white working class resented this threat to their job opportunities.

The British Columbia government tried to apply to the Japanese various pieces of legislation which would restrict both their entry into the province and the kinds of occupations they could engage in once here. But its efforts were consistently negated by the federal government in Ottawa who felt bound to observe the Treaty of

Commerce and Navigation which Japan and Britain had signed in 1894 which, among other arrangements, gave the subjects of both powers the right to "enter, travel, or reside in any part of the dominions and possessions of the other contracting party." However, in 1895 the provincial legislature was successful in barring the Japanese from voting in provincial elections. Because the federal electoral list was based on the provincial electoral list, this action automatically disqualified the Japanese from voting in federal elections. They were further barred from voting in municipal elections or school board elections, or from holding any public office; they were not, however, exempt from paying taxes. But what was even more significant was that this disqualification was to apply to Japanese who were naturalized British subjects and to anyone born in Canada of Japanese origin and resident in British Columbia.

Anti-Oriental feeling continued to increase during the early years of the new century and culminated in a riot in Vancouver on September 7, 1907, when, as the result of a series of meetings called by the Asiatic Exclusion League, a wild mob tore through Chinatown and Little Tokyo, smashing windows, ransacking stores, and terrifying the inhabitants. But the Japanese showed then what they were to show later—a refusal to accept discrimination passively. Tom MacInnes, who wrote a series of anti-Oriental articles in the late 1920s, described the Japanese reaction to the rioters: "On the 7th September, 1907, a mob was led to attack the Chinese and Japanese quarters in Vancouver. The Chinese were smitten, and in a Christian spirit they turned the other cheek to the mob. But the Japanese had the cheek to do quite otherwise; and because of the most un-Christian spirit they showed, the mob was soon ready enough to leave them alone."[4]

One of the major contributing factors to the riot had been the increase in immigration. In 1905 and 1906 immigration from Japan had averaged around 2,000 a year, but in 1907 it increased to 7,601. Similar increases had occurred in immigration from China and India, and fear and hostility turned to violence. As a result of the riot, Canada and Japan entered into what was to be known as the "Gentlemen's Agreement" whereby Japan agreed to voluntarily restrict the number of passports issued to male labourers to a maximum of 400 a year. Since that time the number of Japanese immigrants to Canada has exceeded 1,000 in only 1918 and 1973.

There were still not very many Japanese children attending public schools in British Columbia. The *Vancouver Daily Province* for September 13, 1907, six days after the riot, gave the total figure for Chinese and Japanese children in the Vancouver public schools as not exceeding 150. Of the few Japanese in high school, some had worked their way up through the elementary school system, while others, new to Canada, had been admitted after taking an oral examination which covered their studies in Japan. The newspaper reported, "It was found that these Japanese were well advanced in the schools of Japan, their knowledge covering algebra, Euclid, Latin, English and every branch of study incorporated in a modern curriculum for advanced pupils."[5] Japanese students were already winning for themselves words of praise for their good manners and hard work, qualities for which they would continue to be commended throughout the harsh days which were to follow. M.E. Henderson wrote in *The Canadian Magazine* in 1908, "The Japanese mothers are particularly impressed with the importance of educating their children, and they deny themselves much to have them properly equipped for school, and it is only just to add that the Japanese children in Canadian schools, by their intelligent grasp of their studies and their courteous demeanor, do their mothers infinite credit."[6]

Some young Japanese took employment in Canadian homes as "school boys," that is, they attended school during the day and did general housework in their spare time. In this way they were able to learn English and get some education while being self-supporting. Children were expected to contribute to the meager family income in whatever way they could, such as picking peas, beans, and strawberries on the farms of the Fraser Valley, or assisting their parents in the store.

Over the course of the next twenty years the number of children in the public schools was to increase fairly dramatically, for while the "Gentlemen's Agreement" restricted the number of men who could enter Canada, nothing had been said about limiting the number of women, and there was a large population of single Japanese males interested in marriage. And so the era of the "picture brides" began, a phenomenon which was to continue into the late 1920s. Relatives in Japan would send the prospective bridegroom in British Columbia photographs of likely brides-to-be. Once the bridegroom had made his choice, his relatives in Japan would register his "marriage," thus enabling the woman to come as the groom's wife. This arrangement was perfectly acceptable under the "Gentlemen's Agreement" which allowed for the entry into Canada of returning residents and the wives of residents.

In 1927, Tom MacInnes looked back on the "picture brides" and commented as follows:

> What has since been known as the "Gentlemen's Agreement" was come to verbally, by which it was understood that not more than 400 Japanese thereafter should enter Canada yearly, and that these should be farm labourers...But, unfortunately by some twist in the intelligent heads of our Immigration Department in Ottawa it was construed that because nothing was said in the agreement about Japanese women there was no bar to their entry. What the result of such a ruling would be was pointed out to the authorities; uselessly, of course.
>
> Now twenty years have passed. There is a Japanese woman for every Japanese man who wants one and has the wherewithal. As a result there is a continuous peaceful penetration, by reason of which the Japanese are breeding themselves into possession of a rich share of the business of British Columbia.[7]

For many Canadian-born Japanese children lack of facility in the English language created problems in school. Shortly after the turn of the century the Anglican Church opened a kindergarten on Cordova Street in Vancouver, one aim of which was to teach the children English. A few years later another was started in the Kitsilano area near Granville Street and Second Avenue. In those days the streets were not paved, so a young East Indian boy was paid to carry the small children through the muddy streets to school during the wet weather. In 1910 the Women's Missionary Society of the Methodist Church opened a kindergarten on Powell Street and another on 5th Avenue in 1912. This educational work was carried on during the 1920s and 1930s and extended to teenage students during the 1940s in the interior relocation camps.

Another source of help for the young Japanese-Canadians was offered by the Vancouver Japanese Language School set up primarily to teach the Japanese language and culture to the children of immigrants. Recognizing the difficulties facing Japanese-speaking children in English language schools, it broadened its scope to include a complete education in the primary grades using Japanese as the language of instruction but offering English as a second language. Gradually more and more children enrolled directly in the public schools and after 1920 the school concentrated on teaching the Japanese language and the program in primary education was dropped. As some children still needed help in English, instruction in that subject continued but it was provided after school hours.[8] The school ceased to be in competition with the public schools after 1920 although for a short time it provided supplementary help in English.

For those who did struggle through school and who graduated from university, the doors to employment in the professions were closed in British Columbia. Miss Chitose Uchida graduated from the University of British Columbia in 1916 and took a year of teacher training at the provincial Normal School. As she could not obtain a teaching position in British Columbia, she went to Alberta where she taught in a small town until she returned to her home province a few years later to start her own school to teach English to Isseis, that is, first generation Japanese.[9]

The outbreak of the 1914-1918 war brought a slight diminuation of the hostility meted out to the Japanese population in British Columbia. The white inhabitants now turned their anger on the German and Austrian residents of the province. Many Japanese-Canadians were anxious to prove their loyalty to Canada and to join the war effort. Nearly 200 served overseas during the war and of these over a quarter lost their lives, many were wounded, and thirteen were decorated.[10] But when the more than 140 veterans of Vimy, Ypres and Valenciennes asked for the franchise in recognition of their service to their country they were refused.

The years between the wars were to see a continuation of the resentment of the white community towards the growing Japanese community, and in this atmosphere of hostility increasing numbers of Canadian-born Japanese children entered the public schools of British Columbia.

Worsening Relations, 1920-1941

The two decades between 1920-1941 saw a worsening of relations between the Japanese and white communities. The decline into the depression years and Japan's military expeditions resulted in a variety of anti-Japanese statements such as those of Tom MacInnes:

> We do not want so much Oriental sauce in our stew as to spoil it.[11]

> Both the Chinese and Japanese, however, are fine people if you just have a few of them.[12]

Headlines such as "One in Every Eight Babies Born in B.C. in 1931 Japanese"[13] helped to keep alive the fear of the "yellow peril." Few people were in favour of giving the Japanese the vote; many would have liked to see them sent back to Japan.

The *Report on Oriental Activities Within the Province*, published in 1927, asked that all immigration of Orientals be stopped forthwith, and that the industrial and commercial activities of Orientals in Canada, particularly in British Columbia, be restricted by legislation. The report also made some facts and figures available to the general public which became the topic of many articles calling for action by the provincial and federal governments. Some of these facts which pertained to the Japanese were as follows:

> That the Japanese birth-rate is 40 per 1,000 as compared with a general birth-rate of all races, except native Indians, of 18 per 1,000.
>
> That the increase in the Japanese population through the excess of births over deaths is greater by more than 2 to 1 than the immigration of people of that race.
>
> That the arrivals of Japanese women have greatly outnumbered the arrivals of men for several years past, and that at the present time two women come in for every man that enters.
>
> That of the Oriental arrivals in Canada for the past twenty years British Columbia got...over 98 per cent of the Japanese.
>
> That in three years the number of Japanese children in public schools has increased by 74 per cent, while in the same time the number of white children has increased by 6 per cent.[14]

The report gave the number of Japanese-Canadian children in the public schools of British Columbia during the 1925-1926 school year as 2,477. The numbers continued to increase to over 4,000 in the peak year of 1931-1932, after which they dipped before rising again. But one effect of the furor of the 20s was to stop "picture bride" marriages. After 1928 this practice was discontinued by agreement with Japan.

The strong anti-Japanese feeling which pervaded the province resulted in various attempts to segregate Oriental children from white children in the schools. An early attempt had been made in 1910 by the M.L.A. for Nanaimo but without success. Then in 1914, following the murder of a white woman by her Chinese houseboy who, it was reported, had been mistreated by her, the agitation increased. The anti-Orientalists in Vancouver took advantage of the situation to press their claims that Japanese children were a menace and would have a demoralizing influence on the white children and must therefore be removed from the schools. The Japanese consul protested to the school board, and in time the matter was dropped with no action taken.

In 1921 the president of the Parent-Teacher Association at Henry

Hudson school in Vancouver charged that some of the Japanese children had skin diseases and trachoma and, as they constituted a menace to white children, requested that they be excluded from the school. The charge was investigated by the superintendent of schools who checked on thirty three schools which had Japanese pupils and found that only two principals believed that Japanese students should be segregated from white pupils. The school board therefore refused to exclude or segregate the Japanese children.[15]

Not all schools resisted the call for segregation. In February, 1925, in spite of the efforts of a local minister to stop it, a segregated class of Japanese children was established in Marpole, now part of the Vancouver school district but then a separate school district, with most of the children probably being drawn from David Lloyd George school. Naturally the Japanese community spoke out against this move, and within three weeks the *Tairiku Nippo*, a Japanese language newspaper, reported the Marpole administration as saying that the segregation policy was for educational and not racial purposes, and that when the pupils showed competence in English they would be returned to regular classes.[16] Some days later the paper clarified the situation by pointing out that only twenty-five Japanese children from grades one and two were affected by the policy, but that among this group were some top-ranked pupils and that it did not seem to make sense to segregate these children because of a language problem.[17]

This type of action by school districts resulted in the establishment of a number of kindergartens in various parts of the province, but particularly in the lower mainland, their aim being to teach pre-school Japanese children English and to prepare them to enter the educational system. The kindergartens were run by church organizations connected with the Catholic, Anglican or United Churches. The workers taught the children English through games, songs and activities. The parents were most anxious for their children to do well in school, and during the depression years they did without much themselves in order that their children should be well fed and clothed. Some of the mothers bought sugar sacks which they bleached, dyed, embroidered and turned into dresses for the little girls. Some workers had difficulty finding accommodation; when it was known that they associated with Japanese, doors were closed to them.[18]

In Steveston by 1930, two-thirds of the students in the public schools were Japanese and the kindergartens were thriving. Under the headline "Quaint Japanese Pupils Overflow Steveston School" a reporter gave her sentimental picture of one kindergarten:

> Fifty little black-eyed, black-haired Japanese dolls sitting in solemn circle on the floor; fifty little voices squeaking nursery songs in unison and 100 little feet pounding the floor in steps of English folk dances—that is 1930's contribution to Steveston's school population.
>
> A block or two away you can hear the voices of the kindergarten class of the Japanese children of this community as they sing lustily their interpretation of English songs. These little mites of four and five, that look as if they should be put back on the shelf of a doll shop, attend the kindergarten conducted by the United Church. It takes every Japanese child before it can enter the public school, and it is here that they learn to play and get the first rudiments of the English language.[19]

The kindergartens were popular with the parents who saw the advantages to their children of getting an early grounding in English and in the skills they would need in school. By 1927 the Canadian-Japanese Association was able to report that almost all the Japanese children attended kindergarten, and "according to the opinions of the public school teachers, there is no difficulty in imparting education to them at the beginning, and training is given as easily as to other Canadians; and they in no way hinder or retard the progress of the other pupils."[20]

While the establishment of kindergartens was certainly one answer to the language problems which many of the Japanese children encountered in school, attempts to give the older children additional help in special classes was misunderstood. These were seen as responses to the fact that the children were Japanese rather than a response to the language, and therefore educational, problem the children were experiencing. Discussing Cumberland Elementary school, Mr. George Apps, teacher and principal there for many years, writes: "About 1925 the school adopted a segregation policy for primary grades 1, 2 and 3, much to the distress of the Consulate in Vancouver. The policy was strictly educational and not in the least racial in purpose nor I believe in influence."[21]

Many Japanese-Canadian children were, in fact, doing very well in school and proving themselves to be good scholars once they had overcome the language barrier. The *Survey of the School System*, which was begun in the early summer of 1924, reported the B.C. average retardation per pupil enrolled as 9.03 months. The score for Richmond Municipality was 15.58 months and was accounted for by the presence in the schools of many Orientals, the greater proportion of whom would have been Japanese.[22] However, the results of an I.Q. testing program caused the authors of the report to write:

> The Japanese in B.C. are probably the most intelligent of all the racial groups which make up the total Canandian population today.[23]

There was a rebuttal in the public school reports for 1927. Mr. H.H. MacKenzie, whose inspectorate covered schools in Vancouver, the Fraser Valley and Chilliwack, reported that standard intelligence tests had been given in a number of his schools. "And from these tests," he wrote, "I would boldly state that our native-born, white children are inferior to none, of whatever race, creed, or colour. The men and women who forced the barriers of the Rocky Mountains were no morons, neither are their children nor their children's children."[24]

In 1927 the Canadian-Japanese Society published the resume of an address given by Mr. J.E. Brown, Principal of Strathcona Public school in Vancouver, at the Japanese Parents' Meeting held on May 12, 1925. At that time approximately 30 per cent of the children in the school were Japanese-Canadian; within five years the figure would rise to almost 50 per cent. Mr. Brown told the parents that Japanese-Canadian children ranked first in seven out of sixteen classes and that 56 per cent of the top ten places in all sixteen classes were held by Japanese-Canadian children. "I can therefore say," he said, "that according to the examination results of the children in my school...the ability of Japanese children is above the average." While this was without doubt good news for the parents, Mr. Brown then spoke highly of the general behaviour of the children, their talents for music and their good showing as leaders in clubs and sports. He summed up his remarks with the comment, "In conclusion, I would say it cannot be denied that in my school the children of Japanese origin are above average in ability, conduct, health, companionship, and music."[25]

Three years after his address to the parents, Mr. Brown took issue with the statement in the *Survey of the School System*, which said that the Japanese in B.C. were probably the most intelligent of all the racial groups which made up the Canadian population. He pointed out that no white children had been tested; it had been assumed that the theoretical median score of 100 was correct for white children in British Columbia. Secondly, he felt that the test used, the Pintner-Patterson Scale of Performance, was weighted on the side of manual dexterity. "While few," he remarked, "would probably be disposed to doubt the general truth of this statement, viz., that the Japanese are an excellent selection of immigrants, yet it would impress many as rather a sweeping conclusion to draw on the basis of the evidence."

Mr. Brown then reported on a testing program undertaken in Strathcona school at grade five and eight levels in which comparisons were made between white and Japanese children using the National Intelligence Test and the Stanford Achievement Test, which included sections on Arithmetic Computation and Reasoning, Nature Study, History, Literature, Language, Spelling and Dictation. The results showed that Japanese children were, on the average, five months older than the white children. In all subjects which depended heavily on the English language they rated lower than the white children, but in arithmetic computation they were considerably above the white children. Mr. Brown concluded that the Japanese children were neither inferior nor superior to the white children in ability but they were under a distinct handicap in learning English. This he attributed to three facts: first, that they attended Japanese language schools and were encouraged to retain the language; second, that they spoke only Japanese at home; and third, that the difference between Japanese and English is greater than the difference between many European languages and

English.[26]

In the public school report covering 1941-1942, the median reading level of Japanese children was shown to be two and a half years lower than that of white children. "It is a current belief that Japanese children are superior students, outclassing white children," says the report. "This belief is not supported by the evidence of these test results. In two inspectorates in which there were numerous Japanese children, their scores were separated from the scores of the white children and the two tabulated below. Many of the white pupils are children of foreign language speaking parents." The median for the white children was given as 55.9 and that for the Japanese children as 49.8.[27]

The mid-1930s saw two more reports dealing, in part, with the performance of Japanese-Canadian children in B.C. schools. As part of the research for his thesis, Rigenda Sumida sent a questionnaire by mail to nine elementary schools and six high schools in the province; some were city schools, and some were located in lumbering, farming or fishing areas. Steveston, the town chosen to represent fishing, failed to respond to the questionnaire. Comments from the schools were, on the whole, very positive. Teachers in most schools felt there was little racial tension between the Japanese-Canadians and white children and that the two groups mixed well. The exception was Woodfibre, known at that time as a town split into two communities, the white and the Japanese, where racial intolerance was high. The Japanese-Canadians were seen as well-behaved students of above-average ability provided they had mastered English. A teacher at Britannia High School in Vancouver had a rather novel comment: "Japanese children eat far too much rice," he said, "causing stomach trouble particularly appendicitis."

Sumida also pointed out that the percentage of Japanese attending university was 0.8 per cent compared to a provincial average of 0.99 per cent, which he describes as "a noteworthy fact considering the economic status of the majority of their immigrant parents, who included four fishermen, two farmers, two gardeners, two coalminers, two tailors and dressmakers, two lumber-mill workers, and seven confectioners."[28] He further commented that he felt the education of the second generation Japanese-Canadians in British Columbia had been "remarkably free from discrimination evident in other fields, and as a result the public schools have proven the outstanding force of assimilation in the province."[29]

The second report was written in 1935 by a group of young Japanese-Canadians aged eighteen to twenty-four, who conducted a survey of the group of which they formed a part—the second generation Japanese in British Columbia. They raised funds for their survey by getting contributions from various Japanese individuals and organizations and by putting on a concert. They found that the total number of Canadian-born Japanese in British Columbia, who were therefore British subjects, was 10,965, of whom 135 were third generation. Most of the second generation were between zero and twenty years old; the average age for males was 11.45 years and for females 10.57 years. The oldest male of the second generation was forty-six years old and the oldest female forty years.[30]

What the report showed very clearly was that although the Japanese-Canadian children did very well in school, they were forced into low-status jobs once they sought employment. The majority of the adult second generation, 93.2 per cent of them, were concentrated in the two lowest categories of occupation, semi-skilled and unskilled, which, as the report pointed out, did not accord with their success in school. The report offered two reasons for what it called "this unproportionate spread": the first it described as a lack of initiative on the part of the second generation due to lack of encouragement by white Canadians and older Japanese; and the second, an apathetic passiveness resulting from self-consciousness caused by discrimination in other areas of endeavour. Many second generation Japanese-Canadians with specialized training, the report noted, were forced to go to Japan to obtain work.[31]

Later on, the report pointed out that only about fifteen per cent of the Japanese-Canadian second generation expressed the intention of setting up home in Japan, a figure which the authors of the report felt was "startlingly low, when we consider that the future of the Second Generation is blocked to a certain extent and that they are made to feel on many occasions by the politicians, the press and the public of British Columbia that they are foreigners in

Canada."[32]

In the April 12, 1940, issue of *The New Canadian*, a newspaper put out in English and Japanese, an article entitled "What Do Issei and Canadian Teachers Think of Nisei Moral Standards?" gave the results of a survey conducted by Tsutae Sato, principal of the Vancouver Japanese Language School. He had sent questionnaires to some first generation Japanese (Issei) and to forty-five public school teachers asking them what they thought were the good and bad character traits of the second generation Japanese (Nisei). On the positive side the Issei saw the Nisei as having high moral standards, being lively and cheerful, having a lack of class consciousness, and holding a respect for the female sex. The teachers, however, viewed the Nisei as being studious, well-behaved, careful, hard-working, attentive to detail, respectful, obedient, neat and to a limited degree, ambitious. The bad points of the Nisei, according to the Issei, were disrespect for their elders, lack of manners, lack of perseverance, no ambition, no sense of responsibility, and disobedience. The teachers responded with lack of initiative, tendency to keep their opinions to themselves, aping the defects of their Canadian friends, and emotional reserve. Statistically, however, the Issei made three times as many uncomplimentary remarks about the Nisei as they made complimentary. Teachers, on the other hand, made five times as many complimentary as uncomplimentary comments. Sato pointed out that the different opinions entertained by Issei and Canadian teachers were due to their different value systems, or, as *The New Canadian* put it: "What the Canadians criticize in the Nisei as a lack of initiative, too much reserve and backwardness, conforms to the Japanese ideals of reverence, filial piety and gentleness of spirit. On the other hand, what the Issei would condemn as disrespect, impoliteness and disobedience, the westerner would interpret as indicative of spiritedness, sociability and a co-operative spirit."[33] In a talk to the Fairview Japanese United Church Parent-Teacher Association, Mr. S. Meadows, principal of Simon Fraser Elementary school, had recommended less than a year before Mr. Sato's report was made public that the parents should try and co-operate with the teachers in the following four ways, the first one relating directly to the points made above:

1. to rid their children of extreme shyness that seriously handicaps the average Nisei;
2. to instruct their children not to speak Japanese while in the day schools;
3. not to have the children leave for summer work before the close of the school term;
4. to assist the school nurse as regards dental and medical care.[34]

The difference in language, customs and values between the white and the Japanese communities coupled with the strong anti-Japanese feeling that prevailed did not make it easy for the children to mix on equal terms in school. Sumida pointed out in 1935 that in the Fraser Valley, while the relationships between whites and Japanese were fairly good, the children of the two groups did not associate very much with each other. The reason given in this case, however, was that the Japanese parents felt that the white children might have a bad effect on the morals of their children, an argument used so often in the past by white parents to keep the two groups apart.[35]

The Vancouver Province of December 27, 1937, ran a long article under the headlines "Big Part in B.C.'s School Life is Played by Japanese Group—Students Have Excellent Standing from Scholastic and Disciplinary Views." The article said that the Japanese students in the public and high schools of Vancouver and the Fraser Valley were distinct for three reasons:

First: Their teachers testify that they are excellent students both from a scholastic and disciplinary standpoint.
Second: Their parents evidence a remarkable interest and enthusiasm in education.
Third: In many instances Japanese school children work after regular school hours in their own Japanese language classes.[36]

But in spite of all the laudatory comments made by teachers and others about the scholastic ability and self-control of the children, the second generation Japanese-Canadians were, of course, caught between two worlds, the world of their Japanese parents and their Japanese language and culture, and the world of their Canadian school with its English language and its British-American culture. But the children had a further problem. Although they were Canadian-born, they would not as adults have the right to the franchise which had been denied them back in 1895. And yet they must sit in school and learn about Canadian citizenship and democracy. In 1925 Putman and Weir, in their *Survey of the School System*, had said,

> The development of a united and intelligent Canadian citizenship actuated by the highest British ideals of justice, tolerance, and fair play should be accepted without question as a fundamental aim of the provincial school system. Such an aim has stood the test of time and its application in the daily lives of the British people has enhanced the good name of the British Empire. The moral and patriotic aim is undoubtedly more important, if less measurable, than the other objectives of instruction discussed in this and the following section of the present chapter. It is both cultural and practical, traditional and modern, the keynote of past national progress and the foundation for future advancement.[37]

In 1936, S. Ichiye Hayakawa, later to become well-known for his handling of the troubles at San Francisco State College, described the aims of the young people who conducted the survey on the second generation Japanese as being to "objectively demonstrate their fitness for franchise rights by comparing their own intellectual and social standards with those of other immigrant groups and with those of the general Anglo-Saxon population. By so doing, it is their earnest hope they will be able to make an appeal which British fair play will not be able to deny."[38]

He then went on to talk about the role of the school in the life of the young Japanese-Canadian:

> The Japanese-Canadian who is born in Canada, and who accepts with more than the usual school-boy's docility the patriotic and idealistic sentiments of his Canadian teachers,

(since accepting some kind of idealistic program such as "the kingly way", "the seven-fold path", etc., etc., is almost a racial habit), seems to be a curiously loyal Canadian. In British Columbia he occasionally feels cynical about the people who glory in democratic institutions at the same time as they with-hold from him those common privileges which enable a society to call itself democratic; nevertheless, he accepts with joy any chance that offers of conducting himself as a political being in the political system in which he lives. He enjoys testifying in courts; he loves to be elected to committees and secretaryships and chairmanships in church clubs and high school classes; one suspects that he would even serve on juries, if he were permitted to do so, with conscious dignity and a sense of responsibility. The young Japanese-Canadian, denied the rights of citizenship in all but name, is nevertheless (or, perhaps, therefore) a fervent believer in representative government, parliamentary procedure, and individual rights. Moreover, he is, like other believers in democracy, an optimist. He believes that the society which professes such ideals will ultimately practice them. He therefore doggedly prepares himself for citizenship in Canada as a Canadian.

If this analysis is correct, the Japanese-Canadian has to a great extent his Canadian school teachers and professors to thank for his present admirable attitude. It is they who, for better or for worse, inculcate such political ideals into him, and it is also they who have encouraged him to persevere in those ideals. (For all that is said against the teaching profession, the school teachers are the ones who do the real work in the matter of spreading and perpetuating the ideals of a society among its members.) Consequently, whenever political parties bring misery to the young Japanese-Canadian by pointing him out as the little yellow rat that is gnawing out the vitals of provincial prosperity, it is teacher who reassures him and comforts him, and tells him that democracy *is* democracy, or will be. If, then, Robert Hamaguchi or Lillian Suzuki make an appeal to British fair-play in the matter of a franchise, the British Columbia tax-payer may feel that he has got value for the money he has spent on having Canadian ideals taught to the children of immigrants, however much he may be embarrassed by the consequences.[39]

The children were well aware of the discrimination against their race as this excerpt from a grade 6 essay, written in 1921, clearly shows:

> We Japanese are now facing discrimination. How can we avoid it? We should not do what white people do not like. Before going to school we should wash our hands and faces well. And we should make sure that our necks and ears are always clean. If we eat tsukemono too much we will be disliked for our bad breath. It is also very bad to go out in dirty clothes. We should wear clean clothes but not too fancy. In the school playground it is better to play with white children. This way we can also learn English. In school we should listen to our teachers carefully and get higher marks than white children. Then white children and teachers will like us.[40]

Almost twenty years later a high school student wrote:

> Despite the fact that we have been born and educated in Canada, we are aliens in the land of our birth because we are denied the right to vote. We have been trained to become Canadian citizens and yet citizenship is refused to us. Why does British Columbia hesitate to do what many of the other provinces have done?
>
> . . . It is the duty of the second generation and those to follow to educate themselves. In the school of life we educate ourselves by experiences. The "Niseis' " cry is, "What can we do with an education which we cannot put to its best use? In the business world our hopes and ambitions are cruelly shattered by Canada's refusal to accept us.[41]

While close friendships often grew between white and Japanese-Canadian children during their years together in school, graduation day usually brought an end to these associations. The white student entered the larger world of further education or employment in any one of a variety of occupations; the Japanese-Canadian was frequently forced to work only with other Japanese and to move in a restricted world hedged around with invisible barriers.

Dr. S.I. Hayakawa, who completed his B.A. at the University of Manitoba and his M.A. at McGill, advocated moving out of B.C. "Your belief that it is necessary to get out of B.C.," he wrote in a letter to Mr. Shinobu Higashi of the New Canadian Society, "is one that I strongly share. I would go as far as to say that the kids ought to get out while they are still twelve or thirteen if they can. Of course, few can—but it would be fine if they could, since it is from high school age and on that one really begins to develop the personal maladjustments that social discrimination can cause."[42]

The voices of the teachers were slow in coming and muted. In 1936 *The B.C. Teacher*, the official journal of the B.C. Teachers' Federation, published an article entitled "Subjects—But Not Citizens." This was followed two years later by an editorial, "Isn't It About Time That We Spoke Up?", which stimulated a letter to the editor from Dr. J. R. Sanderson, who said in part: "Fact number one is that there is a Canadian-born Japanese population in British Columbia. Fact number two is that they are going to remain here. What then shall we do about it? We can treat them with friendliness as fellow-Canadians, or we can ostracize them as undesirables. The latter policy, as you point out, is dangerous as well as un-christian. Problems are *made*, not solved that way."[43] But the teachers said little more until the war with Japan started and by then it was too late.

1938 saw further attempts to put pressure on the Japanese through demands for some form of minimum school tax for each child registered. At a meeting of the Richmond School Board, whose boundaries encompassed Steveston, a fishing village with a large Japanese population, the Chairman of the Board, Arthur Laing, informed the audience that of the 1,706 children attending school, 670 were Japanese. Laing went on to state that while the cost of educating a child in Richmond was $30.52 a year, the Japanese parents had contributed only $5.00 a year per child on an average. He suggested that the municipal council should pass a minimum school tax by-law of perhaps $30.00 per child. Discussion then centred around whether the Japanese should be permitted to use the Steveston school building after school to teach Japanese to their children. Mr. Laing recalled that several years ago when the school was built, the Japanese had contributed $20,000 to its construction and the municipality only $7,000; under these circumstances it hardly seemed fair to deny them use of the school.[44]

Halford Wilson then took up the question of school taxes in his "Brief on the Oriental Situation in British Columbia in the year 1938." In a section of the brief entitled "Education Problems Occasioned by Oriental Population" he reminded his readers that education was financed from two sources: land taxation at the local level and provincial aid from consolidated revenue funds. Therefore if tax revenue from Oriental parents at the local level was low, these children became a tax drain on the entire white population of the province.

He quoted figures to show that in Richmond, where whites constituted 66.3 per cent of the total population they paid 91.5 per cent of the school taxes; whereas the Japanese, who constituted 33.7 per cent of the population, paid only 8.5 per cent of the school taxes. He made similar comparisons for Maple Ridge and Vancouver. To strengthen his argument he extrapolated from the birth rate figures and projected that by 1968 almost one-third of the enrolment in Vancouver schools would be Japanese, but he apparently did not take into account the cessation of the "picture bride" era which, coupled with the fact that the brides of the twenties were becoming the matrons of the late thirties, would mean a considerable decline in the birth rate for Japanese-Canadians until the second generation reached child bearing age.

Wilson was particularly concerned that 27 Japanese students were enrolled in three Vancouver schools in one of the best residential districts: Kerrisdale Elementary, Point Grey Junior High and Magee High. He said, "These are not all the Orientals in this school, but we make this point to demonstrate the conditions under which this Japanese population lives, while enjoying the best educational facilities of the City at the expense of the white population. All these children referred to above live in the area known as the Celtic Cannery area, at the foot of Blenheim Street, and we attach a photograph of the residences they occupy.''[45]

It was hardly surprising that the Japanese community was not in a position to pay its full share of school taxes considering that it was not allowed a full share of the provincial economy. As soon as the Japanese became established in an industry, steps were taken to close off the industry to them or at least to reduce their involvement to a token. The number of fishing licences issued to Japanese fishermen during the two decades between the wars was cut very considerably; in 1934 the B.C. Board of Industrial Relations gave the sawmill industry the right to pay one-quarter of its workers only 25 cents an hour, 10 cents below the standard wage of 35 cents an hour, and although it was not stated, it was generally understood that the low rate would go to Japanese workers; when the Japanese moved onto the land as small holders, efforts were made to prevent Orientals from buying land; some Japanese tried running small businesses, often serving members of their own community, but trading licences were harder to come by for the Japanese than the whites; Japanese had not, by law, been employed on public work projects for many years.

Halford Wilson continued his anti-Japanese attacks into 1940, causing *The New Canadian* to retort: ''Apparently his only method of ensuring that Oriental parents pay more school taxes is to campaign for the right to rob them of their legitimate right to earn a daily living.''[46] And a week later, ''If the standard of living for Japanese is lower per capita, does Mr. Wilson believe that it is low from personal choice? Does he believe that the average Japanese family would prefer living in its tenement to living, say for instance, in Mr. Wilson's own comfortable home? Perhaps in his infinite wisdom he conceives of the Japanese deliberately accepting lower incomes so that they might not have to pay their proportionate share of the cost of government.''[47]

Halford Wilson also took issue with the Japanese language schools which he described as ''a menace to Canadian national life, and an indication of an unwillingness to assist in the assimilation of these nationals into our citizenship.''[48] Japanese language schools had been part of the way of life of the Japanese community for many years. One of the earliest had begun in 1906 on Alexander Street in Vancouver, and others had sprung up all over the province wherever groups of Japanese had settled. The annual report of the Vancouver City Schools for 1926 expressed the board's gratitude to the principals of the Japanese schools who had co-operated by being present when Japanese children were undergoing physical examinations and by explaining to the parents the recommendations which were made. The report pointed out that there had been a marked increased in the treatments received for physical defects among the Japanese since this arrangement had begun.[49]

By 1935 there were about forty language schools with an enrolment of over 3,000 students in the province.[50] One of the best-known was the Vancouver Japanese Language School, the largest in the province, administered for many years by Tsutae Sato, an Issei. In 1939 when charges continued that the Japanese language schools were anti-Canadian, Sato stated that while he was accused of teaching his students "things that are inimical to Canadian thoughts and ideals," in fact he strove for one goal "that the Nisei might become good Canadian citizens, that his citizenship will be a broad and tolerant one, one that has breadth and vision, a certain cosmopolitanism." Sato felt that in teaching Japanese to the Nisei he was leaving them with a little of the cultural heritage of their parents and ancestors.[51]

The New Canadian attempted to downplay the charges. "Whether the Japanese Language School is or is not the hot-bed of what has been crudely termed 'Mikadoism' is no longer the issue at stake. It is now a foregone conclusion among sociologists and educators that these schools provide only a fundamental knowledge of reading, writing and composition in the Japanese language and that the chief medium of expression of the Canadian-born Japanese is the English language."[52]

The Japanese Educational Society, which represented 25 Japanese language schools was, according to a report in the November 29, 1940, issue of *The New Canadian,* "unanimous in upholding the strictest adherence to the accepted program of study, designed to inculcate true Canadian citizenship in the pupils." The Society also agreed to "devise ways and means of securing textbooks in line with the life and interests of the pupils themselves and the Canadian scene."[53]

In mid-December, 1940, the Department of Education, through

an amendment to the Public Schools Act, acquired the right to open and close private language schools and to supervise and inspect them. "The measure is designed to guard against possible subversive teaching in language schools," said *The New Canadian*.[54] But charges continued to be laid against the schools: first, by Halford Wilson, who contended that the schools were subsidized by the Japanese government and that the curriculum used was the same as that set by the Japanese educational department,[55] and, secondly, by Dr. H. White, Director of School Health Services, who reported that health workers felt that the children attending the language schools suffered from overstrain caused by the additional work imposed on them. *The New Canadian* dismissed Halford Wilson's charges by saying that "this journal has neither the space nor the patience to re-emphasize the already proven falsity of his charges," but it took seriously the health question raised by Dr. White. "If Dr. White's conclusions were to be the sole basis for a decision on the school issue, there would undoubtedly be good reason for seeking to have these classes abolished." Then the paper pointed out that the problem "embraces far more than only a consideration of the effect of longer hours of study upon the health of children":

> Ninety-nine per cent of Canadian-born Japanese, of an age sufficient to judge, will declare from their own personal experience that a knowledge of the Japanese language is essential for effective and wholesome relationships which in the past have been largely responsible for the most enviably-low rate of juvenile delinquency in the city. And these are the relationships which are in need of even further broadening and deepening, if increasingly grave social problems within the family and community are to be met successfully.
>
> The same ninety-nine per cent will declare from that same personal experience that a knowledge of Japanese language is practically an indispensable asset in seeking employment. With discrimination both in law and in fact imposing very real restrictions upon vocational outlets, it is a recognized and regrettable fact that the vast majority of Canadian-born

> Japanese whatever their talents and education, can find work only from Japanese-speaking buying public.
>
> The simple fact of the matter is that if the people meet with a strain through the study of the Japanese language, it is an unavoidable strain, and is but a part of the whole burden which members of any immigrant group seeking to assimilate into an adopted country must face, endure and overcome. There is no immigrant group which wholly escapes from the conflict between an old and new cultural background, between a new and older group of people. In the case of Oriental immigrants, this universal conflict is simply deepened on the one hand by very diverse cultural heritages, and on the other by intense human prejudice directed against a new people racially very different from the old.[56]

But for some of the children, attendance at a Japanese language school served to emphasize further the dilemma they were caught in the pull of two, as yet, incompatible cultures:

> Japanese school as I experienced it in a small community, if it left any sort of influence on me, was ironically, one which made me more staunchly Canadian than before attendance at that worthy institution. Not that Japanese school forcibly crammed "yamato damashi" down my unwilling throat, or eulogized the glories of Japan to the detriment of my beloved Canada, but simply because I was born Canadian, lived Canadian, and thought Canadian that the learning of anything as alien as Japanese was a necessary duty from which I escaped at every opportunity.[57]

But on that fateful day in early December, 1941, all 59 Japanese language schools were closed by order of the federal government. The effect of the Japanese attack on Pearl Harbour was to uproot from their homes over 20,000 people of Japanese ancestry, 13,300 of whom were Canadian-born, and to change the whole course of history for British Columbia and its Japanese people.

The War Years and After

From the commencement of hostilities in September, 1939, the Japanese-Canadian community sought to prove its loyalty both by its contributions to war bonds and through the efforts of a number of Nisei to join the forces. Their money was accepted but the offers to serve were, except in a very few cases, declined. The following interchange between two well-known politicians of the day was reported in *The New Canadian.*

> R.L. Maitland, Conservative leader, said he was opposed to Orientals having the vote even if they were registered as British subjects.
>
> "But you are willing to let them fight for you," Harold Winch, C.C.F. leader said.
>
> "That is all very well," Mr. Maitland replied, "but the principle of allowing Orientals to vote is wrong. They do not understand Canadian government sufficiently to take part in our legislation."
>
> "They understand it sufficiently to want to fight for it," retorted Mr. Winch.[58]

School children also demonstrated their loyalty. On June 1, 1940, Strathcona School in Vancouver's Chinatown put on a "Pageant of Empire" when "the might and glory of the British Empire was presented in dramatic form and unravelled before the wondering eyes of the students. From the days of Alfred the Great to the present crisis the history of England was portrayed by students of all colours."[59] The parts of Alfred the Great, James Wolfe, and the Duke of Wellington were all played by Japanese-Canadian children, as was—ironically—"Democracy."

In late February, 1942, over two months after the Japanese attack on Pearl Harbour, the federal government anounced that all people of Japanese origin must be evacuated from a 100-mile protected area along the B.C. coast, and on March 4, the B.C. Security Commission was established to plan, supervise and direct the evacuation, though whether the term "evacuation" should be used to describe what was in fact an expulsion is open to question. By mid-March the first group of Japanese-Canadians to be evacuated was taken to Hastings Park Exhibition Grounds in Vancouver which served as the collection centre. From there the evacuees were taken to camps in the interior.

Joy Kogawa, a child at the time of the evacuation, later expressed her feelings in the following poem:

What Do I Remember of the Evacuation

What do I remember of the evacuation?
I remember my father telling Tim and me
About the mountains and the train
And the excitement of going on a trip.
What do I remember of the evacuation?
I remember my mother wrapping
A blanket around me and my
Pretending to fall asleep so she would be happy
Though I was so excited I couldn't sleep
(I hear there were people herded
Into the Hastings Park like cattle.
Families were made to move in two hours
Abandoning everything, leaving pets
And possessions at gun point.
I hear families were broken up
Men were forced to work. I heard
It whispered late at night
That there was suffering) and
I missed my dolls.

What do I remember of the evacuation?
I remember Miss Foster and Miss Tucker
Who still live in Vancouver
And who did what they could
And loved the children and who gave me
A puzzle to play with on the train.
And I remember the mountains and I was
Six years old and I swear I saw a giant
Gulliver of Gulliver's Travels scanning the horizon
And when I told my mother she believed it too

And I remember how careful my parents were
Not to bruise us with bitterness
And I remember the puzzle of Lorraine Life
Who said "Don't insult me" when I
Proudly wrote my name in Japanese
And Tim flew the Union Jack
When the war was over but Lorraine
And her friends spat on us anyway
And I prayed to the God who loves
All the children in his sight
That I might be white.[60]

Miss Margaret Foster and Miss Grace Tucker, members of the Anglican Church of Canada, had worked with Japanese-Canadian kindergarten children for many years, teaching them English and preparing them for public school. They went with the children and their families to the relocation camps in the interior of British Columbia. For many children the presence of two beloved teachers from the happier days of the past helped to ease the trauma of the present.

The evacuation continued over the next nine months and was not completed until October, nearly eleven months after the attack on Pearl Harbour, so that when the public schools opened in September, 1942, there were still some Japanese-Canadian children who had not been moved. But the schools were closed to them. *The Vancouver Province*, under the headline "City's Strangest 'First Day'—Hundreds of Jap Children Turned Away From Schools," reported as follows:

> Vancouver children returned to school today after summer holidays and it was the strangest "first day of school" ever seen here.
>
> ...In most schools teachers took on the task of telling Japanese boys and girls that they were not wanted at schools this year. Nearly 1,000 Japanese youngsters are still in the city and most of them turned up for school opening.
>
> At Strathcona School, where more than 600 Japanese were students last year, teachers were busy singling out the Japanese

children as they entered the school and informing them that they could not be admitted.

The older children generally understood the reason they could not attend school, but the youngest tots just stared dumbly when their last year's teacher told them to return home.

"We are not taking Japanese youngsters because we have been assured they will all be evacuated from Vancouver by the end of October at the latest," declared H.N. MacCorkindale, Superintendent of Schools.

"We are not refusing them the right to attend school because of their Japanese racial origin but because they will only be in the city a short time. If any other group of children, regardless of their racial origin, planned to attend school for only a month or six weeks, we would advise them to continue their summer holidays for that time.

"If we enrolled the 1,000 Japanese who are here, it would mean employing an additional 25 teachers for a month and then firing them. That would be highly impractical."

At Strathcona School, which last year was attended by more than 600 Japanese, there were empty classrooms for the first time in years.

"It would cut your heart to see these Japanese youngsters turned away," declared a male teacher at Strathcona. "They are darned nice students. They are real little sportsmen. It hurts me to have to send them home. I am sure many of them do not understand the real reason we are not taking them and feel they are being persecuted. The Japanese going through this school are real Canadian citizens."[61]

Not all parents took the superintendent's advice to let their children continue their summer holidays until they were evacuated. Education was far too important to be dropped, and who knew when the schools in the relocation camps would start? Emergency classes were organized at the Japanese United Church on Powell Street, but one mother enrolled her eight year old daughter in a nearby Catholic private school. Miho had been to the Buddhist Temple with her father and had attended an Anglican kindergarten, but when it came time for her to kneel before the statue of the Virgin Mary she was at a loss to know what to say. The only Christian prayer she knew was "Our Father"—hardly appropriate for a lady! So she counted quietly up to 300 and returned to her seat. The next day she counted up to 500, and feeling that this too was inadequate, asked Sister Gloria what she was supposed to say. Sister Gloria taught her the "Hail, Mary" and in an effort to help Miho understand a little of the Catholic religion told her that she was married, that, indeed, all the sisters were married, and to the same Person—God—a statement which thoroughly shocked Miho who saw it as an example of polygamy in the extreme!

The evacuation was devastating to some schools. In Vancouver, Japanese-Canadian children numbered 2,216 or 5.9 per cent of the total school population,[62] but in parts of the province the percentage was far higher. Mr. George Apps, teacher and supervising principal at Cumberland Elementary School on Vancouver Island for many years, recalled that the school lost one-third of its population when the Japanese left, ultimately reducing the school from thirteen classrooms to seven. Mr. Apps has his own memories of the evacuation:

> The Cumberland Japanese were first sent to a concentration camp in Hastings Park. On our way to Mission, Mrs. Apps and I went to the park gates to visit them. The guard refused us permission. When some of the children saw us outside the gates such a crowd pressed against the gates that the guard called us in to say our farewells inside.
>
> A few years ago I visited Toronto, so I wrote to a couple of ex-pupils and phoned one after arrival. He suggested we meet some of them at a Sunday tea at the Japanese Canadian Cultural Institute which they had organized at Don Mills. We expected to meet perhaps half a dozen. We found they had contacted as many as possible in the surrounding area and over forty were gathered to what turned out to be a banquet. A wonderful evening was spent answering questions about former teachers and classmates.[63]

A school of sorts was set up in one of the buildings in the Exhibition Grounds. The United and Anglican churches opened a kindergarten; the room allotted to them was large, cold and bare, and the sound reverberated like thunder. Young Japanese-Canadians, themselves either just out of school or still in school tried, with totally inadequate supplies, to work with the other children. The school population was naturally in a state of constant flux as families were moved to the interior and others took their place. Between May and September, 1942, there were usually around 700 to 800 students receiving instruction.[64]

Those families which elected not to move to other parts of Canada were housed in camps at Greenwood, Kaslo, Slocan Valley, New Denver, Sandon, Tashme and one or two other places. At one time these camps contained over 12,000 men, women and children, a large percentage of whom were Canadian citizens by birth. Ghost towns became alive again. Kaslo, which had dropped from a population of around 6,000 at the turn of the century to 500 whites, received nearly 1,000 Japanese-Canadians. Sandon, with a very small population took in over 700 evacuees, while the Slocan area, with 350 whites, took in nearly 5,000.[65]

Wooden cabins were erected, often requiring two families to share the same kitchen; small hospitals were built, and barns or other buildings were transformed into schools. A three-page school newspaper called "The Sandon Spotlight" contained the following description: "Our little gray schoolhouse is constructed over a carpenter shop. We study the whole day through the humming of the electric saw, the pounding of the hammer and the running waters of the toilet and the tap. Students in grade one, two and six study at the former City Hall, while the rest of the grades attend the gray brick schoolhouse."[66] People used to the rain of the coast had to learn to cope with the snow and frost of the mountain areas. To add further to the general unhappiness and worry, some husbands had been separated from their wives and children and were in road camps elsewhere in British Columbia or as far away as Ontario.

Families were expected to support themselves either by obtaining employment or from their own resources. For those who were in need, the B.C. Security Commission provided some income for food and clothing. The rates for maintenance were slightly higher than those provided by the provincial government, but not as high as those provided to whites in Vancouver which gave higher relief rates to whites than to Orientals.

Because the families had been ordered out of the protected area by the federal government, the B.C. provincial government decided that the senior government must take the responsibility for the education of the children, along with the responsibility for housing, health and other matters. The B.C. Department of Education consequently refused to provide teachers or facilities for the education of the many Japanese-Canadian children in the camps in the interior, estimated to be as high as 5,500.[67] For some children this meant that there was no school ready for them when they reached camp and the summer holidays had to continue into the fall. The official opening of the school at Sandon did not take place until November, 1942.[68] In mid-January, 1943, *The New Canadian* reported that the opening of the school program at Tashme had been delayed as the heating equipment had not yet been installed in the classrooms,[69] but it was April before the school buildings in the Bay Farm—Slocan City—Lemon Creek areas were ready for occupation.[70] During these weeks of enforced vacation one mother arranged for a young university student to tutor her daughter in the evenings after he had finished work. She scrupulously saved the one candle allowed to the family each day, so that on the evenings when he came she could burn ten candles to provide a decent light by which teacher and student could study.

In some parts of the province elementary school children were allowed to attend local schools as fee paying students, but the provincial government would like to have prevented them from doing this. The Hon. H.G.T. Perry, Minister of Education, announced his intention of introducing legislation which would make it legal for school districts to bar Japanese children from B.C. schools, a move which Harold Winch, C.C.F. Opposition Leader, referred to as "a definitely retrograde and uncivilized step, contrary to the high ideals for which we are supposed to be fighting."[71] The editorial writer of *The Vancouver Daily Province* felt that it was quite in order to expect the federal government to pay the cost of the education of the children while they were in the relocation camps, but he found it difficult to understand why Mr. Perry thought it necessary to outlaw Japanese children from the public schools of British Columbia. He went on: "This would be to visit upon innocent children born here, all the consequences of the war in the infammation of public sentiment against their race and of all the explosive implications of the unresolved Oriental problems in Canada and especially in British Columbia."[72] The legislation was never passed.

Two Japanese-Canadian certificated teachers, Miss H. Hyodo and Miss T. Hidaka, were put in charge of the B.C. Security Commission schools which served about 3,000 children in grades 1 to 8. Since it had been extremely difficult for Japanese-Canadians to obtain teaching posts once they had graduated from Normal School, few had tried to enter the profession, and of those who had, some had gone to Japan and others had become teachers in the Japanese Language Schools. (Miss Hyodo, after completing her teacher training some years before the war, had applied for a job at Richmond Public School which had been experiencing problems with its fairly large population of Japanese-Canadian children, a number of whom did not speak English. The trustees hired Miss Hyodo on condition that she taught only Japanese children.[73]) The Hon. H.G.T. Perry, Minister of Education, made it clear that there would be no help coming from his Ministry by announcing in mid-August, 1942, that "white teachers will not be provided to instruct Japanese students in British Columbia so long as the present shortage of teachers exists in the province."[74] Intensive teacher training programs for young untrained Nisei, largely girls, who would, from now on do much of the teaching, were therefore held in July, 1942, and for the following three summers. In an address to these young teachers at the 1943 summer school, Mr. H. W. Pammett of the federal Department of Labour is reported to have said, surely with some irony:

> You teachers have done and are doing a big job in educating nearly 3,000 children, two-thirds of all the Japanese children in Canada.
>
> Make it your chief goal in all your teaching, to lead your

> pupils to think and talk and act as Canadians. If you succeed in this, you and they will win back all the privileges of Canadian citizenship which this war has curtailed.[75]

The Commission did not provide instruction at the high school level; this was left to the churches who helped approximately 1,000 students to enrol in provincial correspondence courses and to study under supervision. In a few instances high school students were permitted to attend local schools. In addition, the various Christian churches organized and ran kindergartens for pre-school children.

A Royal Commission set up to enquire into the conditions in the relocation camps reported in Janauary, 1944, that the natural lighting in the improvised classrooms was inadequate and that there was some overcrowding.[76] Six months later, in August, 1944, a report of the Department of Labour made the following comments on the Commission schools:

> The fundamental weakness of the Commission schools is the lack of association of these Japanese-Canadian children with Canadian children of British and other racial origins. A secondary defect is the home influence of parents who, in many cases, speak little English, but this is a defect shared with children of a number of other foreign minorities in Canada. Its retarding effect, however, is magnified by lack of association with British Canadian children. Every effort is being made by Occidental staff and teachers alike, nevertheless, to encourage these children to develop upon thoroughly Canadian standards.[77]

The question of the quality of the education being received by the Japanese-Canadian children was publicly aired in mid-1943 when the Minister of Education, H.G.T. Perry, was reported as saying that the Japanese children had opportunities in education similar to the almost 5,000 white children in the province who were taking the province's correspondence courses, and that as the Japanese had arranged for competent instructors from amongst their own university graduates to assist and supervise the education of the children, it seemed that the Japanese children had additional advantages not enjoyed by white children. Mr. Perry's comments were written up in the *Vancouver Daily Province*, under the headline, "Japs' Chances for Education Better Than Whites."[78]

It was hardly to be expected that the spokesmen for the Japanese community would remain silent, and a week later the following editorial, reprinted here in its totality, appeared in *The New Canadian*:

We are Bewildered

When we had finished reading the *Daily Province* report, "Japs' Chances for Education Better Than B.C. Whites," as explained by the Hon. G.T. Perry, provincial minister of education, we wondered whether to take it as a high compliment to our schools, or to give one of those things commonly known as the "horse laugh."

We do not know if Mr. Perry stated the whole of the report which explained to great lengths, the "advantages enjoyed" by Nisei students in the interior towns. It was a pleasant surprise for us for we did not know we even had an "advantage." The minister, we presume, stated that Japanese children have all the advantages of the B.C. correspondence courses but also "competent instructors from among their young men and women who have graduated from Canadian universities, to assist and supervise the education. Thus, the Japanese children . . . have the advantage not enjoyed by white students of the same courses . . . they have personal direction and instruction."

Mr. Perry, we presume again, also explained carefully that "Japanese students may subscribe for high school correspondence courses and pay for them in the same way that white children are doing." Here again, exultantly trumps the report, they (the Nisei) have the advantage over the white children, for they receive personal direction from university graduates of their own race.

After some research and thinking, we believe that the above facts are slightly in error. We hope that the public is acquainted with the fact that Lemon Creek teachers, according to our latest report from that centre, have no desk and there are only eight classrooms in that school with blackboards, six using tiny bulletin boards and six with nothing at all. We also hope that some inkling of the struggle and long hours put in by Nisei teachers on a low basic wage, who on the contrary from being university trained, are 99 per cent just out of high school is known.

We sincerely trust that some time in the future it will be most carefully explained to newspaper reporters that "the personal direction from university graduates of their own race," which the high school correspondence students may enjoy, are from young men and women, who, after a full day of work, teach and instruct and prepare lessons far into the night. . .*at no salary at all.*

As far as we have been able to ascertain, Japanese students do not pay the same amount for correspondence courses as the white students are doing. . . they pay more, the total running up to a large sum. And in most cases, we understand, for white children in out-of-way places, the course is entirely free except for a registration fee of two dollars. The fact that Japanese parents are dipping into their slender savings to pay a monthly fee for their children who are lucky enough to attend local schools, we hope is also known.

Perhaps it would be better if we did give a loud laugh, not of bitterness, not of anger but one of sheer wonder how and why such statements appear in the paper. Perhaps, we are totally in error in our facts, or we have not the right slant on this subject. It seems that since the Nisei students are not getting the same educational facilities as thousands of other B.C. students, the good minister has kindly pointed out that anyway, the evacuee children are better off than 1400 elementary students enrolled at the High School Correspondence School in Victoria. As one evacuee put it, someone seems to be trying to make two plus two equal five.[79]

At a meeting in mid-July, 1943, of the Kaslo Community Council, Mr. H. T. Pammett, a representative of the Deputy Minister of Labour, when asked why Nisei on the prairies could go to regular schools while those in the interior towns had special schools and untrained teachers, explained that it was due to the shortage of trained teachers in B.C. and the hostility of the B.C. government. Mr. Pammett pointed out that it was not the intention of the government to force people out of the towns, but it was evident that if parents were really anxious to secure the best possible education for their children they should seek it east of the Rockies.[80]

One community found the presence of the Japanese-Canadian children beneficial according to the local high school principal who, after referring to "our present guests, the Canadian-born Nisei," wrote in the school paper, "They have made possible a better education for the present residents of Greenwood; without them we would have no high and very little elementary school. They are giving this real gift—and paying for it—courteously and quietly. We will ever be grateful."[81]

For the children life was very different from what it had been and many adjustments had to be made. The younger children found a greater freedom in the camps and enjoyed the countryside, but for some of the older ones the move to the interior was traumatic; everything they had known had been ripped from them, and their future was in grave doubt. One wrote:

> With the mocking realization that our citizenship was not to be acknowledged, came the summons to evacuate. To me, as to others, it meant tearing myself away from the cheerful city, and only home I'd ever known...It meant turning my back on an accustomed life, even though a suddenly rather hostile one because of my race, to go where? Some God-forsaken hole away up in the mountains. I was bitter.

She went on to describe the futile existence at Tashme in the early days—chopping wood and hauling water—until, through the United Church missionaries, she was able to pick up her education by correspondence courses and gradually the pain eased:

> Since coming to Tashme the feeling of bitterness and hurt, that I first felt, has gradually grown dim, and I hope by now is

> completely erased. Being able to walk about without the diffident fear of someone looking at me with disdain, "Another dirty Jap," has helped.[82]

For the older students school meant more than just reading, writing and arithmetic. It was the place where fundamental questions regarding life, liberty and the future could be asked. For the parents it offered opportunities to get involved in a variety of activities such as sports, plays, crafts, parent-teacher meetings, and other social occasions. Girl Guide companies and Boy Scout troops were organized in some centres to provide out-of-school programs.

By 1944 some members of the British Columbia Teachers' Federation were showing real concern regarding the treatment by the provincial government of the Japanese-Canadian children. The Central Mainland District Council prepared three resolutions which it submitted to the 1945 Annual General Meeting of the Federation. One hit at what it called "the unfair discrimination in the matter of Correspondence School fees," accusing the Department of Education of charging considerably lower fees for all the other children in the province than it charged Japanese students, and pointing out that this was not compatible with the ideals of democracy. It must be remembered that the cost of these fees was born by the parents rather than by the B.C. Security Commission.

A second resolution got to the heart of the matter with its second "whereas":

> Whereas Japanese students resident in some school districts are being discriminated against in the matter of school fees; and
>
> Whereas just treatment to minority groups is one of the boasts of democracy;
>
> Be it resolved that Japanese students be accorded the same treatment as all other British Columbia children in the matter of school fees.

The third resolution called for the Department of Education to "assume its full responsibility...for the education of Japanese students now debarred from some schools or obliged to pay discriminatory fees in others."[83]

The end of the war did not bring an end to the harsh treatment of the Japanese-Canadians who were given the alternatives—either disperse across Canada or be repatriated to Japan. Some left the camps to join friends or relatives in eastern Canada, but by November 21, 1945, 10,347 had made "voluntary" requests for repatriation. Of these, one-third were children born in Canada, while three-quarters were Canadian citizens.

But many Canadians were sickened by the treatment accorded the Japanese-Canadians and voices were raised in protest. Edith Fowke took issue with Mr. Mitchell, Minister of Labour, who had said that no coercion or force or any pressure of any nature was used.

> If by coercion and intimidation you mean putting a pistol to a man's head or compelling action by threat of physical violence, then no coercion or intimidation was used. But if by coercion and intimidation you mean threatening individuals with the loss of their livelihood, with imminent separation from their families, and with the danger of being considered disloyal, then coercion and intimidation were used. Mr. Mitchell may prefer to find another name for it, but by whatever name it is called the type of persuasion used was unworthy of a society that claims to be democratic.

She quoted from a number of sworn statements such as this one:

> I was willing to go East but my wife is confined in the New Denver Sanitorium and at that time I was told to go East and work on a farm. I have three small children with no one to look after them. I refused to sign at first, but the Placement Officer threatened to cut me off the Department of Labor, Japanese Division, payroll and also refused to give me maintenance. With no other alternatives I had to sign for repatriation.[84]

The protests continued. One writer pointed out that any child under sixteen whose father signed the request for repatriation automatically lost his/her Canadian citizenship which the writer termed "an outrageous interference with the rights of people who were born into Canadian citizenship and who have no possible claim to any other citizenship." He wondered whether the parents realized that by signing the repatriation document "they were consigning their Canadian-born children to the fate of never being able to return to Canada, and of becoming stateless in a world in which the ability to claim the protection of some reasonably powerful government, or one with powerful friends, is a prime condition of personal safety."[85] Finally, in Janaury, 1947, MacKenzie King, Prime Minister of Canada, repealed the deportation order, but by then 4,000 people had left for Japan, one-third of them Canadian-born children.

Meanwhile the Commission schools closed down, but as not all the people moved away from the camps a severe strain was placed on some local school boards who now had to find places for these children. In the Slocan and New Denver school districts the enrolment practically doubled overnight forcing the use of temporary accommodation.[86]

Attitudes were changing. On June 16, 1948, a Japanese-Canadian woman voted in the school board plebiscite in Greenwood, and so took the first step towards the acquisition of equal rights by Japanese-Canadians in British Columbia.[87] In 1949 they won the right to vote in municipal, provincial and federal elections. Some of them moved back to the coast. Japanese-Canadian children were accepted in schools all over the province, and a few Japanese Language schools opened up. The number of Japanese-Canadian students in university increased steadily. In 1951 the first Nisei was appointed to a teaching position in Vancouver.

The last few years have seen much public debate on the treatment of the Japanese-Canadians during the war. Some feel the Japanese brought it on themselves by becoming "an isolated, aggressive, self-sufficient, hard-core community"[88] in the years between the wars. Some agree with Mr. Halford Wilson that the evacuation "was a good thing in the long run because the dispersal worked out so well for all," a comment which he is reported to have qualified by saying, "The ends justified the means, though I admit the means were harsh."[89] Some feel that what occurred "is the skeleton in the closet that stalks out to haunt discussions on civil liberties and it has prompted Canada's last three prime ministers to make public statements, firmly condemning what had happened."[90] But if anyone had looked closely at the skeleton in the closet they would have found that the bones were not five years old but seventy years old, for the treatment meted out to the Japanese during the war was the culmination of seventy years of discrimination, seventy years during which the lives of thousands of Canadian-born Japanese children were shaped by the forces of bigotry and self-interest.

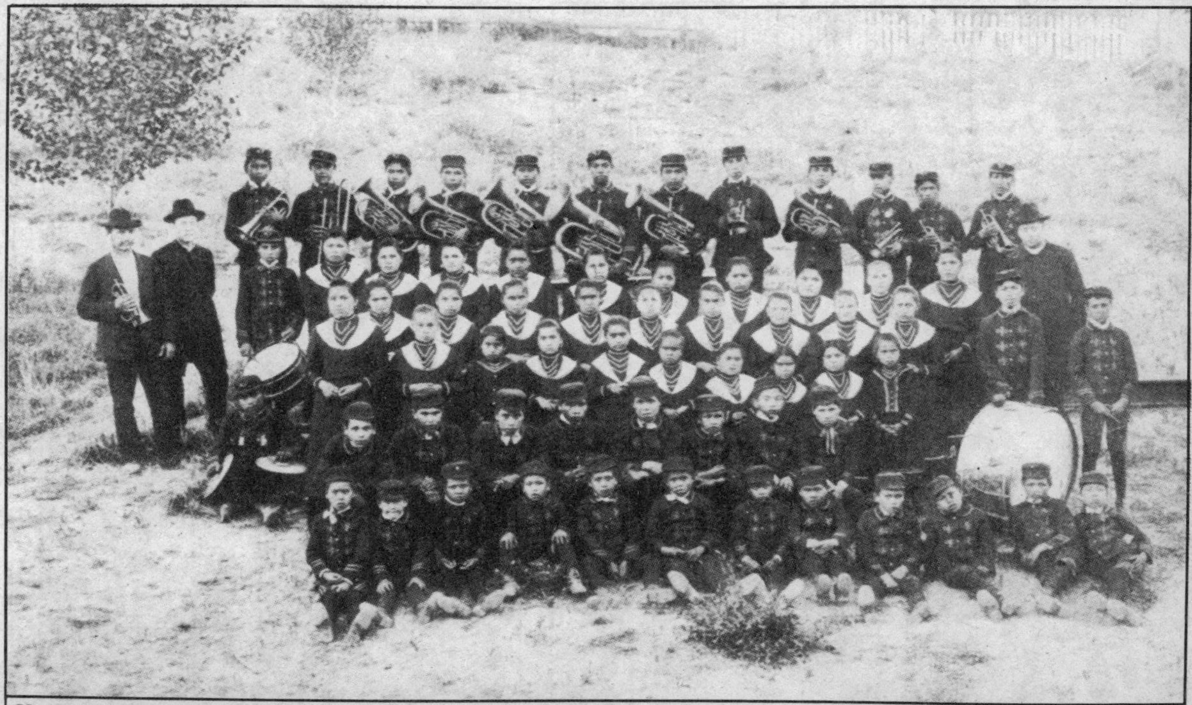

Kuper Island Industrial School Brass Band. Department of Indian Affairs Annual Report 1901-1902.

School for Indian Girls at Alert Bay, 1897. Vancouver City Archives.

Metlakatla Industrial School (Boys). DIA Annual Report, 1902-1903.

Anglican Kindergarten for Japanese Children, Vancouver, 1932. Photo by Margaret Foster.

Boys Farm Relocation Camp, 1943. Photo by Margaret Foster.

Slocan, 1942. Photo by Margaret Foster.

Out of School. 1945, Barnet, B.C. Photo by Hardev Teja.

Off to School. Lake Cowichan, 1945. Photo By Nirmal Bawa.

Class Photo. Paldi, B.C., 1935. Photo by Baljinder Siddoo.

Inside New Denver, 1953. Photo by Diane Waldron.

School Boys. Champion Creek School, 1926. Photo by Muriel St. Denis.

Doukhobor children, around 1953. Photo by Diane Waldron.

Amor de Cosmos, premier of B.C.: Coolies, go home!

Girls at Champion Creek School. Photo by Muriel St. Denis.

Graduating Class, Strathcona School, 1933. Photo by A. White.

Chapter 4
The Doukhobors

Thirty women once descended on the office of Dr. Campbell, the Deputy Minister of Education. Campbell told them that if they agreed to send their children to school they [the children] would be promptly returned home. "We can't change the laws of the country," he explained. Mrs. Mary Popoff, a Doukhobor spokesman, replied, "We can't change the laws of God either. We won't accept your schools—they're in conflict with the teachings of Christ."

SIDNEY KATZ
"The Lost Children of British Columbia"

Emigration

A few days before Christmas, 1898, the *S.S. Lake Huron* left Batum at the eastern extremity of the Black Sea with its human cargo of over 2,000 Doukhobors bound for the prairies of central Canada. The calm of the Mediterranean gave way to an eight day storm across the Atlantic, until a month after leaving Russia the ship docked at Halifax and the passengers began a four day train journey to Winnipeg. Three more shiploads followed bringing to Canada a total of over 7,000 people who had decided to leave their Russian homeland to escape the persecution they had been subject to since the founding of their religious sect in the middle of the eighteenth century.

The name "Doukhobor" had been given to them in 1785 by Archbishop Ambrosius of the Russian Orthodox Church as a derogatory term. *Doukho-bortsi* means "spirit wrestlers" and was intended by Ambrosius to mark these dissident Russian peasants off as a heretic sect who were wrestling against the Holy Spirit, but they adopted the name, broadening the concept, for they believed that they wrestled *with* the Holy Spirit and *for* the Holy Spirit. The practices of the sect grew out of their strong belief in the immanence of God.

> Doukhoborism is a Life-Conception fundamentally based on belief in God, and on the teachings of Jesus Christ. This Life-Conception brings out that God is the All-Creative Spirit-Life-Force, by Which everything that is was created and through Whom it exists. In a human being God is manifested through one's love for one's fellow humans and likewise for all creation. Herein lies the basis for our multiple explanation—God is Spirit; God is a Word; God is Truth; God is Love; God is Man.[1]

The Doukhobors acknowledged no authority other than God. Years later when the principal of an institution to which some Doukhobor children had been taken announced that he was in charge, a boy looked up and said, "Jesus Christ our boss." There were no priests, for all were equal in the sight of God; laws which required one person to acknowledge the superiority of another were seen as bad; naturally they were pacifists.

To the Russian authorities their strange behaviour, particularly their refusal to serve in the army which culminated in the burning of all their weapons on June 29, 1895, made them appear as lawbreakers. Persecution and torture was their lot for many years as they moved from place to place in Russia seeking the right to live according to the dictates of their religious beliefs. Finally with the help of Leo Tolstoy and others arrangements were made for the sect to take up land in Saskatchewan and Manitoba, and funds were raised to pay the costs of the long journey.

Initially three colonies were established near Yorkton and Prince Albert; villages were built and the land broken and tilled. The arrival of so many people with strange ways and speech soon caused resentment amongst the other settlers. The local authorities also experienced difficulties: the Canadian government had granted the Doukhobors exemption from military service in accordance with their pacifist beliefs, but they expected them to obey the laws dealing with such matters as the registration of land ownership, the registration of births, deaths and marriages, and, later, the education of their children, but for the Doukhobors obedience to God's laws took precedence.

The first clash came when under the Homestead Act the Doukhobors were required to register title to their land as individuals. In addition, in order to acquire crown lands, it was necessary for each title holder to take an oath of allegiance to the crown. For a people whose only allegiance was to God such an action was unthinkable. While a few took the oath and gained title to their land, becoming known as Independent Doukhobors, the majority followed the advice of their leader, Peter Verigin, and refused to sign, with the result that the Minister of the Interior revoked title to much of their land.

Settlement in British Columbia

As land was essential to their existence, the Doukhobors looked elsewhere, and in 1908 after travelling through the Rockies Verigin agreed to purchase over 8,000 acres in the Kootenay area of British Columbia in the name of the Christian Community of Universal Brotherhood, in this way hoping to vest the ownership of the land in the Community rather than in individuals, thereby avoiding the necessity of individuals having to take the oath of allegiance. There were four main parcels of land at Brilliant, Grand Forks, Pass Creek and Slocan Junction. As the years passed more land was acquired so that by 1924, when Peter Verigin lost his life in a train bombing, the Community owned over 21,000 acres in British Columbia.

The Doukhobors set to work to irrigate and clear the land and to plant orchards; they built sawmills and brick plants and acquired a jam factory; to supplement the community income some men took outside employment; and in a remarkably short time they had paid all their debts and the land was theirs. But Paradise it was not.

In the early days when the sect first moved to Saskatchewan the failure of parents to send their children to school was not an issue. There were very few schools and attendance was not compulsory. There was little tradition of schooling amongst the Doukhobors; education was a matter for the home and for religious meetings. The Quakers sent teachers, but these reached only a small number of children. Later, when the group moved to British Columbia they ran into trouble with the provincial government and its compulsory school attendance laws.

For some time no attempt was made to force the Doukhobors to send their children to school; however, in 1911 as the government began to exert pressure, the Community agreed that children in the Grand Forks area should go to the local school and that they would build a school at Brilliant. Things began well, but the school at Brilliant was closed after one term and the children at Grand Forks were withdrawn at the end of one year. The reason for these actions probably lay in the arrest of four men for failing to register a death. After each was sentenced to three months in gaol, the Doukhobor children were withdrawn from school. When the Community made clear its intention not to comply with the registration laws, the government countered with the first of a number of commissions of enquiry into the "Doukhobor problem."

William Blakemore, an English mining engineer who was chosen to conduct the enquiry, had for the last few years edited a newspaper in Nelson, a small town close to the Doukhobor land holdings. He travelled throughout the Kootenays and the Prairies hearing evidence and collecting information. His 1912 report is a valuable document on the early days of the Doukhobor community in British Columbia. He began by tracing the history of the people from their persecution in Russia up to their settlement in British Columbia. In writing on education Blakemore pointed out that in a letter to the Community in Saskatchewan before he left Russia in 1902, Peter Verigin had advised them to submit to education; however, he did not seem to have put much force behind his words according to Blakemore who wrote " . . . it is hard to believe that leaders who were able to exact such implicit obedience from their followers in other matters could not have secured a reasonable compliance of the law in this respect."[2] It is possible, however, that Verigin might have been afraid of losing some of his authority in the Community had the people been educated. "The fear was well based," wrote a member of the sect many years later, "a liberally educated mind could readily search and learn that the principle of human equality is dominant within Doukhobor roots and that tribute to the conscience (not to the leader) is primary."[3]

Blakemore recognized that the years of persecution the sect had undergone in Russia might have caused them to lack confidence in all forms of government. He went on: "It must not, however, be supposed that because this misguided people refuse elementary education for their children, they do not give them the best of home training. The children are intelligent, respective, and observant. The home life is almost ideal. They are taught all the cardinal virtues with which most of us, as children, were acquainted, but which are now too often regarded as old-fashioned—such as obedience, reverence, industry, and thrift; and it is not a little to the credit of their parents to find that the chief objection they entertain to education is the fear that secular teaching may undermine the religious spirit."[4]

With the move to British Columbia, the Doukhobors began an experiment in communal living which did not finally die out until the late 1940s; today in the Kootenays very few of the large square houses designed by Verigin remain. A village consisted of two houses each containing downstairs a large kitchen and a common living room and upstairs eight small sleeping areas for single people, old people, and young married couples with small families. Outside, linking the two houses, was a further row of sleeping rooms for larger families, store rooms, washrooms, a sauna, a blacksmith's shop, and any other areas necessary for the running of the farm. The daily chores were shared by all members of the community.

While the young children had plenty of freedom, rules were formulated around 1912 to govern their behaviour.

1. In the morning it is obligatory for all children to wash and

pray to God, then to read the Lord's Prayer and other psalms.

2. All children must obey their grandmother and grandfather and fulfil their demands with good service, and then they must do all that their father and mother tell them to do.

3. When at home you must strictly follow the accepted rules; take off your shoes and go barefooted in the house at all times.

4. Indecent mischievousness, cries, and fights are not permitted under any circumstances.

5. All children must be brought up in the spirit of Christian peaceful life; and with the growth of the body one must try and develop a reasonable soul in tune with God which brought us Christ and his sacred teachings.

6. A devout life of the first order must be encouraged for the children in the medium of toil in agriculture and in justice (in everything). All the necessities—clothing and food—are to be derived from personal toil on the land and one must maintain a reasonable adaption to the conditions of the day. One must strictly understand the will of God.

7. The denial of greed and envy in children is to be looked upon as a high and necessary virtue.

8. Modest clothing, moderate diet of fruit and vegetables, and simple living quarters with clean air must always be maintained amongst the children.

9. In summer, the costume of girls must consist of one long dress, while boys up to 12 years old must wear one long shirt. All must go barefoot and bareheaded.

10. All children, without exception, must come every day to the

sobranye to sing prayers and hymns and to read psalms.[5]

According to a census of Doukhobors taken in British Columbia up to October 22, 1912, there were a total of 1,736 children in the six communities of Brilliant, Champion Creek, Glade, Pass Creek, Crescent Valley and Grand Forks.[6] Blakemore tried to find out why the parents of these children would not send them to school. One woman objected to the fact that the lady teacher "curled her hair and wore ribbons" and that after the girls had attended school for a few weeks they followed suit. This she saw "as an evidence of vanity, that on no account would she be willing to subject her children to such degrading influence."[7] Others objected because they felt that once educated their children would leave the land and enter commerce which Blakemore describes as "a conclusion which it is impossible to combat whatever one may think of its wisdom."[8]

The Community gave Blakemore a statement outlining their position. While the English is poor, the substance of their argument is clear.

> The School teaching Doukhobors same did not accepted while being in Russia, and very seldom the children were thought to read and write, and if it had happened it was at home-school. We educate our children by means orally, so as not to have expense for the paper and printing matter. The School education we turned aside by many reasons and the most important of them are:
>
> 1. The school education teaches and prepares the people, that is children, to military service, where shed harmless blood of the people altogether uselessly. The most well educated people consider this dreadfully sinful such business as war, lawful. We consider this is great sin.
>
> 2. The school teaching at the present time had reached only to expedience for easy profit, thieves, cheaters and to large exploitation working-class laborious on the earth. And we ourselves belong to working-class people and we try by the path of honest labour, so we may reap the necessary

> maintenance, and to this we adopt our children to learn at wide school of Eternal Nature.
>
> 3. The school teaching separates all the people on earth. Just as soon as the person reached read and write education, then, within a short time leaves his parents and relations and undertakes unreturnable journey on all kinds of speculation, depravity and murder life. And never think of his duty, respecting his parents and elder ones, but he looks opposite, turning themselves, enslaving of the people for their own licentious and insatiableness gluttony.[9]

As a result of his investigations Blakemore concluded that the Doukhobors were "desirable settlers from the standpoint of their personal character, farming skill, devotion to agriculture and general industry." He had failed to establish any valid objection to them except their non-compliance with the registration laws and the Schools Act. He recommended that "bearing in mind their strong religious views, their honesty of purpose, and their ingrained obstinacy, no drastic steps should be taken to force their immediate compliance, but that suitable representations be made to Peter Verigin, their head, of the determination of the Government to insist on compliance." He suggested that if it became necessary to resort to prosecution and conviction that the imposition of fines would be more effective than imprisonment. He also recommended that "in order to give the Doukhobors confidence and secure their sympathy some arrangements might be made under which Russian teachers could be employed in conjunction with Canadian teachers, and the curriculum modified so as to include only elementary subjects." Then he struck right at the heart of their beliefs with a recommendation which must have destroyed any feeling of trust which he might have built up during the months of investigation. "That it is in the best interests of the country that the Order-in-Council granting exemption from military service should be cancelled."[10]

The Doukhobors, through their spokespeople, continued to speak out against the evils of the public schools: their preparation of the children for militarism and war, their seduction of the children from the land to the cities and therefore to money-making activities, and their failure to teach spiritual values. Alexander Evalenko in his book *The Message of the Doukhobors* published in 1913 wrote:

> In the matter of rejecting the Government schools we reject this kind of education for a number of reasons:
>
> First: The way school is taught to children of the present generation, with boy-scouting and military drill and rifle practice, we consider all this the most pernicious and malicious invention of this age. The manner of educating the childish mind renounces the teaching of Jesus Christ, who brought peace, love and equality to this earth, which should be instrumental in bringing about the Kingdom of God . . .
>
> Second: The school teaching is primarily a matter of easy lucre, from the Emperor and down to all officials, lawyers, doctors, and all manner and species of commercial buy-and-sell men, who have a great need of arithmetic and rapid reckoning, in their insatiable greed for easy money and luxury . . .
>
> Third: Being of Russian birth, we yet dwell in our own community and consider ourselves citizens of the entire earthly globe and therefore we cannot regard our residence in British Columbia as fixed for all times. Today we happen to be here, after some time we may find ourselves in another country altogether . . . Well, then, the conclusion therefrom is that all the time we have nothing else to do but educate ourselves—here in English ways and manners and in some other country after their ideas. And how about something of our inner own, of the fundamental Christian, shall we tend to acquiring this, or not?[11]

The Doukhobors had cause to be concerned about military drill and rifle practice. In 1910 the provincial Department of Education had signed an agreement with the Lord Strathcona Trust which would provide money "for the encouragement of physical training and military drill in public schools." One of the Trust's stated aims was "the fostering of a spirit of patriotism in the boys, leading them to realize that the first duty of a free citizen is to be prepared to defend his country—to which end all boys should, so far as possible, be given an opportunity of acquiring a fair acquaintance, while at school, with military drill and rifle shooting."[12] By 1913 there were 25 active cadet corps companies including one at Grand Forks.

The provincial government, which had had little experience of dealing with communities of people, put through in 1914 some anti-Doukhobor legislation known as the Community Regulation Act. This placed an obligation on the Doukhobors to provide vital statistics and to send their children to school; failure to comply would result in a fine. A clause, however, was inserted in the act whereby if an individual failed to pay the fine, goods and chattels of the rest of the Community would be liable to seizure and auction. The entire Community would therefore suffer in the event of non-payments of fines which were set at not less than $25 and not more than $100.

During 1914 and 1915 no Doukhobor children attended school. Then the Attorney-General, William Bowser, promised that the children would not be subjected to any para-military exercises or religious teachings and Verigin agreed to send some children to school up to the capacity of the schools to accept them, for at this time there were not sufficient schools to accommodate all the school-age Doukhobor children. And so in January, 1916, the school at Brilliant was reopened and over the years more were built at Krestova, Outlook, Pass Creek, Spencer, and Champion Creek. By 1922 there were 11 schools operating, two built by the government and the rest by the Doukhobors.

The Burning of the Schools

For a few years there was relative peace in the Kootenays. While by no means all the Doukhobor children were in school, average attendance rose from 41 during 1916 to a high of 209 during the peak year of 1920-1921 when 414 children actually enrolled.[13] Then a decline set in.

The end of the First World War saw a worsening of relations between the Doukhobors and local residents, some of whom wanted the pacifist Doukhobors expelled from their land which they felt should be given to returning veterans. In 1919, the right to vote in provincial elections was taken from the Doukhobors and a sense of martyrdom and persecution was aroused once more in the Community.

In 1920 changes were made to the Public Schools Act which placed the Community schools under an appointed trustee who took the place of the more usual Board of School Trustees and who had the power to assess and tax the local people for the support of the schools. If the enrolment at a school declined unduly, the government could force the Community to pay the full cost of the school, including the teacher's salary, and the usual government grant would be withheld. These changes gave the government greater control over the Community schools.

Restlessness grew in the Community. In 1922 some parents began keeping their children out of school, and average attendance fell to 153 from 209. In December, 1922, the authorities charged eight parents with failure to send their children to school and fines were levied. When it became obvious that the police intended to seize Community goods, the fines were paid. In February, 1923, A Doukhobor father was fined $50 for keeping his children out of school. He refused to pay. Court officials seized his motor truck and advertised it for sale. There was commotion in the district and the threat of a general withdrawal of children from school. Peter Verigin went to Grand Forks, and just before the sale the father decided to pay the fine and send his children to school. The truck was returned.[14]

In April, 1923, the Doukhobors began burning the schools. The first to go was Outlook. Miss Spence, the teacher, who lived in an apartment at one end of the school heard the arsonists. She hurried over to a neighbour, clad only in her night attire, and gave the alarm, but the school was lost.[15]

As the months passed, the burning of the schools continued,

often following the attempt of the police to seize property for the non-payment of fines. Verigin's house as well as some sawmills and a poleyard owned by the Community came under the hands of the arsonists. The Minister of Education, the Hon. J.D. MacLean, made it clear that the Doukhobors would have to pay the cost of rebuilding any schools which were burned down. By April, 1925, fines levied on Doukhobor parents were running at a few thousand dollars. Goods were seized from Community warehouses and sold, and the effect brought about a temporary truce. In May the children started flocking back to school in such numbers that all available accommodation was soon taken and another round of school building began.

While the majority of British Columbians agreed with the government's handling of the Doukhobor school problem, a visitor to Canada, probably from England, in a letter to the editor of the *Victoria Times* posed a series of rhetorical questions to his readers:

> Do you really think that it is essential that the Doukhobor acquire an education such as your laws insist upon in order that he may not become a loafer, a robber, a thief, a pick-pocket, a murderer, a wanton, a pervert, a drunkard, a tobacco slave, a dope fiend, or a wastrel? Is he any of these things because he has not acquired an education such as your laws insist upon? Is the lack of education making him a lawbreaker to the extent of imperilling your safety, your morals, your future happiness or peace of mind? Are you able to do more with your education than he is with his?
>
> . . . Are you sure that your education is better than that which they can receive from their parents? Are you positive? Are you certain your children are better behaved than theirs?
>
> . . . Good people of British Columbia, do you wish to be Pharisees, Philistines, killers of the Christian spirit? Can you not be quite happy to leave the Doukhobor to follow his simple, kindly life? Cannot you permit him to educate his young by using his own teachers and his own methods as do all other religious sects?

The letter was signed "A Stranger Within Your Gates" and in

parentheses came the comment "England always respects religious beliefs."[16]

In the same month, the Minister of Education made a statement about the Doukhobors as follows:

> We have imprisoned them, fined them, and exerted continuous pressure on them for the last four or five years. If they won't learn any other way, they have got to be made to know that it doesn't pay for them to burn down Canadian public schools as they have been doing.
>
> The schools will be rebuilt and the whole cost of this work will be charged to the Doukhobors. Perhaps they will be able to understand our laws when they are thus given to them in terms of dollars and cents. They are pretty stubborn but when they have to pay the bills for their foolishness they will be more inclined to go easy.[17]

The truce continued during the summer of 1925 when a number of new schools were built. Mrs. Muriel St. Denis (nee Gurney) applied for and got the teaching position at Champion Creek school, largely, she thinks, because her father had been a lighthouse keeper and it could therefore be expected that she was used to isolation. She was met in early September, she recalls, by a large Doukhobor who drove her by horse and cart to her schoolhouse on the banks of the Columbia River. It was a wooden building with the schoolroom at one end and the teacherage, consisting of a small bedroom and living room which doubled as the kitchen at the other end. Water had to be carried in, and there was an outside lavatory.

Her one room school averaged around 30 children from grades 1-8, but in addition Mrs. St. Denis taught English three nights a week to adults. The children spoke English with varying degrees of fluency. They were interested in their lessons and came to school clean and well cared for. All those who should have attended school did attend.

Mrs. St. Denis got on well with the local people. They asked her if she believed in war and if she would teach anything about war; she replied No to both questions. She involved herself in the local community and helped with such activities as the yearly picnic and

Christmas festivities, and the local people reciprocated by lending her an old horse until such time as her husband-to-be, whom she met up there, gave her a better horse. They also gave her vegetables, fruit and bread which, added to her salary of $120 a month plus $35 a month for the adult class plus the rent-free teacherage, gave Mrs. St. Denis a very good living for a single woman teacher in those days.

When Mrs. St. Denis felt the need to visit a larger town for the weekend, on Fridays after school she climbed into the little boat tied up on her side of the Columbia and drifted down stream and across the river to the small settlement of Blueberry from where she could catch the train to Trail or Nelson.

One evening in the winter, a small group of local Doukhobors knocked at her door and after telling her that one of the old men had died, asked if they might put his body in her woodshed over night. Next day they would dig the grave in the cemetery which was adjacent to the school. Unfortunately the ground was frozen so hard that the old man spent three nights in her woodshed during which time his relatives prevailed upon Mrs. St. Denis to take his photograph so that they would have something to remember him by.

On another occasion, Mrs. St. Denis answered a knock on the door and a Doukhobor woman slipped furtively in out of the dark. Because her religion forbade it, she had never tasted meat but she said bacon smelled so good, would Mrs. St. Denis let her taste it and not tell. In 1927 when Mrs. St. Denis left to get married, the local people gave her some embroidered material and a sack of potatoes. She remembers them with affection.[18]

1927 was also the year when the new leader, Peter Verigin, sometimes called Peter the Purger, arrived from Russia to take up his duties. His father, Peter the Lordly, had died in 1924 when a train he was travelling on in the Kootenays was dynamited. In response to a question from reporters when he landed in New York in mid-September as to whether he intended to see that Doukhobor children went to school, Verigin said, "Yes, we will take everything of value that Canada has to offer, but we will not give up our Doukhobor souls. We will educate our children in the English schools, and we will also set up our own Russian schools and libraries for which I brought with me Paul Ivanovitch Biriukov." But in late December the Minister of Education rejected the Doukhobor request that they be allowed to introduce Russian into their schools. The Premier said that there was no objection to the Doukhobors studying their own literature in their own homes. "The government, however, will not tolerate, and I am sure the Legislature would not approve, the use of any foreign language in the public schools of this province. Should we grant such a concession to the Doukhobors, people of many nationalities here would be entitled to ask for the use of their language in the schools and we should have a real dual language question on our hands."[19]

The latter part of 1925 was sufficiently quiet for the *Victoria Times* to write in April, 1926, that the Doukhobors had at last embraced Canadian education with amazing enthusiasm: more new schools had been built and attendance was up. "These facts," the article went on, "have convinced officials of the Department of Education that the Doukhobor school problem, for long one of the most serious difficulties which they have had to face, has finally been solved and that there will be no further trouble among the Russian colonists."[20] But in 1928 the zealots were parading and proclaiming that the schools were turning the children into "the slaves of Satan."[21]

Every religious sect produces its zealots, those who see it as their duty to purge the religion of corruption and heresy and to keep it pure. During the early leadership of Peter the Lordly this group, known now as the Sons of Freedom, were small in number, but in the 1920s they attracted others to their ranks. Their protests usually took the form either of parades at which they frequently stripped off all their clothes and returned to the simple state of Adam, or of burning or dynamiting schools, government and Community property to show their disapproval of education, authority, and materialism.

In mid-January, 1929, militants drove Doukhobor children out of the schools at Carson, Spencer, and Outlook. At Grand Forks they camped near the school, but were banished outside the city limits. Some stripped. During the summer at least six schools, a warehouse, and a flour mill burned to the ground. In early August a group marched down the Slocan Valley towards Nelson. About

300 camped at the roadside and when the police and Peter Verigin visited them to persuade them to withdraw, they stripped, and 104 were arrested and given sentences of six months in gaol each. Eight children, seven girls and a boy, who were taken into custody with their parents, were sent into the care of the Children's Aid Society in Vancouver. Some days after arriving there they escaped hoping to join their parents in Oakalla, but they were apprehended and sent to the Boys' or Girls' Industrial Schools, used for delinquent children, where they remained until their parents were released in February of the following year. There is little evidence that the experience did anything other than increase the resentment of the children towards authority.

Attorney-General Pooley announced in late August, 1929, that in order to put an end to the troubles caused by unruly Doukhobors, the government proposed "to sequestrate a number of their younger children by proper court action under the Neglected Children's Act and place them with such bodies as Children's Aid societies for education." He continued, "If the Doukhobors behave themselves for a period they will get their children back. If they persist in disorderly habits they will lose more children until we have them all under training in institutions."[22] Pooley's statement brought some public protest. W.D. Calvert, M.D. wrote letters to the editor of the *Victoria Times* in which he referred to the proposal as not only savage but grotesque. "If taken seriously, it savors of the barbarism of the middle ages."[23] In an open letter to the Attorney-General he pleaded, "Recall your inquisitor before he perpetrates his ugly task of selecting and abducting these children."[24]

The activities of the Sons of Freedom continued to grow during the early 1930s. Peter Verigin tried to eject the group from the Community, but they moved to Krestova where the poorer land gave them more cause for discontent. The government amended the Criminal Code so as to provide a mandatory three year gaol sentence for nudity in a public place. But these measures did not deter the Sons of Freedom who were not ordinary law-breakers but religious fanatics concerned with ideas and not penalties.

In May and June, 1932, the Sons staged a series of nude marches along the road to Nelson. In total over 600 adults were arrested and sentenced to the mandatory three years' imprisonment, and 365 children were either arrested with their parents or left without someone to care for them.

Custodial Care of the Children

As the federal penitentiary at New Westminster would not hold all the Doukhobor prisoners, a special penal camp was built on Piers Island in Haro Strait off Vancouver Island. But for the 365 children, no such solution was possible. They were brought by train to the coast where some of them were put in foster homes and the others, about half, were put in various institutions: the Boys' Industrial School; the Girls' Industrial School; the Loyal Protestant Home, New Westminster; the Protestant Orphanage, Victoria; the Alexandra Orphanage, Vancouver; and the Children's Aid Society, Vancouver. Every effort was made to keep brothers and sisters together.

It was, of course, a traumatic experience for the children, particularly for those who were sent to an institution which must have seemed to them to resemble the prison currently holding their parents. The 75 girls who were sent to the Girls' Industrial School engaged in various forms of passive resistance. They sang hymns at the top of their voices all the way to the school in the bus from the railway station, and refused to enter the building on their arrival at 6:00 a.m. They were pushed gradually through the door and up to the third floor dormitories where they were asked to undress and bathe before going to bed. One girl, pretending not to understand, got into bed with her clothes on. Her clothes were removed and she was led to the bath tub; the others then followed. Throughout the next few weeks they continued to protest, first by holding a nude demonstration and then by going on a hunger strike.[25] At night they took off their clothes and piled them in a heap in the middle of the floor; in the morning they put on anything, whether it fitted or not, forcing the staff to spend some time sorting out the confusion as they tried to find dresses and shoes more appropriate to each girl than what she had taken.[26] Gradually, under protest, the girls took on some of the daily chores such as cleaning the dormitory, working in the laundry, or baking bread. In September school opened and again they resisted: they stood by their desks and refused to sit down until forced to, then they refused to pick up their pens. In the evenings and on Sundays they gathered together and sang hymns, and remained during their stay in the institution a very close knit group. According to R.H.C. Hooper writing in 1947 on the custodial care of the Doukhobor children during this period, the girls appointed a leader each day whose task it was to decide which regulations or orders were acceptable or contrary to their beliefs. "So unobstrusive was this leadership," says Hooper, "that the staff was often unaware of the identity of the particular girl in authority."[27] But one of the girls, now a grandmother, gives no credence to Hooper's statement: the girls simply acted together as a group, with the aim of their resistance being to try and force the authorities to let them go to Piers Island to join their parents.[28]

The boys at the Boys' Industrial School put up a similar fight. According to Hooper, when the boys who were over the school leaving age of 15 refused to work on the school farm, the superintendent stationed them at intervals in the fields to scare away the birds. After two or three days of monotony in the heat of the sun, the boys asked to work. There was resistance among the younger boys regarding school, but when a teacher threatened to make the boys who refused to study live in cottages with the regular inmates of the institution, juvenile delinquents, the boys picked up their pens.[29]

In the early days of their imprisonment the parents were allowed to write and receive letters in Russian, but the flow of letters between parents and children was so great that the heavy demand on the interpreters, who had to translate everything into English for the censors, was such that long delays ensued. The Doukhobors were therefore asked to use English. The number of letters dropped to a trickle as people had to find someone who could write in English, and the resultant breakdown in communication between parents and children caused such discord and unhappiness that the officials relented and allowed Russian to be used. Attempts were made to keep the parents informed as to their children's health and well-being: a few visits were arranged and foster parents wrote and sent photographs of their foster children.

Allegations of serious ill-treatment of the children in the Girls' and Boys' Industrial Schools resulted in an investigation of conditions by officials of the John Howard Society and the Children's Aid Society. It was said that the girls were beaten, placed in "black holes," and subjected to forced feeding after a two day hunger strike; of the boys it was said that they were strapped, placed in "black holes," given corporal punishment for bed-wetting, and forced to stand before a picture of the king for hours.[30] Officials of the two societies exonerated the institutions and explained that the "black hole" was a room where children were placed for a few hours after some misdemeanour.

But was the exoneration justified? In an interview a Doukhobor woman recalled with passion but with little bitterness the extent of the physical mistreatment she, a girl of twelve, in 1932, and her friends endured in the Girls' Industrial School. She admitted that the girls deliberately disobeyed the authorities, seeking only that they should be reunited with their parents who, after all, were not detained in a real prison but were living as a group on an island. The girls tried to draw attention to their request by disobedience. In return they were, she said, struck by straps and blackboard pointers on their hands, arms, shoulders, legs and heads. When they refused to sit down in their desks they were hit with heavy books. When they clutched the underarm seams of their jackets and refused to let go, they were struck repeatedly on their forearms raising a line of welts. But when visitors came to inspect the school, the girls who showed signs of bruising were hidden from sight. Girls who refused to pick up a pencil had it forced into their hands sometimes point first so that it penetrated the skin. Some days the punishment for an offence was to stand outside in the hot sun. She recalled seeing girls faint from abuse and remembered her own tears. One girl stubbornly refused to cry because she would not give "them" the satisfaction of seeing her breakdown. One worker who was kind to the children was ostracized by the other workers. During the months they were there the girls cried a lot, sang a lot, and asked repeatedly to be sent to their parents.[31]

In his evaluation of the custodial care of the 365 children, Hooper concluded that the physical care provided was most satisfactory, that emotional well-being was maintained within the capabilities of the particular organization, and that thc program was therefore successful in providing care while the parents were in prison. He stated, "This care was so designed that on returning to the colonies and reuniting with their parents, the children could re-enter the communal way of life without creating any major adjustment problems." However, he noted that a secondary purpose of the government was "to alter those manifestations of the Sons of Freedom faith which involved a non-recognition of man-conceived government. In this it was not effective." In summary he said: " . . . later religious teaching and the passage of time have combined to create in the minds of many the impression that this episode in their lives had been merely another form of persecution. It is known that some of these children are actively participating in the quasi-anarchistic activities of the present day." He ended by pleading that if direct measures should again prove necessary, children should only be separated from their parents as a last resort.[32]

Claudia Lewis, writing in 1952 in the *Report of the Doukhobor Research Committee* and looking back on the episode said: "Of course, for scores of Doukhobor children of all ages there was the disrupting Piers Island experience of twenty years ago, when the solid structure of home life was completely shattered by the removal not only of parents but of the children themselves from all their familiar associates and anchorings. The bitterness engendered by this experience, for children and parents alike, is still feeding into the resentful tide among the Sons of Freedom."[33] Another section of the same report adds these words:

> Removal of the children is not the magic answer to the Sons of Freedom problem. Not only would it be disruptive to the total Doukhobor community, but there are also definite limitations to foster-home and institutional care in British Columbia.
>
> Psychiatrists and social workers have grave concern about removal of children from their homes. No matter how the home may appear to the outsider, it may have values to the child much superior to those offered by a foster-home even of

> high standard. The emotional impact of removal is severly traumatic to the ordinary child; it will be much more severe to the Doukhobor child who would not only leave his family but in such circumstances go and live with the "enemy."
>
> . . . Finally this is a moral question surrounded by heartbreak. Removal of the children would doubtless be marked by Doukhobors as the greatest injustice that the government ever visited on their group.[34]

While the incarceration on Piers Island lasted for three years for some of the parents, custodial care of the children terminated in the spring of 1933. The provincial government came under political pressure when it became known that during these depression years the government was spending $17.50 a month to support a Doukhobor child while a widow with one child received only $16.10 relief. A delegation from Independent and Community Doukhobors by offering support helped the government to make up its mind to return the children to Doukhobor foster-homes where they would be maintained at no charge to the government. Parental consent to this plan was not required, and by the end of May, 1933, all but four of the 365 children in care had been placed in Doukhobor foster-homes. While this may have seemed a more humane way to treat the children, difficulties lay ahead for some of them: they were placed with Orthodox Doukhobors who largely disapproved of the activities of the Sons of Freedom and who were therefore interested in reforming their foster children with the result that the children were once again subjected to a conflict of values; and, as the foster parents received no financial support for the children, they required, in some cases, that the children work for their keep. Slowly, as their parents were released from Piers Island on parole, this unhappy period ended for the children as they returned to their homes to try and pick up their disrupted family life, but from their ranks were to come many of those who were to cause disturbances in the Kootenays during the late 1940s and the 1950s.

The report on the public schools for 1932-1933 stated that as the bombing and burning of schools had been stopped due to the imprisonment on Piers Island of the faction responsible, much better progress had been made in the schools than in previous years.[35] But in the report covering the years 1935-1936, Inspector F.A. Jewett of Nelson expressed his concern.

> In the community schools and in those schools in which there is a major proportion of Doukhobors, no great progress has been made in Canadianizing this people. The persistence of the Doukhobors in maintaining their identity as such and in resisting Canadian influence is a strong as ever.
>
> While the children seem to be happy at school, they quit at the earliest possible date and at the present time there are many of school age who, supported by their parents, are defiantly absenting themselves from school. Trustees and teachers find great difficulty in getting proper books and supplies for Doukhobor children.
>
> I cannot see that force is likely to accomplish much with this people who take a pride in thinking themselves martyrs. For many generations they have followed a leader and think in communistic terms. For these reasons, it seems to me these people must be reached through their leaders. If the government can co-operate with the leader and get his co-operation in return, the united influence could not be otherwise than good. This suggestion may have been followed before with poor results; but in these days when disintegration of the community seems under way and the attendant problems of debt and insecurity face the individual Doukhobors, a conference with the leader might result in a better understanding and a guarantee of better support to Canadian institutions. There are, no doubt, misunderstandings and misconceptions that have no real foundations. If co-operation cannot improve present conditions, it would seem that forceful, direct action cannot be delayed for long.[36]

Ewart P. Reid, in his concluding remarks to a study of Doukhobor education in British Columbia prior to 1932, made these comments: "Much of the Doukhobor opposition to public schools arose not because school per se was opposed but because of the course content and methodology employed. Many of these difficulties arose because of the educational theories and practices which prevailed at that time. Insistence by the schools on dividing children into grades, or using military drill, using competitive tests and comparative grading, on teaching history with military and political orientations, and refusing to allow the teaching of Russian did nothing to make schools more palatable, even to the Independent Doukhobors." Reid went on to point out that British Columbia had had during those years a highly centralized education system run by an ultra-conservative government and there was little flexibility. In addition the Community schools were controlled by an official trustee and there was no provision for the Doukhobors to exercise any measure of control over the schools. Hence the schools never became a part of the community but were simply institutions imposed upon them. As a further criticism Reid said, "Canadian public schools in most provinces have, at one time or another, made some provision to accommodate the educational wishes of minorities. British Columbia is the only province which has never made such provisions and from the time the Doukhobors arrived in British Columbia the government attempted to enforce uniform educational regulations."[37]

Financially, during the few years which remained before the outbreak of the Second World War, the Community was in serious trouble. Not only had the Community lost some of its assets through bombings and burnings, the depression hit it hard as, indeed, it was hitting many Canadians, and it also suffered from internal problems. Acts of violence continued during this time, but lessened considerably during the war years only to increase in number once again as soon as the war was over. While Doukhobors were not required to serve in the armed forces, a few volunteered and were accepted.

Post-War "Solutions"

The British Columbia Teachers' Federation, which had been

growing in strength during the years between the wars, suggested in 1939 that what was needed was to break down the prejudice and hostility of the Doukhobors by helping them to establish intimate contacts with "lovable Canadians." The way to do this was to put a real Canadian home "radiating the best things in our Canadian mode of life" into the heart of every Doukhobor community so that the people would realize that here in Canada they were among friends.[38] Two years later the federation gave its opinion that "the supervision and administration of all Doukhobor schools should be vested in a single official, a trained and experienced educator of vision, initiative and wide sympathies, whose contacts with the Doukhobors will justify affection and confidence, and that it would be part of wisdom to entrust such a man with authority to adjust the curriculum and management of these schools to their primary objectives."[39]

In late December, 1944, in a brief to the provincial government on teachers in Community schools, the B.C.T.F. made the following recommendations paraphrased here:

1. that teachers for Community schools should be carefully selected, that is, they should have had at least two years teaching experience, be over thirty, and possess high professional and personal qualifications,
2. that their salary rate should be at least three increments higher than the basic salary rate,
3. that their living quarters should be separate from the school, should be well designed and furnished, and that a telephone should be installed in all teacherages,
4. that insurance should be placed on the teachers' books and personal effects without charge to the teacher,
5. that the teacher should be allowed wide liberty in adapting the curriculum to the needs of the Community,
6. that suitable school and playground equipment should be provided,
7. that attendance regulations should be enforced more consistently, and that failure to comply should result in a fine, not imprisonment.

These were the B.C.T.F.'s short-term recommendations; in the long term they felt that consolidation of Community and local schools was the ideal to be aimed at for this would serve to solve the problem of living conditions, provide a Canadian environment for the pupils, speed language learning, solve the teacher shortage, and promote more efficient teaching in a graded school. They suggested as a first step consolidating Outlook and Fruitova schools with Grand Forks.[40]

Maxwell A. Cameron in his *Report of the Commission of Enquiry into Educational Finance* in 1945 agreed with the teachers that every effort should be made to get the Doukhobors into "the ordinary scheme of things" and he therefore made no special provisions for the Doukhobors, treating their schools in the same way as other schools.[41] Consolidation was not, however, likely to be popular with the Freedomites who did not want to see their children taken out of the community by bus to a school in which they were the minority.

In September, 1947, the government set up another commission to enquire into the problems of the Doukhobor community. This time it was a one-man commission—Judge Harry Sullivan. In January, 1948, out of frustration and exasperation he resigned. He felt that although he had devoted much thought and hard work to try and find a solution, he had failed to win the confidence of the Doukhobors but he believed that drastic action was necessary. Florence E. Lebidoff in a statement to the Sullivan Commission wrote: "Schools, forced upon the Doukhobors by the government, were destroyed by fire because schools are propogators of a false conception of civilization, patronizing the beast, militarism. We need no specific evidence to prove this, for a glance at the schools and its results clearly shows that every important weapon of destruction, including the atomic bomb, could be traced to the school door-step and the teacher's desk."[42]

Following an outburst of arson, the provincial Attorney-General in the spring of 1950 asked the President of the University of British Columbia to set up a research project which would look into the Doukhobor situation and make recommendations for its improvement. The chairman was Dr. Harry Hawthorn, a well-known social scientist and then head of the Department of Anthropology. Other members of the Doukhobor Research Committee had backgrounds in law, social work, psychology, Slavonic studies, agriculture, economics and Doukhobor religion. For two years the committee collected its data in May, 1952, brought out its report which covered both the past history of the sect and the present tensions. The report clearly distinguished between three groups of Doukhobors: the Society of Independent Doukhobors; the Union of Spiritual Communities of Christ; and the Sons of Freedom who had lately accepted Stefan Sorokin, a recent immigrant and displaced person, as their leader to fill the vacuum left by the death of Peter the Purger in 1939.

In a section on schooling the report pointed out that "a majority of young men and women have merely been enabled to go beyond bare literacy in English." The committee felt that "education for Sons of Freedom children, if only through the elementary grades, would help greatly to break down the feelings of difference and inferiority that must accrue to them now through their ignorance, illiteracy, and language handicap when in contact with the 'outside world.'"[43] Few had attended high school and fewer still university. The report listed the main grounds of opposition to schooling as:

1. The belief, especially noticeable in recent developments of Sons of Freedom philosophy, that education is synonymous with propensity for evil, and that it drives out "natural" good sense as well as good moral qualities. This poses a sharp dilemma for the present leaders of the Sons of Freedom, who are effective as leaders largely by reason of their own schooling, but who are by pressure of this belief enjoined from sending their own children to school.
2. The fear of the assimilative processes of education in public schools along with other children has existed from the early days of Doukhobor residence in Canada, and was one of the reasons for the move to British Columbia. This fear was once fostered by the leadership, who saw the possibility of losing the identity of the group, and is now held most intensely by the Sons of Freedom, who see relocation as a

retreat from this threat.

3. The objection to national history in so far as it fails to condemn wars, and in so far it glorifies governments.
4. The objection to schooling, some say, where pure discipline is an aim of the classroom, where equipment is inadequate and activity and learning minimal.
5. The feeling that Doukhobors are treated with discrimination.
6. The need of assistance from children in gardening, child-minding and housework at the times when school claims them.[44]

Elsewhere the report tried to put the Freedomites' objections to education into an historical and philosophical framework:

> The Doukhobors came from peasant stock at a time when only the elite were exposed to education. The majority of the sect identified formal education and its project, literacy, with government and church. Furthermore, education and literacy were not valued possessions; they were not considered necessary for "quickening the spirit," which was basic to their religious faith. The early leaders discouraged the sectarians from acquiring any education other than that of their religion itself, for education was not only anti-spiritual, but could also lead to undesirable outside contacts which might draw members away from the group. Education by the state, furthermore, handles national history in a patriotic way; the Doukhobors, denying the authority of the state and abhorring militarism, did not care to expose their children to such an education. In Canada, Peter Vasilivich Verigin discouraged school attendance, and currently the Sons of Freedom maintain this tradition, refusing to allow their children to attend schools.[45]

In a chapter entitled "Doukhobor Childhood and Family Life" Claudia Lewis concluded that the home atmosphere surrounding the child was authoritarian and that a high value was placed on controlled, submissive and obedient behavior. Younger children, however, had a fairly high degree of freedom, while older children were allowed to take part in various aspects of adult life. Lewis spoke against removing children of the Sons of Freedom from their parents and suggested that schooling should be made more acceptable to them by including Doukhobors on local school boards, providing superior teachers, doing away with saluting the flag and singing patriotic songs, teaching the Russian language, dispensing with the graded school readers and supplementing the reading program with excerpts from Tolstoy, and improving the social studies and music programs.[46]

The report, which estimated that approximately 300 children were not attending school in the Kootenays and that many others were attending only sporadically,[47] devoted a number of pages to a discussion of education before producing its recommendations which called for the co-operation of local school boards in the strengthening of the educational program; an increase in salary for teachers working in areas which resisted education; a lowering of the work load of teachers in selected areas so that they would have time to engage in community organization activities; the prosecution of parents for the habitual truancy of their children; an increase in the number of people providing counselling and guidance in schools attended by Doukhobor children; and the development of a flexible program of studies for use in areas resistant to education.[48]

But the Sons of Freedom were considering another solution: in 1952 their leader, Stefan Sorokin, went to Uruguay ostensibly to find land on which to settle the militant group. But the migration never materialized, and in 1953 more acts of arson were committed than in any preceding year, and the government took drastic action, which over the years has received both praise and condemnation.

Early in September, 1953, their homes burned and their hopes centred on yet another migration to another promised land, a group of the Sons of Freedom gathered together at Perry's Siding and erected a tent village. On September 9, 148 adults were arrested and imprisoned for parading nude outside the one-room school at Perry's Siding. They denied the charge: one who was there as a young teenager said the demonstration took place about half a mile from the school. But the charges held, and while the parents were moved to Vancouver and sentenced to the mandatory three years in gaol the children were taken to the old sanitarium building in New Denver where they were to receive, whether they or their parents like it or not, an education.

New Denver

The New Denver operation lasted from 1953 to 1959, for not only were the children of the adults arrested at Perry's Siding taken there, but those children whose parents habitually kept them out of school were from time to time rounded up and committed to care in the institution so that over the years approximately 170 children spent some time in New Denver.

The first group of children placed in the institution resisted both actively, by letting the bath tubs overflow, and passively by stripping or lying on the ground. In early December, Mr. John Clarkson, who had been working at the dormitory as a volunteer, was hired full time to educate and socialize the Doukhobor children. A report by Nelson Allen, Superintendent of Schools for the Nelson area, tells the story of Mr. Clarkson's efforts, problems and successes.

Mr. Clarkson began by insisting that all children must observe regular school hours in a room to which they had been assigned; the children might do what they wished during that time but they must be in the room. The children resisted, but once they realized that the rule was inflexible they obeyed it. In mid-January an educational program began and the children were given pencils, paper, and books. Again the children resisted in various ways on the first morning, but within two hours all the children were working. When the bell rang for school after lunch, all the children were in their seats. Classes continued until the end of June and for half days during July and August in order to prepare the children to enter the local public school in September. As some of the children did not speak English when they arrived at New Denver and others were behind in their studies because of their intermittent schooling, not all the children were ready to be integrated in September, but as the months passed more and more were ready to sit alongside the English-speaking children from the surrounding area.

In 1956, in addition to being in charge of their education, Mr. Clarkson was also made superintendent of the dormitory. He immediately released some of the old staff and hired new people; he also laid down some firm rules covering care of property and behaviour. He instituted various recreational activities and took some of the children on summer holiday trips to Vancouver, Banff, and Calgary, giving them the opportunity not only to see something of British Columbia and Alberta, but also to get an understanding of the different jobs and professions open to them if they got an education.

When the children reached school-leaving age or when their parents promised to send them to school, they left New Denver, but non-attenders who were apprehended took their place so that numbers in residence were usually in the order of 80-85 children.

The dormitory was open to inspection. During Mr. Clarkson's three years as superintendent from 1956-1959, 610 people visited the institution; of these, 196 were government officials, 16 off-duty R.C.M.P. officers, 39 journalists or radio broadcasters, 10 were from church groups, and 349 were simply classified as "other."

Finally in mid-summer, 1959, the parents of the 77 children currently in the New Denver Dormitory appeared before the local magistrate and promised to send their children to the local school in September. In early August all the children were released and the dormitory closed.[49] Not only did all 77 children register for school in September, 13 who had been in hiding accompanied them.

Dr. J.F.K. English, Deputy Minister of Education, paid tribute to Mr. Clarkson with these words:

> That the problem of providing education to these Freedomite children has been successfully solved is in good measure due to the untiring efforts of Mr. John Clarkson. Because of his understanding, patience and self-sacrifice, the Freedomite parents have been brought to the point where they

> realize that public education is not the Satanistic and militaristic monster they had formerly imagined it to be.
>
> Thus, because of the outstanding work of Mr. Clarkson, a problem which has bedevilled and frustrated every government of the Province of British Columbia for the past forty years has been brought to a successful conclusion; and the objectives of the project, which seemed at the beginning to be so idealistic that they appeared to be impractical, have been successfully attained.[50]

Naturally public opinion regarding the apprehension of the children and the custodial care accorded them was highly polarized. There were strong outcries against the forcible removal of children from their parents. Peter Maloff, a Doukhobor lawyer, felt that taking the children with the alleged purpose of educating them only deepened the crisis, and for the children the memory of the separation might instil a life-long feeling of hatred towards the authorities which no amount of education could eradicate.[51] He spoke also of the fallacious belief that formal education is based on the principle of freedom pointing out that "interests of the State will predominate in a controlled formal education, while interests of each pupil [will] be considered as of secondary importance." Then he outlined what he believed would be the system of education that would meet the requirements of the Doukhobors:

> It must be an education which will seek to develop human nature in its widest scope. It should be alive to the most vital life problems. It should be an education which is primarily concerned with man himself, not only material things; education must be a leading force in establishing a new and saner social order; it should lead us to a better understanding of our position in the Universe, our relation to Cosmic Laws, to the whole human society, to the fuller understanding of ourselves. In short, an education that will be a succor in the realization of man's nobler dreams.
>
> But if we want our education to be all that it must be free of control of all political doctrines; free of any particular group and all kinds of authority.[52]

Periodically the R.C.M.P. raided Sons of Freedom strongholds to pick up truants. The first raid occurred in November, 1954, and the largest in January, 1955, when about 50 police and welfare workers moved into Krestova early one morning and took about 40 truant children from their homes. It was not a pleasant job for the police who received a lot of verbal abuse through the media, but for the parents the apprehension of their children was deeply distressing, and while some accounts may well be exaggerated, the agony they felt as their children were taken was very real. A signed statement from one mother after an unsuccessful attempt was made to apprehend her child reads as follows:

> In the morning of January 18, 1955, a group of R.C.M.P. pushed into my house without permission or a knock at the door. I was all alone in the house, such an approach scared the life out of me. Search is not the word for it; they just made one big mess of the house. They said they are looking for school children. I said there are no children present. One of them spoke in Russian: "You are lying." Soon this group left the house, then another group came in to finish messing the house, after which they tore into the other buildings in our yard: bathhouse, woodshed, cow barns and root cellar. They broke the lock on the root cellar door and helped themselves to apples.
>
> They sure made a very poor example for well-educated people with such brutality. Now they want my child to attend the same school as they did, and make the same brutal and Godforsaken person out of her like they are themselves.
>
> May God help me to keep my child away from such schooling and help us to make an intelligent, loyal, peace and God-loving person out of her.[53]

In an open letter nine mothers accused Attorney-General Robert Bonner of repeating the same barbarous acts of King Herod who had killed 40,000 infants in his attempts to stop the coming of Jesus Christ. They described how the police threw parents into the snow and dragged the helpless children from their beds.[54]

Some people, however, saw the New Denver operation as the

only way to break the pattern of violence in the Kootenays. But as in any experiment involving human behaviour no one could be quite sure how the New Denver children would turn out. When the institution finally closed, Mr. Clarkson wrote: "At this time it is difficult to foresee what will be the final outcome of the children's sojourn at New Denver. I would gamble on most of them turning into law-abiding citizens who will raise their children, send them to school with the same pride as other Canadian parents have in seeing their children learning and preparing for life."[55] In fact, a number of the New Denver children did continue their education and some entered the professions, but in 1963 one writer said, "Many of the young zealot offenders now at Haney Correctional Institution and at Agassiz are former New Denver graduates."[56]

In the mid-seventies, S.D. Cameron, who had taught eight Freedomite children from the dormitory in the junior high school in New Denver during the fifties, decided to find out what had happened to them in the intervening years: one had been killed in the 1965 Hope-Princeton slide disaster; another had had personal problems which had affected both his marriage and his job; the third had married an orthodox Doukhobor and still adhered to the faith, while the fourth had become a Jehovah's Witness; the fifth had gone on the trek to Agassiz and after living in Vancouver for ten years had returned to the Kootenays; the sixth had married a Doukhobor who spent five years in Agassiz prison; while the remaining two of the eight had each spent time in Agassiz for conspiracy to commit arson.[57]

Reports in the press on life in New Denver varied greatly. Bert Whyte in a series of articles in the *Pacific Tribune* in 1957 did not have words bad enough for the institution describing it as a disastrous failure. He spoke of the children as being unhappy, and quoted from a janitor who had worked there for three months in 1956 who said the food was not fit to eat and that the only time the children ate well was when a visitor came.[58] He reported the death of Mrs. Mary Gienger whose body was found hanging from a beam in her home in Krestova with a note beside it from her nine-year old daughter Patsy in New Denver which read, "Mommy, I am lonesome for you—come and visit me. I love you. Goodbye."[59] Other journalists were not so harsh and found some positive things to say about New Denver, but the brightest picture of all was painted by the *B.C. Government News* which in 1958 ran an article giving the government's side of the story. It began by reminding its readers that it is the birthright and privilege of every Canadian child to receive an education, therefore when it had become apparent that the Sons of Freedom were determined not to send their children to school the government had had no alternative but to make them wards of the Superintendent of Child Welfare. The writer pointed out that of the approximately 12,500 Doukhobors in British Columbia, only about 2,500 belonged to the Freedomite group and of these only 46 families, involving 66 children, were currently refusing to send their children to school. The children in the New Denver Dormitory were reported as living "under conditions that would be difficult to match in any private school." The buildings were described as being well lighted and heated and attractively decorated, and the food as excellent.

The government saw the strengths of the program as being more than simply the acquisition of literacy skills by the children and listed the following items as proof of success.

1. There has been less difficulty with the adult Sons of Freedom since the educational program became effective.
2. The majority of the Freedomite children are now voluntarily attending school at the various home centres in the Kootenay area.
3. The Sons of Freedom appear to have recognized that there is a strong Government policy being implemented respecting education, and, except for some half-dozen parents of the most fanatical group, they are gradually beginning to accept it.
4. The younger Freedomite children in the schools at New Denver have now become almost fully integrated with the other Canadian children.
5. Only forty-six Freedomite families have children now involved in the New Denver School program, where formerly there were twice this number.
6. The majority of the Orthodox Doukhobors and many of the Sons of Freedom are supporting the Government plans for

the handling of these few Freedomite children.

7. A considerable number of Sons of Freedom have moved from the Krestova area to get away from the pressure of the fanatical group, and in many cases their children are attending school voluntarily.
8. The educational program has received almost unanimous public support from the people and press in the Kootenay and all Interior areas where those concerned are directly acquainted with the Sons of Freedom problem.[60]

Support for the government's action ranged from condemnation from some: " . . . one's view of whether the good results were worthwhile must rest on one's willingness to accept a government's right to coerce people for what appears to be their own good. In our view, that right is unacceptable"[61]; to praise from others: "One courageous rescue-attempt was made by the British Columbia government—the first enforced education of the children."[62]

One inmate of New Denver who was with her parents at Perry's Siding in 1953 at the age of 13 and who remained in New Denver until 1955 feels that the New Denver experience tended to produce one of two results in the children: a few became activists and are part of the small core still from time to time causing trouble today; but some, she feels, simply turned their backs on the whole Doukhobor situation. This does not mean they have embraced any other creed, but rather that they have cut adrift from the Doukhobor world without coming to anchor in the Anglo-Saxon world, and these, Diana feels, are the ones who have suffered the most.

Diana took part in one real life adventure story, what she believes to be the only successful escape of any children from New Denver. One late spring morning, Diana and two other girls, all aged around fourteen, told the authorities in the Dormitory that they were going to walk up the mountain and have a picnic. They packed a lunch and once they were out on the road some distance from the buildings they hitched a ride with a travelling salesman heading south. A mountie watched them get into the car, waved to them, and immediately phoned the registration number of the car through to the detachment at Crescent Valley. Diana, who knew the country and was taking the group to her aunt at Winlaw stopped the car when there were still five miles to go because she felt they would do better to walk along the railway tracks rather than stay on the highway, so they set off down the hill to the tracks. Shortly afterwards the car they had been travelling in was stopped and the driver admitted to letting them out. The police backtracked and met a car coming up the hill with some person or persons in the back seat hidden from view behind a large newspaper. The car was stopped and searched, and although the occupants, Doukhobors, had seen the girls they denied it. The girls meanwhile had had time to hide along the tracks.

The girls reached Diana's aunt's house only to learn that the police were close behind. Immediately scarves were tied around their heads, their blue jeans covered with long skirts or coats, and they were sent into the fields. As they made their way slowly to the high raspberry canes, the police not far behind, they heard an old grandmother berating the police, "Why are you wasting your time looking for the girls here? They are probably halfway to Creston now to pick strawberries." The police left, and the girls moved deeper into the bush where they lived for a week in a tent. The two other girls were quietly collected by their relatives, and Diana, whose parents were in gaol, lived with her aunt. Several times the house was raided but they never found the built-in hiding place behind the trap door. Diana turned fifteen in the fall and could therefore leave school, but that summer her mother was released from gaol and they moved to Vancouver Island. Today Diana lives in a comfortable, well furnished apartment in Vancouver and has a good job. Her experiences as a Sons of Freedom child have made her sensitive to the hopes and aspirations of others. When asked if the bombings and arrests which took place frequently in her childhood days upset or frightened her, she replied, "No, unrest was simply a part of our life style."[63]

Even for those Doukhobor children whose parents sent them to school regularly during the 1950s, life in the classroom was not always easy or comfortable. Sam Fillipoff, now an elementary school teacher in Vancouver's Chinatown district, recalls his own school days:

When I entered grade one, I spoke no English. Though English language acquisition came quickly and easily many other problems ensued. The English speaking students made fun of me and occasionally attempted to provoke me to fight. My parents forbade me to fight and warned me that I would have to endure the abuse if I were to continue at school. The teachers offered little protection since they considered this part of the assimilation process in becoming a Canadian. There was conflict between home and school also. My parents had instructed me not to take part in any militaristic activities at school. This included singing "O Canada", raising the flag, marching or drill in physical education and paying homage to the monarch. This "disrespect" annoyed some of the more nationalistic teachers who had just returned from the war. As a result they ignored the abuse some of my friends and I were receiving.

By seventh grade the English language handicap had been largely overcome. Parental encouragement helped grade achievement in school. However, the parents still considered reading a luxury when there was many a chore to be done in maintaining the farm. My parents really wanted me to be a teacher who lived on a farm. This caused some conflict revolving around values that differed from those of the farm. Extra-curricular activity was such an area. Organized sport was the focal point since it demanded a considerable amount of scheduled time that conflicted with farm work. Also, by high school I aspired to be a dentist. Though my parents were encouraged by this prospect, they also saw that economically that this would be very difficult. The subject was rarely mentioned and the reality prevailed. High school teachers were generally big city people just passing through to a better position after a little experience at our expense. They did little to raise our aspirations. There were a few other teachers who really cared and they made the difference. Several of these teachers became models for me. They respected our beliefs and encouraged us to strive for higher learning so that we could come back and teach and improve the social situation of our people. These teachers I shall never forget. They helped me become what I am today. They were few but their influence was beyond measure.[64]

The March to Agassiz

1961 and 1962 brought more acts of violence in the Kootenays, more trials, and more imprisonments. In late July, 1962, the government opened a new fireproof prison, Mountain Prison, near Agassiz in the Fraser Valley to house the 104 prisoners. Back in the Kootenays the Sons of Freedom led by Fanny Storgeoff, known on account of her size as Big Fanny, burned their homes and set off on yet another protest—this time to march to Agassiz where at the gates of the camp they would draw the attention of the world to the "Doukhobor question."

About six hundred people moved off from Krestova on September 2 but by the time the group left Grand Forks twelve days later the number had doubled. By the end of September they were encamped in the Seventh Day Adventist Camp near Hope, and in early October the younger children were registered to attend classes at the Coquihalla Elementary School. As there was not enough space for the over one hundred Sons of Freedom children expected to attend school, classes were at first set up from 4:00 to 6:00 p.m. after regular school was over; the parents would not permit the children to be out later as it would mean walking home in the dark. But by the end of October a proper full-time elementary school had been established for the children in the buildings owned by the Seventh Day Adventist Church. One difference for these students was that they could not be integrated with the local children as were their older brothers and sisters who were attending the local high school.

In mid-January, 1963, the marchers moved to Vancouver where they found lodgings in halls, inexpensive hotels, rented houses, or private homes. A delegation of the sect met with Dr. Sharpe, Superintendent of Schools for Vancouver, and asked that all their children be put in one school to prevent assimilation. When Dr.

Sharpe explained why this could not be done they accepted his answer and the children were enrolled in a number of schools in the city. They were not required to sing "O Canada" but were expected to stand during the singing, otherwise they took part in the normal school program.[65]

The last move of the marchers came in mid-August, 1963, when in order to support the prisoners who were in the midst of a hunger strike, the group camped outside Mountain Prison. The provincial government gave financial help to the local school authorities to meet some of the costs of enlarging the local school and increasing the teaching staff. At first the Doukhobor children were segregated from the other children while the teachers determined the grade level of the children, procured the necessary supplies, and made whatever administrative changes were necessary. One report written in 1964 said that none of the children were doing poorly in school and none had displayed behavior or discipline problems; the most outstanding characteristic of the school was that a child of the age of a sixth grader might be found in the fourth grade. The children appeared to mix well and not to show any signs of feeling "different." Numbers, however, slowly dropped: in September, 1963, there were 80 Freedomite children in school; in January, 1964, only 64.[66] Gradually over the years as the prisoners were released the camp outside Mountain Prison dwindled away. Some of the marchers returned to the Kootenays, some settled in Vancouver, but the promise made in 1959 by the Freedomites that they would send their children to school has been kept with very few exceptions.

While a small core of militants still remains, the process of education and therefore assimilation has continued. Some of the younger Doukhobors do not speak Russian and in an effort to counteract this trend Russian classes are offered in some secondary schools and after school. Woodstock and Avakumovic feel that while many younger Doukhobors are being assimilated, there is consolation in the fact that "many young people from the non-Doukhobor world have moved closer to the ideals of human living that peasant prophets began to preach in the Ukraine almost three centuries ago."[67]

But history has a way of repeating itself. In 1953, twenty years after the children had been released from institutional care, fires blazed in the Kootenays; in 1979, twenty years after the children were released from New Denver, the fires were blazing again.

Chapter 5
The East Indians

One mission of education is to help men see foreigners not as abstractions but as concrete beings, with their own reasons, sufferings, and joys, and to discern a common humanity among the various nations.

Learning To Be: The World of
Education Today and Tomorrow

"Let the Sikhs Stay At Home"

The English have always been obsessed by the weather, but never more so than on the evening of June 21,1897; for the next morning the old queen, who had both delighted and disappointed her subjects during her long reign, would delight them once more by driving through the streets of London in what the *Times* would later describe as a pageant "of wonderful splendour and variety, and not to be matched by any of which history holds the record."[1] When the morning light broke through there were clouds in the sky but a confident young police constable announced that it would be fine because Victoria was a good queen[2]—and fine it was!

For sixty years Victoria had reigned over a steadily expanding Empire and on this June morning near the close of the nineteenth century, Londoners waited as heads of state from all over the world and troops from every corner of the Empire assembled in the parade grounds to form up into the long column of pomp and pageantry which would wind its way through the well-known streets, past the well-known buildings, in celebration of Victoria's Diamond Jubilee. When the procession came in view, there were the Canadian Hussars and, of course, the Mounted Police, and the New South Wales Lancers and Mounted Rifles; there were the Natal Mounted Troops and the Rhodesian Horse—and many, many other mounted regiments from the British Isles and the colonies, too numerous to mention. Behind them came the foot soliders, the Malta Militia and Artillery, the Canadian Active Militia, the Canadian Highlanders, the Borneo Police—regiment after regiment marching along at a steady pace interspersed by bands or by carriages containing the dignitaries from home and abroad. That night a tired queen wrote in her journal, "My escort was formed from the 2nd Life Guards and Officers of the native Indian regiments, these latter riding immediately in front of my carriage."[3] Victoria's matter-of-fact statement did not do justice to the enthusiasm with which the crowds cheered the troops from India, an enthusiasm which caused the sober *Times* to write, "But there could be no sort of question that in this part of the procession the deputation of officers of the Imperial Service Troops attracted the public most. Their dark-bearded faces, their upright carriage, their strange and rich uniforms, were a delight, and Sir Partab Singh, in his showy uniform, excited roars of applause at many points upon the route."[4] And a little further on, "the foreign and military attaches and the Indian native officers were received with a roar of applause."[5] And once more, "Next to the splendid reception which Her Majesty herself received—a reception which appeared to gratify the Sovereign exceedingly—no demonstration of warm affection and patriotic loyalty could have exceeded that which was accorded to our Indian and Colonial troops and statesmen."[6] And yet again, "After Her Majesty had gone by the enthusiasm flagged somewhat until the Indian and Colonial troops appeared, and then the cheering was continuous so long as the representatives of our dependencies remained within view."[7]

And then it was all over. "The tumult and the shouting dies;/The Captain and the Kings depart" wrote Rudyard Kipling in a hymn composed especially for the Diamond Jubilee. The heads of state returned to their countries, and the troops made their way back to their own parts of the British Empire, an Empire which during the next sixty years would change beyond anything the old queen, bobbing from side to side in her well-sprung carriage, could possibly have contemplated as she drove through the streets of her capital on that memorable day in 1897.

Some of the soldiers from India made their way home across Canada and saw in British Columbia a green land, and a land moreover very sparsely populated, with a climate at times somewhat like that of the Punjab, the region from which the majority of them came. These were not the only men from India to visit British Columbia; some Sikh soldiers who had helped stem the Boxer Rising in China remained behind in Shanghai, Peking, and Hong Kong, and from there took ship across the Pacific. As these various adventurers returned to India or wrote letters home, knowledge of British Columbia's potential for growth, its natural wealth, its reasonable climate, and its need for settlers became known in the Punjab, that area of India lying to the north and west of Delhi and reaching up to the mountains of Kashmir. Manual work in this young Canadian province was easy to obtain, and wages, while perhaps not as high as those of white workers, were high enough to permit one to save a fair sum and to send it home to enable others of his family to join him. Or so it was reported.

It took time for the news to spread. By 1904 there were around 250 East Indians in British Columbia. In 1905 the number increased a little, but in the latter part of 1906 they started to come in the hundreds so that between 1906 and 1908 almost 5,000 landed at British Columbia ports, and this influx was more than the white population, already hostile towards Orientals (in which category it placed the Hindus as they called them), would tolerate. Part of the cause of the sudden increase lay in the activities of certain East Indian entrepreneurs who saw an advantage to themselves and others in bringing over large numbers of labourers to work in the logging camps, sawmills, and mines, or on the farms, or along the railroad tracks. Dr. D.R. Devichand said in July, 1906, that Hindus were gradually supplanting the Japanese and Chinese in the local sawmills. "I am," he went on, "now negotiating with parties in India with a view to drawing attention to the grand opportunities which await the sober and industrious Hindu in British Columbia." He added that he expected the vanguard of the Hindu invasion to begin in early September.[9] Dr. Devichand's announcement was followed by a sober editorial the next day in the *Vancouver Province*:

> The Hindu population of the East is turning its gaze towards the Western Hemisphere and sending out its pioneers to report on the possibilities. Already several hundred brawny people are domiciled in our town and an influential man among them is authority for the statement that some thousands will be here before a great time. What their advent in large numbers to the province will mean can only be surmised but it may mean much during the next few years. The Hindu labourer is a man of skill and intelligence as well as of much strength and endurance and will be a most valuable ally of the rancher in clearing the land and making the country a farm instead of a forest. The conflict in the labour market between him and the Chinese and the Japanese may place the employment of workmen within the means of all who are in possession of property and may thus accelerate the progress of the province and of all the industrial life of the country. How the invasion will be regarded by the white labourer remains to be seen. As the Hindu is a British subject, however, it seems impossible that any steps can be taken to exclude him from the country.[10]

The white labourer was not going to regard the influx of Hindus with any favour whatever, but before he had time to give any thought to the matter the headlines read, "Hindu Invasion Has Commenced"[11]—forty-eight men had arrived in Vancouver on the CPR liner Athenian, but this was a mere handful compared to the numbers which followed. In late August 300 arrived, and there was nowhere for them to stay. Banner headlines blazed "Hindu Hordes Make Themselves At Home—Annex Choicest Portions of the City—Motley Crowd With Pots and Pans, Turbans and Trunks, Invade Vancouver—Mayor Buscome Wires Ottawa For Help."[12] About 100 of the men set up camp in Stanley Park; others moved into houses near False Creek which had already been condemned as unfit, but which at least provided better shelter than the open air. In mid-November many of them still had nowhere to live so a large tent was pitched at Granville and Beach Avenue to provide cover for some of them; and at least one citizen took a few Hindus into his home saying as he did so, "I am against the Hindus being allowed in the vicinity at all, but in the name of humanity we must keep them from freezing to death."[13] The citizens of Vancouver held a mass meeting and sent telegrams to Winston Churchill, at that time the British Colonial Secretary, and to Sir Wilfred Laurier, Prime Minister of Canada, but before measures could be taken to control the flow of immigrants from India, hundreds more landed seeking jobs they had been told were readily available.

A year later they were still coming. "The Hindu invasion has recommenced in earnest," reported the *Vancouver Province* in the fall of 1907, "and nine hundred turbaned men from India will arrive in Vancouver this afternoon at 2 o'clock on board the Canadian Pacific steamship Monteagle."[14] The next day the paper described the disembarkation. "The scene in Vancouver's Oriental melodrama late yesterday afternoon shifted from the Flowery Kingdom to the coral strand. Little Japan and Little China were severally and jointly eclipsed by Northwest Bengal in British Columbia. And the final act has yet to come. The only element that seemed to make the bewildering kaliedoscopic scene of yesterday unnatural was the absence of the heroine. Seven hundred and ninety-eight physically fit and handsome dark-eyed bronzed Romeo homebuilders and not one Juliet."[15]

With unemployment on the increase in the province, hostility towards East Indians grew. Articles appeared which showed an ignorance of India and its people (there was, for instance, confusion in the minds of many people over the terms East Indian, Sikh, Hindu, Punjabi) and these helped to stamp in certain unfounded stereotypes: because East Indians were faced on arrival with both a housing shortage and a strong reluctance on the part of the whites to rent rooms to them, they were forced to crowd together in dilapidated buildings, and then it was said that this was how they liked to live; because they were unable to find jobs to earn money to buy warm clothes and had to "wrap themselves in blankets, which scarcely covered their shaking bodies"[16] it was said that they were not able to cope with a temperate climate and should return to the tropics.

Legislation was enacted to keep those that had landed in a position of inferiority and to control the influx. In March, 1907, the provincial government disfranchised East Indians even though they were, by right of their membership in the empire, British subjects. This move effectively barred them from voting in federal elections. Less than a year later, on January 8, 1908, through an order-in-council, all immigrants unless covered by a special treaty were required to come to Canada by a continuous journey from their country of origin. As there was no special treaty with India and as there were no ships which sailed directly from India to Canada, immigration of East Indians was effectively stopped. The drop in numbers was dramatic: for two years in a row over 2,000 East Indians had entered Canada; once the new regulation was in force the figure dropped to ten and never exceeded a hundred until 1947.

The situation was a difficult one for the federal government. It was easy to bar the Chinese from entry as they had no special claim on Canada; it was less easy to bar the Japanese because of the existence of a treaty between Great Britain and Japan which, among other measures, allowed for free movement of nationals in the other country; but it was very difficult to bar East Indians because as members of the empire they were, like Canadians, British subjects and therefore presumably had some rights in other parts of the empire. It was left up to the future prime minister of Canada, William Lyon Mackenzie King, to justify the federal government's action in cutting off immigration from India by the "continuous journey" regulation, which he did. After visiting England where he conferred with members of the British government and with those concerned with the government of India, he submitted a report in which he said, "It was clearly recognized in regard to emigration from India to Canada that the native of India is not a person suited to this country, that, accustomed as many of them are to the conditions of a tropical climate, and possessing manners and customs so unlike those of our own people, their inability to readily adapt themselves to surroundings entirely different could not do other than entail an amount of privation and suffering which render a discontinuance of such immigration most desirable in the interest of the Indians themselves."[17] Mackenzie

King then dealt with the manner in which large numbers of East Indians had been persuaded to leave their country; he described the outflow as having been not spontaneous, but owing its existence, among other influences to:

> 1. The distribution throughout certain of the rural districts of India, of glowing accounts of the opportunities of fortune-making in the province of British Columbia, visions of fields of fortune so brightly hued that many an Indian peasant farmer, to raise the money for the journey, had mortgaged to the lender of the village his homestead and all that it contained at a rate of interest varying from fifteen to twenty per cent.
> 2. The activity of certain steamship agents who were desirous of selling transportation in the interest of the companies with which they were connected and of themselves profiting by the commissions reaped.
> 3. The activity of certain individuals in the province of British Columbia, among the number one or two Brahmins, who were desirous of exploiting their fellow-subjects; and certain industrial concerns which, with the object of obtaining a class of unskilled labour at a price below the current rate, assisted in inducing a number of the natives to leave under actual or virtual agreement to work for hire.[18]

Mackenzie King reported that certain steps had been taken. First, the Government of India had been warned about the risks involved in emigration to Canada. Second, the steamship companies had been informed of the regulation prohibiting the disembarkation in Canada of immigrants who had not travelled by a continuous journey from their native country. Third, the governments of both Canada and England were reminded that it was, in fact, unlawful under the Indian Emigration Act of 1883 for a native of India to leave the country under an agreement to labour for hire unless he was going to Ceylon or the Straits Settlement. The Act had originally been brought in because Indian labourers overseas had been taken advantage of and had suffered great hardships and privations. "It is, therefore, to be said," continued Mackenzie

King, "that emigration (in the sense defined) to Canada from India, is not lawful under the India Emigration Act, and cannot be made lawful except through the action of the Canadian government in making the necessary laws, to the satisfaction of the government of India, for the protection of Indian emigrants."[19]

In his final statement under the title "A Harmony of Policies," Mackenzie King summed up:

> Whilst effective as a means of restricting a class of immigration unsuited to Canada, it will be apparent that the arrangement as herein set forth is one which finds its justification on grounds of humanity as strong as are the economic reasons by which it is supported. . . . Nothing could be more unfortunate or misleading than that the impression should go forth that Canada, in seeking to regulate a matter of domestic concern, is not deeply sensible of the obligations which citizenship within the empire entails. It is a recognition of this obligation which has caused her to adopt a course which by removing the possibilities of injustice and friction, is best calculated to strengthen the bonds of association with the several parts, and to promote the greater harmony of the whole. In this, as was to be expected, Canada has had not only the sympathy and understanding, but the hearty co-operation of the authorities of Great Britain and India as well.[20]

Mackenzie King was to remain opposed to immigration from Asia for the next forty years.

The order-in-council requiring immigrants to travel to Canada by a continuous journey from their country of origin was renewed in May, 1910, and was made to apply not only to labourers but to the wives and children of those men already in Canada, causing further hardships. "Many Hindus had their wives and families awaiting embarkation in Calcutta when the order was made," wrote one person, "and the women and children are still in India living on such remittances as their men-folk may send them and anxiously awaiting the removal of the restriction which keeps them from enjoying the company of their husbands and fathers as the case may be."[21] Representations were made to the government to have the regulation lifted, at least for wives and families, or if not lifted, then clarified. "Naturally, people in British Columbia are wondering what 'continuous' can possibly mean if a journey from Calcutta upon a through ticket, making the closest possible connection with the steamship of Hong Kong, is not a continuous one."[22] A petition was sent to the Imperial Conference in London, England, in 1911, but with no result. At the end of the same year a delegation went to Ottawa where the Hon. Robert Rogers, Minister of the Interior, said that the government would not object to the wives and children coming provided they came in accordance with the regulations. The East Indian community considered chartering a ship, but nothing came of the scheme.[23]

But while one group sought to have the wives and children of East Indians resident in British Columbia admitted, another group sought to keep them out. H.H. Stevens, Member of Parliament for Vancouver, argued that those who pleaded for bringing in the wives of Hindus were suggesting that "chastity is an impossible virtue,"[24] and in his view "foolish fanaticism" was blinding people's judgement. "As a matter-of-fact," he went on, "this question of bringing in their wives never entered into the minds of the Hindus until very recently, and then only as a means to rouse sentimental support from a certain type of moral busybody, and how well the wily Hindu succeeded is evidenced by the hub-bub which has resulted."[25] Stevens then examined what the admittance of wives and children would mean in numbers. "First, they ask that the wives and families of those now in the country be admitted, which, according to their own statements, would number about 2,500 or 3,000 families. Taking five as the average family, and this is small, it would mean that there would be an immediate increase of the Hindu colony of about 12,000 to 15,000 souls."[26] Stevens claimed that the Hindus would congregate around the cities where they would work for lower wages than whites and that they would not farm or pioneer.

Meanwhile the *Vancouver Province* reported on its front page on January 13, 1911, that the first Hindu baby had been born in New Westminster, the child of a fairly well-to-do shopkeeper at Fraser Mills.[27]

In 1912 the "continuous journey" restriction received its first serious test. Two men, Bah Singh and Balwant Singh, one a priest at the Sikh Temple, on their return to Vancouver from India brought back with them their wives and children. As returning residents the two men were permitted to enter, but because their families had not come direct, they were ordered to be deported. On April 30 the women and children were arrested with the intent of returning them to Asia on the *S.S. Monteagle* due to sail shortly, but a writ of Habeas Corpus was obtained in the Supreme Court of British Columbia and they were released. The case was discussed in the press across Canada. Towards the end of May the federal government relented and gave the wives and children permission to remain in Canada as "an act of grace without establishing a precedent."

The East Indian community continued to press its claims for the right of all residents to bring in their families, but public opinion in the west was against them. "We in British Columbia are sorry for the people who live apart from their families," commented an editorial writer in the *Vancouver Sun*, "but we have to look to the future, and no question of mere sentiment can be allowed to interfere with what are the best interests of our people. We have only to look abroad and see how the Chinese have monopolized the Malayan Peninsula, and how the Japanese are trying to plant their feet in every genial clime where they think there is room for them, to realize the danger of the Asiatic scourge. Let the Sikhs stay at home."[28] Ten days later the local East Indians gathered together and passed the following resolution: "We, the Hindustanis of Canada, assembled in a mass meeting at the O'Brien Hall, Vancouver, B.C., on this 15th day of June, 1913, request the Dominion Government of Canada, that the promise given to our delegates on December 15, 1911, by the then Minister of the Interior, Hon. Robert Rogers, that families of the Hindustanis domiciled here shall be admitted into Canada, be given effect to in a suitable manner without any further delay."[29] A *Vancouver Sun* reporter who was present remarked, "Accidently, perhaps, but with very marked effect on the meeting there were present the members of the one Hindu family in Vancouver by special act of grace. The tall turbaned husband, a fine looking man, carried his baby daughter into the hall, and beside him walked, attired in spotless white Indian dress, his wife."[30] But the following day the editorial writer carried on where he had left off, saying that the answer to the resolution passed at the mass meeting should be "firm and unmistakeable in its denial of the request made."[31] And it was. Not until 1919 would the Canadian government make any concession towards the admittance of the wives and minor children of East Indian residents.

But some East Indians did not see the government's action in admitting the two wives and their children as an "act of grace"; they regarded it as a small but significant breakthrough in their struggle to obtain fairer treatment under the immigration regulations. And so in 1913, when thirty-six East Indians arrived in Vancouver aboard a freighter from Singapore and were, of course, immediately ordered to be deported, they took the case to court and applied for a writ of Habeas Corpus on the grounds that the men were being illegally detained pending the deportation. The judge threw out their application, but they tried again, and to the amazement of everyone, Chief Justice Hunter overturned the first judgement declaring certain orders-in-council ultra vires and ordering the men to be released, thereby enabling them to enter Canada. The news of the successful appeal soon reached India where there were many who still dreamed of emigrating to Canada. Gurdit Singh, a Sikh, decided to test the new ruling. He chartered a steamship, the *Komagata Maru*, and took on passengers at Hong Kong, Shanghai, Kobe, and Yokohama. With 376 East Indians aboard, the ship sailed for Vancouver where it arrived on May 23, 1914.

There was strong opposition amongst the citizens of Vancouver towards allowing the men to disembark. The ship was forced to anchor out in the harbour, and no one was permitted to land except the captain and Gurdit Singh and two assistants. Then the legal arguments began and the days dragged by one after one. Twenty men who proved that they were returning residents were taken off. Food was supplied as stocks ran low, but the prospective immigrants remained cooped up on the ship out in the inlet away from the dock. At last the matter went before the Court of Appeal and on July 6 the judges declared, contrary to the findings of Chief Justice Hunter, that the orders-in-council lay within the powers given by the immigration act to the government of Canada, and that the Court has no jurisdiction to interfere. The writ of Habeas Corpus was refused, and the deportation order was declared legal and enforcible. Conditions on board deteriorated as some of the men, deeply frustrated, tried to take over the ship. Police and immigration authorities steamed out to the *Komagata Maru* aboard a tug, the *Sea Lion*, to take possession of it, but they were repulsed. H.H. Stevens, who was on the *Sea Lion*, arranged with the premier to bring *H.M.S. Rainbow* from Esquimault to Vancouver, and finally on July 23, the *Komagata Maru*, escorted by the gunboat, left Burrard Inlet and sailed for Asia taking with it its cargo of disappointed immigrants, some of whom were so embittered by their experience that they joined the movement to throw the British out of India and over the years various violent disturbances were attributed to these people. Later that same year William Hopkinson of the Calcutta Police, who had been brought to Vancouver to investigate seditious activities by East Indians on the pacific coast, was shot dead by Mewa Singh after he had given evidence in a murder trial that had resulted from his use of East Indian informers during the course of his enquiries. The effect of these two incidents upon the white and East Indian communities in British Columbia was to increase the hostility and suspicion between them and to provide a legacy of mistrust which was handed down.

With immigration now completely cut off and with war raging in Europe, the East Indian population in British Columbia scattered and grew smaller over the years. Some men moved out to the sawmills and lumber camps along the Fraser River or on Vancouver Island; some went to the States; and some, when they could, returned to India. In 1909 a Sikh Temple had been built in the 1800 block West 2nd Avenue in Vancouver and the Khalsa Diwan Society was organized with branches at Victoria, New Westminster, Abbotsford, Fraser Mills, Duncan, Coombs and Ocean Falls; throughout the years to follow the Society provided the East Indians with leadership and a sense of community. There were very few East Indian women and children in the province, but contrary to the newspaper reports which spoke of overcrowding and dirt and disease, those families which were able to get decent accommodation proved that given the right conditions they could live as well as working people from any other country. James E. Dobbs said in 1917, "I visited the home of one Sikh family in Vancouver, who succeeded in getting into Canada after waiting for about 18 months in Hong Kong before being permitted to proceed. This family consists of father, four sons and grandmother. Through the industry of the father a large lot was purchased, a neat cottage built, and the family life today would be a credit to any immigrant laborer establishing a home in a new country."[32]

Rajani Kanta Das, writing in 1922 on the conditions of Hindustani workers on the Pacific coast commented:

> The most important problem, which the Hindustanees on the Pacific Coast have to solve, is that of their domestic life. Practically all of the immigrants are male. Most of them are married, but left their families in India. As soon as they became successful in business, they sent for their wives and children. Some of them came to join their husbands and fathers, but were not allowed to land on the Pacific Coast.
>
> One of the objects of the policy adopted by the Canadian Government was to prohibit the arrival of the families of the Hindustanees domiciled in Canada so that they would be compelled to return to India sooner or later. This policy was also adopted by the United States Government.
>
> The Hindustanees vigorously protested against such policy. They could not abandon their successful industrial careers in the new country, nor could they leave their wives and children in the old for good. Nothing has so much embittered them as this policy of exclusion; for it is not only injustice to them, but also to their innocent wives and children. This embitterment is fully shared by all educated men and women in India today.[33]

However, at the time Das was writing the Canadian government had already relaxed its regulations. At the Imperial Conference in 1918 it had been decided by the Commonwealth leaders that Indians already domiciled in other British countries would be allowed to bring in one wife and her children. By order-in-council the Canadian government in 1919 implemented the policy, but few came, the cost of bringing them being more than many of the men could, in the post-war days, afford. The 1927 *Report on Oriental Activities in the Province* showed that between 1906 and 1925 only forty-five women and forty-one children had entered Canada compared to 4,909 men.[34] Of this number, thirty-six women and twenty-four children had entered since 1920.[35]

In the spring of 1922, Sadhu Singh Dhami, "a turbaned teenager" as he described himself almost fifty years later, arrived in Vancouver from the Punjab and enrolled in a high school: "My most meaningful introduction to the new world," he wrote, "began in the John Oliver High School, South Vancouver. The first Sikh boy with long hair and turban to be seen in the area, I was received with a warmth of feeling which masked curiosity. If the teachers' encouragement made learning easier, the gay, youthful atmosphere made life most enjoyable; only the inordinate attention of the girls embarrassed me. They would ask me to write their names in Urdu or Gurmukhi, persuade me to tattoo these in ink on their fore-arms, and stretch out their hands to know what the future held in store for them. Curious and inquisitive always, they asked one day, with shocking impudence, whether I was a boy or a girl. And the reply blurted out by the provoked Punjab manhood in me produced blushes that giggles could not conceal. Everybody called me "Sheik" which I took as a forgivable mispronunciation of "Sikh", and a gesture of goodwill. It was much too late to shake off the nickname when I learned that it had, in fact, originated in a mistaken identity with Rudolph Valentino, the popular, romantic star of exotic films about the East. Yet when I went to see one, flamboyantly advertised by a picture house on Hastings Street, the heavily powdered blonde in the glass cubicle refused to sell me a ticket. 'With that turban,' she said with curt finality, 'you can't get in.' 'But Valentino is wearing a turban,' I replied, 'and he is very much in.' 'Ah,' she sighed dreamily, 'Valentino can do anything he likes!' "[36]

It was necessary for Dhami to take his lunch to school each day. "As chappatis and vegetable curry, our regular food, were clumsy to carry and inconvenient to manipulate in public," he continued, "my compatriots made pinnies (a preparation of flour, ground nuts and sugar, fried in butter and rolled into balls) for me. With the cold weather, however, they became hard as baseballs and acquired a dark, ominous look. Fortunately, an abundance of thick brush-wood around the school promised privacy at noon. But one bright day the boys surprised me in the process of disintegrating my lunch with a stone. After a most hilarious interlude, they all wanted to taste the grim-looking fragments of my 'energy bolus,' and relished them with such gusto that my lunch problem was solved. The embarrassing ordeal was a thing of the past, for now I received dainty sandwiches for bits of my bolus, and enjoyed the western food in the boisterous company of my classmates."[37] That year Dhami was one of only sixteen East Indian students in British Columbia schools. The following year the numbers mysteriously rose to thirty only to drop back to twenty by 1925.[38]

During the 1920s and 1930s the size of the East Indian community remained virtually static. While each year a handful of wives and children entered Canada to bolster the small number of births, emigration and deaths kept the population down. At the outbreak of World War II, it was estimated that there were only fifteen East Indian families in Vancouver,[39] and in 1941 the Vancouver School Board reported a total of fifty-one Hindus in the city schools representing .1 per cent of the school population.[40] Small communities had also become established in other parts of the province, but until the Second World War was over there was little the East Indians could do to win rights of immigration and enfranchisement equal to those accorded immigrants from Europe.

"Halleluiah!"

The post-war years brought many welcome changes for the East Indian community in British Columbia. The fight for the franchise was finally won in 1947, the same year in which India obtained its independence from Great Britain. In 1951, 150 East Indians a year were allowed to enter Canada; in 1957 the number was raised to 300. And then, ten years later, the breakthrough came: "Halleluiah!" wrote the editor of *The Indo-Canadian*. "We, INDO-CANADIANS, are no longer second-class citizens. Not from October 1, 1967, when the new immigration laws came into force. We now enjoy the same privileges as ethnic groups hailing from Europe and other selected countries."[41] Following the relaxation of the regulations, the increase in immigration from the Indian sub-continent and from other parts of the world where East Indians had settled, such as East Africa and Fiji, was swift and very dramatic. The 1961 census gave the total number of East Indians in Canada as a little under 7,000, with about 4,500 resident in British Columbia; in 1977, Norm Buchignani, who had made a careful research of the sociological and historical literature dealing with East Indians, estimated that there were now over 150,000 East Indians in Canada of whom not more than a quarter lived in British Columbia.[42] The effect of this high immigration was naturally felt by the school system.

The relatively small number of East Indian children in the schools of the province until the influx of 1968 and subsequent years had caused few problems. "Sikh children take part in every school activity; there is no segregation of any kind," wrote Lyn Harrington in 1948.[43] Indeed, in 1947, an East Indian student had been elected president of the student council at Victoria High School, the first of his ethnic group to hold the position. The *Victoria Daily Times* applauded the action in an editorial by saying, "There is a healthy reaffirmation of the democratic ideal in the election of a Canadian of East Indian extraction, Baghat Singh, to be president of the Students' Council of Victoria High School for the coming school year. Here, in essence, is a concrete recognition by a large group of Victoria youth of the principles for which this country recently fought and which it is now struggling, with the other nations of the globe, to establish as a way of life for the world —a world in which a youngster, irrespective of his race, creed or religion, will be judged and accepted for what he is and for what he holds true."[44] A month later, the *Vancouver Sun* announced that two Canadian-born Sikh sisters, after spending two years at the University of British Columbia, were now studying medicine at the University of Toronto.[45] Jennifer Munday in 1953 provided more detailed insights. "According to the principal of Henry Hudson Elementary School in Vancouver," she wrote, "where several very young East Indians attend, there is no marked difference between their conduct and adjustment and that of their classmates. A few of them have difficulty with the language when they first begin school, but the majority are Canadian-born, and English is known by other members of their families."[46] Munday was concerned that a large percentage of the East Indian students, both boys and girls, left school as early as possible, that only a small number graduated from high school, and very few went on to university. She pointed out that in the year in which she was writing (1953) out of fifteen East Indian students at the University of British Columbia only six were Canadian residents, and that the first East Indian woman student would graduate from the university that year. She felt that the failure on the part of students to continue their education was largely due to pressure from home, the school being seen as one of the major factors in the disintegration of the old traditions.[47] In any case, for girls in particular, job opportunities seemed somewhat limited. Parents discouraged their daughters from taking jobs in factories or restaurants, and while both the Hudson's Bay Company and the T. Eaton Company denied that they had any hiring policy which excluded East Indians, neither company had in their employ any East Indian salesclerks. Munday reported that no girls had attended Normal School, two were taking nurse's training, and the great majority found jobs in offices.[48] For boys the opportunities were better and were increased by a good education: two were in medicine, and some in other professions, but although East Indians had been allowed since 1947 to enter the legal profession, none were currently enrolled in law school at the University of British Columbia.[49] She also remarked, "It is seldom that any close relationship exists between Sikhs and other Asiatics. The second generation is striving to prove that they are not an unassimilable minority and they do not want to draw attention to their differences, racial and cultural, by allying with another minority group....I think the general opinion of the second generation is that there is no active discrimination directed towards them." Some proof of that lay in the fact that East Indian boys and girls had been elected presidents of their student councils in high schools in Victoria, North Vancouver, Mount View, Cloverdale and Mission, and girls had become cheer leaders.[50] For those children whose parents wanted them to read and write Punjabi, classes were offered at the Sikh temple.[51]

Between 1966 and 1969 immigration from India to British Columbia tripled; in 1974 it was almost nine times the 1966 figure and this did not include East Indians who entered Canada from any other part of the world. Approximately a quarter of these newcomers were likely to attend school either on arrival or when they turned six. In early 1971, it became apparent to both the Vancouver School Board, who received the largest number of immigrants of any school district in the province, and to the Sikh community that additional help must be given to the newly arrived children to assist them in mastering the English language and in adapting to the new way of life; so a meeting was held at the Sikh Temple between representatives of the two groups and other interested people. The result was the establishment of a summer program for elementary school children which culminated a year later in the setting up of a special Punjabi-English primary class in a nearby school.

A survey had disclosed that there was a high proportion of East Indian children in the schools close to the Sikh Temple on Ross Street in South Vancouver. Of the total population of Sir Walter Moberly Elementary School, fourteen per cent were East Indian, while at the primary annex the figure was twenty-five per cent. But of greater concern was the age-grade retardation noted. Twenty-five per cent of the East Indian pupils were one year behind in their grade placement and fifteen per cent were two or more years behind. The teachers considered that only fifty-one per cent were making satisfactory progress. Not all the children were immigrants: forty per cent had been born in Canada. There seemed to be three major causes of the children's poor progress: first, their previous educational experiences had not equipped them to cope with the British Columbia curriculum; second, they lacked facility in the English language; third, the Indian and Canadian ways of life were sufficiently different to set up cultural conflicts.

Sir Walter Moberly Elementary School was therefore chosen as the site for the 1971 summer program called "Under the Mango Tree." It was a co-operative venture of four local organizations: the Vancouver School Board, the Vancouver City Social Planning Department, the Khalsa-Diwan Society, and the Metropolitan Health Board. The aims of the program were to improve the children's English; to help the children and their parents to become more familiar with the city, with its resources, and with Canadian ideas and programs; to encourage the children to socialize more with Caucasian children and children of other nationalities; and to involve them in recreational activities.[53] The program was under the direction of two young East Indian unversity students; the group leaders and assistants, largely high school students, were either East Indian or Caucasian; all were paid by the federal government through the Opportunity for Youth scheme. A total of 112 children from kindergarten to grade seven enrolled in the program, sixty-two per cent of them being East Indian, the others being of Japanese, Chinese, Greek, Portuguese and other European backgrounds. The children attended from 9:00 a.m. to 3:00 p.m. four days a week for six weeks. Various activities were arranged which were intended to stimulate language development and at the same time to increase the children's knowledge and understanding of the Canadian way of life and of their own neighbourhood and city in particular. At its termination the program was judged to have been successful, and consequently it was mounted again in succeeding summers. Gradually the Vancouver School Board developed an extensive summer program for immigrant children in various parts of the city and took over most of the organization.

Partly as an outcome of the summer program, the Vancouver School Board decided to set up an experimental primary class in Moberly School Annex consisting of 5 to 8 year old Punjabi-speaking children under the direction of Mrs. S. Sandhu, a bilingual Punjabi-English-speaking primary teacher who was trained to teach English as a second language. Twenty children were enrolled in the class in September, 1972. The aims of the program were much like those of the summer program with regard to language development, but in addition attention was also focussed on improving the children's self-concepts and in helping them to understand and appreciate the Canadian culture without losing their esteem for the East Indian culture. The teacher was free to use Punjabi whenever she felt the situation called for it, such as in explaining a new concept, or coping with the distress brought on by the loss of a lunch bag. An evaluation at the end of the first year recommended that the class carry on for an additional two years.

A more comprehensive report at the end of the second year presented some specific recommendations. The author raised once again the question of the federal government's responsibility for the education of immigrant children. "The Canadian Federal Government," wrote Moody, "when granting permission for young East Indian immigrants to enter Canada, should provide a certain sum of monies for their education, thus allowing school boards to hire extra teachers, purchase special material, and so on. This would help these children to progress more quickly, and would not hinder the learning of English-speaking children."[54] But between the British North America Act which placed the responsibility for education firmly on the provincial governments and the failure of the provincial governments to initiate discussion on this topic when the federal government opened the way in 1971, there was no likelihood that the government would intervene at this time to assist in the language training of immigrant children. A number of other recommendations concerned the parents, particularly the mothers. The author wanted the parents to be encouraged to speak English and to become more involved in the life of the school. She felt that mothers should place their young children in nursery school and should attend the nursery school themselves part-time in order to become more familiar with the Canadian culture and to receive information on nutrition and health care. The author suggested that the children should spend longer in school before being taught to read, and that greater use should be made of Punjabi in the classroom as she felt that the children's lack of fluency in their first language might be impeding their progress in English. Moody also questioned the school board's objective (which was also a directive of the Ministry of Education at that time) that the majority of the children should be ready to be placed in a regular class after one year in the Punjabi-English class. "One has high expectations," she commented, "if he anticipates that an 8-year old immigrant child can receive only one year of intensive language instruction and then function successfully in a regular class. Perhaps the child should extend his length of stay in the East Indian class, but at the same time increase his integration time into regular class."[55] Moody recommended that the class should continue, but for personal reasons the teacher had to leave the employ of the school board and with discrimination against East Indians on the increase the wisdom of segregating these children from the Caucasian children was questioned and the class was in time disbanded and no final report issued.

At the close of 1974 the Vancouver School Board made a survey of the number of children within the district who spoke English as a second language and in 1977 it repeated the survey. The results showed that in 1974 there were 1,344 East Indian children in the elementary schools and that by 1977 the figure had risen to 1,875. The number of East Indian students in secondary schools rose from 368 in 1974 to 597 in 1977.[56] What the numbers were in school districts in other parts of the province it is not possible to say as similar surveys were not carried out either by the districts or by the Ministry of Education, but many of the districts in the Fraser Valley and those in the interior where logging operations and sawmills formed an important part of the local economy experienced a sharp increase in the number of East Indian children in the schools.

Teachers were, on the whole, unprepared for this new wave of immigrants and few had any detailed knowledge of the culture from which they came. It was not long before stereotypes of East Indian children became popular: boys were seen as aggressive and girls as passive. Remarks such as the following were common:

> East Indian boys have difficulty adjusting to the demands for non-aggressive social behavior. The young male seems to be indulged and has difficulty adjusting.
>
> East Indian girls—their whole cultural training has been to be passive, non-questioning and non-aggressive. Teachers feel frustrated because these students are reluctant to speak out in class, to suggest ideas or initiate projects.[57]

While the teachers were undergoing a period of adjustment, so were the East Indian families. As early as 1968, before the East Indian community had felt the effects of high and rapid immigration, Michael Ames and Joy Inglis commented in *The*

Indo-Canadian on the changing relations between elders and young people. "The elder members of the community complain that the young, especially those Indians born or educated in Canada, are no longer respecting their elders as they should and as the elders believe they would were they still living in India. Young people, on the other hand, complain that the elders are too old-fashioned and repressive."[58] In a later article written after they had conducted a detailed survey, Ames and Inglis reported that young Sikhs had indicated that they found it increasingly difficult to live up to the traditional ideals,[59] and that they considered the attempts of parents to prevent young couples from establishing their own independent households as old-fashioned and repressive,[60] yet strong family bonds existed. "On the one hand, the Canada-born believe they should govern their own lives, and on the other, they regret the loss of parental favour that this independent "rebelliousness" frequently entails. In several cases where young people were cut off by their parents for choosing unacceptable spouses, the Canada-born expressed deep regret and actively sought readmittance to parental favour."[61] Like so many others before them the young people were caught between the pull of two cultures.

But in addition to the difficulties they faced in school and at home, East Indian students and their parents began to form the butt of racist jokes and grafitti. Name calling—"raghead, rugrider, Punjabi"—increased, along with acts of violence directed at both people and property, and the local press which had over the years paid little attention to East Indians began to devote far more space to their affairs, but, according to one researcher ". . . it was evident that throughout this period [January to August, 1975] vandalism and minor crimes against persons, when the victims were East Indians, were consistently transformed by the press from specific incidents in a rising Vancouver trend of petty crime into necessarily racial incidents."[62] Later she went on, "Throughout this period there was almost a remarkable consistency in the press' theory of story placement, the violent, the assertive, and the unusual about East Indians commanded large formats in prime places, while "normal reality," if it was covered at all, was buried in the newspaper's outback."[63] She pointed out that while there was "nothing conspiratorial about this situation it helped to shape white opinion by reinforcing past images."[64]

The British Columbia Teachers' Federation was sufficiently concerned about the rising discrimination in the small and large towns in the province that at the meeting of its Representative Assembly in the spring of 1975 it passed two resolutions, one condemning discrimination on the basis of race in the communities or schools of the province, and the other establishing a Task Force on Racism which was charged with the responsibility of working with other groups to find a solution to the mounting racism. A major contribution of the B.C.T.F. Task Force was a slide/tape show depicting a number of discriminatory acts against members of minority groups in British Columbia during the last century and this. Some school board trustees reacted negatively to the slide/tape show but in the majority of school districts it was well received.

In addition to the B.C. Teachers' Federation, other groups were also trying to combat racism both within the schools and outside them. In 1975 the Immigrant Services Society of British Columbia, in co-operation with the three levels of government, established the Immigrant Services Centre at the junction of Main Street and Marine Drive in South Vancouver, close to the Sikh Temple and in the heart of the largest East Indian community in the city. The centre was staffed largely by bilingual East Indians and consisted initially of a co-ordinator, a crisis worker, a nurse, along with social workers, interpreters and receptionists, and for a while it was the headquarters of a two-man police unit, one of whom was East Indian. The centre was very successful in providing a good information service and in giving prompt and efficient help to those in trouble. The Immigrant Services Society also gave assistance to some of the small towns in the interior which were experiencing racial problems such as Quesnel and Williams Lake, and it provided a fulltime worker in Surrey where a number of incidents occurred. In most instances communities needed assistance in adjusting to the rather sudden influx of East Indians, an ethnic group with which they had had little experience and of whom they had little knowledge. It was unfortunate that districts which could, with a little foresight, have predicted a movement of East Indians into their area, did so little to prepare teachers, parents or the general public, so that they could meet the newcomers with understanding. "A few new strategems should be added to those on which Canadian school regulations are founded," wrote Vincent D'Oyley, Associate Dean of the Faculty of Education at the University of British Columbia. "The introduction of any ethnic cluster of immigrants to an area requires preparation of the receivers, with articulation between the different levels of bureaucracy—federal, provincial, municipal—of strategies for the achievement of schooling rights. Where educational professionals have a history of failure in motivating a linguistic or cultural group, or where the general public is ignorant of particular ethnic or racial presence, federal-provincial ad hoc arrangements should be introduced to promote public acceptance of the group and to facilitate equality of educational opportunity. Such arrangements should involve teacher retraining and the adoption of special curricula aimed at fostering minimal literacy and quantification skills."[65]

There was a measure of opposition to the growing negative forces of racism through the federal government's promotion of the concept that Canada is a multicultural society embedded in a bilingual framework. This concept had grown out of the ideas contained in Book IV of the *Report of the Royal Commission on Bilingualism and Biculturalism* entitled "The Cultural Contribution of the Other Ethnic Groups." The federal government established the Canadian Consultative Council on Multiculturalism which in its first report recommended that programs specifically designed to assist alienated teenagers to overcome conflict between cultures be introduced;[66] it also came out in favour of the teaching of ethnic languages and cultures in schools.[67] While some provinces set up special ministries or special departments within established ministries to promote multiculturalism, the British Columbia government gave little support to the program, and it was left to local citizens and concerned groups to do what they could in terms of their own interests. The Immigrant Services Society of British Columbia and the Canadian Council of Christians and Jews, after running some trial projects, decided to sponsor a Multicultural Resource Team whose role would be to work with teachers and other school workers to increase their knowledge of and sensitivity towards different aspects of multiculturalism so that they, in turn, could work better with the students and their parents. In April, 1976, the two sponsoring agencies together with the Vancouver School Board approached the federal, provincial and municipal governments for financial support. The federal and municipal governments quickly allocated funds but the provincial Ministry of Education delayed giving an answer for so long that the sponsors had to decide whether to cancel the whole project or gamble on the Ministry ultimately granting the funds. Having received some verbal reassurance from officials at the Ministry, the sponsors gambled and the project got started in the fall of 1976. Members of the team made a thorough survey of the needs of schools and set up various pilot projects, but on February 2, 1977, the Ministry responded negatively by saying that they had come to the conclusion "that a precedent would be set which could have significant economic ramifications on a province-wide basis," but the Associate Deputy Minister did not elaborate on what the ramifications might be. He continued, "It is our opinion that the type of problem you are dealing with is more appropriately dealt with by the local educational, and municipal, authorities."[68] The team was forced to disband in the early spring for lack of money with its work half done.

Due to the efforts of these and other groups, such as the B.C. Civil Liberties Association and the Human Rights Council, racial tension gradually subsided although it was never far from the surface and was ready to explode over such matters as an application to build a Sikh Temple in Delta, and wherever unemployment was high there was a danger of physical violence breaking out between whites and East Indians. But within the schools East Indian children became a more familiar sight and teachers, through workshops, and day-to-day experiences, learned more about them and about racial attitudes, their own and those of others. With the reduction in immigration from 1975 on, the potentially volatile situation slowly died down although a 1977 report showed that throughout Canada East Indians were generally held in low esteem.[69]

As a reminder of all that had gone before, the *Vancouver Sun* on

October 15, 1977, reported the death in Vancouver of Mr. Giani Kartar Singh.[70] Mr. Singh was one of the last survivors of the *Komagata Maru* incident. In 1914 he had been forced to return to India with the other would-be immigrants, but in 1976 he finally landed in British Columbia having come to join relatives. With his death another living link to the past had been broken, but the memory of the *Komagata Maru* and all that led up to it and all that followed it is a legacy inherited by all British Columbians.

Afterwords

> *Children's dependency renders them uniquely vulnerable to becoming the invisible casualties of institutions and systems which assume that by responding to the needs and demands of adults, they simultaneously and adequately address the needs of the children who depend on adults.*
>
> Admittance Restricted

The forces which shaped the lives of the children of ethnic minority groups in British Columbia from the mid-nineteenth century on were no different from the forces which shape the lives of children today: educational, religious, social, economic, and political. But shackled as they were with limited knowledge and limited power, few parents and few children could stand up against the negative effects of those forces, and few public institutions paid much serious attention to the effects those forces had on the children.

It has been many years since the first native Indian child walked into William Duncan's school in Fort Simpson or since the first Chinese child sat at his wooden desk in one of Victoria's public schools, many years during which many children have been both physically and emotionally abused on account of their race or the beliefs of their parents. Who spoke up for these children, who argued their case, and who listened? Within our society there are various groups of people, any one of which might, had it been both able and willing, have changed the nature of the treatment meted out to the minority groups' children over the past 120 years, but in general their responses were weak and tardy—too frequently those who would have acted could not and those who could have acted would not.

Parents

It is customary for parents to speak up for their children and, indeed, one of the reasons that the Japanese were considered more aggressive than the Chinese during the years between the wars was because far more of them had young children for whose future they were prepared to fight. But the parents of children of the various ethnic minorities were limited in what they could do, for over the years they were forced into a state of political and economic subservience.

One of the first actions taken against each of the minority groups as their numbers began to build up was to disfranchise them. It was not until the end of World War II that Asian Canadians in British Columbia were permitted to vote in school board, municipal, provincial and federal elections, to hold public office, and to enter the professions. Until they were allowed to have a public voice of their own, the parents of Asian Canadian children had to rely on the courage of their own spokesmen—largely in the ethnic press; on the occasional conscience-stricken editorial of an often hostile press; and on those leaders of the white community whose concern prompted them to speak out on behalf of the children. A second action taken against these minority groups was to drastically limit their involvement in the economy of the province by measures which made it difficult for most of them to earn more than bare subsistence wages; for self-interest has been rampant in this century and, as Barbara Ward has said, "No one should underestimate the degree to which conscience can be silenced when conscience and self-interest conflict."[1] For the parents of Chinese and Japanese children the years between the wars were hard years; job opportunities diminished, welfare rates were in some cases lower for them than for whites, and there was the indignity of being told that they liked living in poverty. But the parents hung on and helped their children through school and today they must marvel at the success of their children in a world they were not allowed to enter. Perhaps these parents spoke loudest by their actions as they supported their children through the lean and hungry years.

For Doukhobor parents the situation was no better; they had no way in which they could enforce changes which would make the schools more acceptable by bringing them into closer harmony with their beliefs and no way in which they could prevent the government from seizing their children, for they, too, lacked power. Today they are enfranchised and economically more secure but there has been a weakening of the sense of community and an erosion of the faith which prompted the exodus from Russia.

But for the native Indian parents, progress along the path from poverty and political impotence has been slow—a low standard of living is still the only way of life that far too many Indian families know. Their leaders have spoken with eloquence on the need for a better system of education for their children, a system which they feel should be based on their needs and values. But people whose main source of income is welfare do not have either the economic or political clout to bring about more than minor changes in educational policies. The honourable settlement of land claims without further delay is vital to the health and happiness of the children, as is a recognition of the value of the native cultures to Canada.

The success of a child's education depends very much on good co-operation between the school and the home. Over the years the degree of parental involvement in the education of the children of ethnic minority groups has been minimal due not only to the parents' lack of voting power but also to their lack of facility in English, and, in some cases, to the failure of schools to help parents understand an educational philosophy different from their own. There are times in the lives of most children when school and home must work closely together for the good of the individual; often the adolescent years for minority children can be harsh years when the values taught in the home and those taught, overtly and covertly, in the schools are in conflict. It is hard for children to be criticized in school for behaving in ways which would earn them praise at home; it is also hard for them to be denied by their parents the opportunity to engage in activities enjoyed by their peers. The need for understanding by all parties of both points of view is great. The dilemma for parents is not an easy one for them to resolve: what will they teach their children?—the old values they were brought up with or the new values, some of which are not attractive; and if they permit the new values to supersede the old, will they have cheated their children out of their heritage? For the schools and for society in general, problems concerning value systems are the most difficult to resolve involving as they do gut feelings about what is "right" and what is "wrong." To move people from hostility towards another culture to toleration of that culture and eventually to appreciation of that culture takes time and patience.

It has not been easy for parents to articulate exactly what they want for their children or, indeed, for them to achieve a consensus: on the one hand, many parents mistrust the schools which they see as creating a barrier between themselves and their children, and between their children and their ancestral language and culture; while, on the other hand, they recognize that the schools can provide their children with the tools they need if they are to succeed in the larger society. Schools have to be seen by parents as an integral part of the local community, concerned with the needs and hopes of the local community, if parents are to trust them.

If through economic and political weakness parents of minority group children were largely denied the opportunity to modify the educational system, what role did government play?

Government

Until very recently the Ministry of Education largely ignored the presence of children of different ethnic groups in the school system except when circumstances forced it to take notice and then its actions were, to say the least, contradictory and insufficient. For example, during the first and second decades of this century the Ministry (then the Department) of Education was on the one hand trying to force Doukhobor children to attend school while at the same time ignoring the efforts of the Victoria School Board to keep Chinese children out of its schools. Briefs and reports, sometimes commissioned by the government, which were submitted to the Ministry over the years on the education of Doukhobor children in particular and immigrant children in general had little influence on Ministry policy. The failure of the Ministry to accept any responsibility for the education of British Columbia-born children of Japanese ancestry during World War II brought it little honour, and its apathy since the war towards the education of non-English-speaking children in the public schools, a group which probably now represents about 10 per cent of the school population, has further confirmed the image of a disinterested public institution. Although, in more recent years, the Ministry has made funds available to school districts for the setting up of classes to teach English as a second language, the funding formula has been such that the school district which received the greatest number of non-English-speaking immigrant children, namely, the Vancouver School Board, was granted an inadequate sum of money for the task it had to do. It was not until the mid-1970s when the Vancouver School Board counted the number of non-English speaking children in its schools and the size of the ethnic vote became apparent that the Ministry responded with additional funds which enabled the school board to double its program.

In 1971 the Minister of Education for British Columbia along with the Ministers of Education for the other provinces, who together form the Council of Provincial Ministers of Education, chose to ignore an offer by the federal government to discuss aid to the provinces for the teaching of the official languages to children of immigrants. This was unfortunate as our system of government, which allocates certain powers to the federal government and other powers to the provincial governments, has over the years enabled both parties to play political football with the education of native Indian and immigrant children; for while education is under provincial jurisdiction, the federal government is responsible for native Indian affairs and immigration. Collaboration between the two levels of government could have been highly beneficial. As it is the division of responsibilities has placed school boards in the frustrating position of having requests for additional sums of money needed to mount good programs turned down by both parties on the grounds that the other institution is the responsible funding agency.

Another neglected area has been multiculturalism. It was not until April, 1979, that the British Columbia government turned its attention to the federal government's policy that Canada is a multicultural society in a bilingual framework. This it did by sponsoring a two day conference entitled "Toward a Multicultural Policy for British Columbia." Many recommendations resulted from the discussions including a number concerned with multiculturalism and education and the teaching of languages, but whether any positive action will result from the conference only time will reveal.

But governments do not lead, they follow, and one might expect that leadership would come from professional organizations related to education.

Professional Organizations

The record here is again a sad one until recently. The Parent-Teacher Association, a voluntary organization, and the British Columbia School Trustees' Association, a body of elected citizens, have had little to say over the years apart from the occasional article or minor report. An exception has been the Vancouver Board of School Trustees which, particularly during the last decade, has submitted a number of well-documented briefs to both the federal and provincial governments, but with limited success. The British Columbia Teachers' Federation remained silent until the late 1930s when it slowly found its conscience and its voice which resulted in 1975 in the establishment of its Task Force on Racism, an action which very quickly plunged it into controversy.

The terms of reference of the B.C.T.F. Task Force on Racism were as follows:

1. To create awareness of racial and cultural prejudice within schools and society.
2. To implement B.C.T.F. policy relevant to the Task Force on Racism program.
3. To make recommendations to the B.C.T.F. Executive Committee on matters affecting race relations.
4. To develop teaching materials on racism.
5. To establish communication with community and government organizations working in the area of race relations.
6. To gather examples of various programs or practices that have been used successfully in schools to deal with racism and to make these programs available to teachers in B.C.[2]

The Task Force was concerned with various aspects of racism in schools including name calling or physical violence on the part of the students, racist jokes in the staffrooms, or bias in textbooks. The Force prepared bibliographies and other materials to increase teachers' knowledge and self-awareness of the subtle ways in which racism can be manifested and to provide teachers with ways of combatting racism in the classroom and the community. One of the Task Force's major productions was a slide/tape show which posed, and then graphically answered, the question, "Do we have racial discrimination in B.C.?" As evidence it pointed to a number of discriminatory acts against native Indians, French Canadians, Chinese, Japanese, Doukhobors and East Indians during this century and the last. While many teachers reacted favourably to the slide/tape show, which was called "Racism in B.C.," the B.C. School Trustees' Association asked the Secretary of State's office, which had provided some funds for the project, to have the show destroyed because they felt it would probably exacerbate the problems of racism, a request which the Secretary of State's office quite properly turned down. The show became a public issue. The *Victoria Daily Times* described the B.C. School Trustees' attitude as disappointing saying, "The association refused to co-operate with the B.C.T.F. in making the package because it refused to accept that there is racism in the schools of B.C. and outside them. Ostrich-like the trustees' association suggests that merely using the package in the schools may promote racism. That is a weak and simplistic answer that simply won't hold water. Refusing to acknowledge the problem, or simply ignoring it is not going to make racism disappear. Doing nothing in the face of virulent and vicious racism that sprouts up in B.C.—see Vanderhoof, Richmond, Quesnel—from time to time is going to aggravate it. Trying to deny racism in B.C. is like an elephant trying to hide behind a sapling. The B.C.S.T.A. should come out of its idyllic unreal world and face facts."[3]

School trustees throughout the province deliberated on the advisability of allowing the slide/tape show to be used in schools in their districts, and those who banned it—few in number—were usually castigated by their local press. The first school board to ban the show was Surrey. The trustees felt that it presented a biased view giving only the negative aspects of racism. The *Surrey Leader*, however, after attending a public showing, described the presentation as "glossy and provocative" and as one which might foster discussion.[4] After the Sechelt School Board delayed making a decision on whether to approve the show, the *Peninsula Times* wrote, "Discrimination does exist. It exists on the Sunshine Coast, and the only method of dealing with it is through education and understanding. It would be a grave mistake for the trustees to follow the convoluted thinking of Surrey and ban the documentary from our schools."[5] A trustee in Saanich, a district which also banned the show, who had spent some years in the immigration department felt the show was incomplete and suggested that it should include information on Canada's present immigration regulations which he considered to be the fairest and least discriminatory in the world, and that it should acknowledge the generous assistance given to immigrants in Canada.[6] The *New Westminster Columbian*, commenting on the actions of districts which banned the show, wrote, "In doing so they fail to recognize the value of jogging a child's sensibilities. Like the defensive driving course that shows motorists the tragic pictures taken by police of car accidents, the presentation in our mind brings the point home that B.C. has a long historical record of racial hatreds. Few people after seeing the presentation can fall back into the comfortable position of saying the problem doesn't exist here."[7] Karenn Krangle, the education reporter for the *Vancouver Sun*, described the decision of the Langley trustees to follow the example of Surrey with the words: "If Surrey's silly, Langley must be looney. . . Langley, Surrey and the B.C.S.T.A. all believe that the presentation may spark discriminatory attitudes in children rather than prevent them, and therefore should not be shown in schools. That attitude seems to imply that children are either innocent lambs with no parental or peer influence to begin with or are so stupid that they will miss the point of the whole presentation—that discriminatory acts are not a good thing. The people who believe this and who are afraid to take the risk of what they believe will be poisoning young minds, are, in effect, burning the history books—denying that discrimination did exist and still takes place."[8] Surrey, Langley and Saanich were, however, in the minority. The B.C. Teachers' Federation reported that during 1977-1978 sixty-five workshops on racism had been held and "Racism in B.C." had been shown 250 times.

During the 1970s various citizens' groups such as the Immigrant Services Society of British Columbia, Directions ESL, the Council on Immigrant Children and the B.C. Multicultural Society all took a stand on a number of complex issues relating to children, while various native Indian organizations clearly indicated the direction they felt education should go if their children were to be adequately prepared for their adult years. But these are very recent developments. Who spoke for the children during the first half of the century? Surely the schools, whose first responsibility must be for the children in their care, did not remain silent?

Schools

Within the schools, then as now, there were good teachers and poor teachers, sensitive teachers and insensitive teachers, knowledgeable teachers and ignorant teachers; and the good ones supported and helped the children and the poor ones harmed them. Many teachers felt frustrated by the failure of the children to learn, whether the cause lay in large classes, different learning styles, home backgrounds, or poor facility in English. Some were frustrated by the restraints imposed on them by the administration, whether at the school, district, or provincial level, which made it difficult for them to help the children in the way they would have liked. The obvious inequities they saw around them caused some teachers to speak out, not always a wise move bearing in mind the climate of the times, both political and economic; but others became apathetic and were a source of concern to H.B. Hawthorn whose reports on Doukhobor and native Indian children stressed the importance of good, well-trained teachers for children of ethnic minorities. Public school principals, on the whole, took the side of the children and with few exceptions, did not permit flagrant discrimination to occur. The position of native Indian children in the church-run segregated schools was entirely different, and the damage inflicted on the children in residential schools and on their children in turn through the suppression of their languages and cultures can never be measured nor repaired.

Teacher training institutions largely ignored any suggestions that student teachers should be sensitized to the needs of children who did not belong to the dominant group. Even before the turn of the century the Deputy Superintendent of Indian Affairs pointed out the need for superior teachers for native Indian children, a point reiterated later by H.B. Hawthorn. But it was not until 1972 that any attempt was made to ensure that teacher training programs were available to native Indians, and the preparation of teachers to work in multicultural classrooms is only now just beginning.

Ethnic Groups

Most ethnic groups were held together by a formal association, be it a benevolent society, a religious group or a semi-political organization. Individually these associations tended to be weak; had they spoken with a united voice perhaps they might have been heard in the provincial and federal capitals. But unity would not have been easy to attain as the attitudes of the various ethnic groups towards education were not identical. The Chinese, Japanese and East Indians usually saw education as a way of moving up the economic ladder, but as many high school graduates discovered during the first half of this century, even a good education would not guarantee them a job if their skin was the wrong colour. The officials of Indian Affairs and the missionaries believed that education could cure barbarism, particularly if the children could be separated from their home. (What the Indians thought about education was not considered relevant until recently.) The Doukhobors, on the other hand, saw education as the cause of barbarism and pointed to the 1945 explosion of the atomic bomb at Hiroshima and Nagasaki as the epitome of all barbaric acts; they objected strongly to certain facets of education which they felt were contrary to their belief in the supremacy of God's law over that of elected governments and contrary to their fervent adherence to pacifism. Part of the difference in the attitudes of these ethnic groups towards education lay in their traditions: in China, Japan and India formal education had for many years been an accepted part of the culture though not necessarily available to all; for the native Indians or the Doukhobors formal education was either not known or was not seen as relevant.

Each group therefore sought changes in the operation of the schools and in the curriculum which would ensure that the kind and quality of education their children received would be more in harmony with their beliefs and goals. The Chinese and Japanese people opposed the segregation of their children on the grounds of race and asked that better English language instruction be provided for their children so that they would not be handicapped by poor facility in the language of instruction. The Doukhobors wanted to see an end to any activities which smacked of militarism; they requested that no emphasis should be placed on the study of government or wars; and they asked that Russian should be taught in the schools, it being the vehicle through which their culture was transmitted. The native Indian people have made it clear that they are seeking a recognition of their languages and their cultures, and that they expect the schools to prepare their children to live successfully and with dignity in the years ahead. Both the native Indians and the Doukhobors have opposed the emphasis placed on competition in the schools preferring co-operation, as both groups see co-operation as providing a better foundation for social harmony than competition. Most of the requests made over the years were quite reasonable, but most were ignored, and the same curriculum was taught to all children regardless of their backgrounds and their parents' wishes; but there were exceptions as individual principals made individual responses to local needs.

One of the most fundamental issues which both the schools and society has to grapple with is that of language. We are living in an era when the divisive nature of language is all too apparent: it will be sad indeed if Canadians continue to feel that languages must divide them. The average Canadian attitude to languages was nicely summed up by Keith Spicer at a conference in Vancouver when he said, "We are the only nation in the world which thinks that learning another language is a pain in the neck instead of an opportunity." Our history unfortunately bears that out, for the support given to the learning of languages in general in the schools of the province and to the learning of minority ethnic languages in particular has been negligible. For a century the native Indian languages were slowly strangled and now belated attempts are being made to revive them: but for some Indian languages relief has come too late and they are in their coffins; others have found the strength to breathe for a little while longer but death is near; only a few are alive and well. The languages spoken by the immigrant groups did not receive the same oppressive treatment; the children continued to speak their first language in their homes and, as the groups were to some degree ghettoized, in their local communities. The Japanese and Chinese third language schools were well patronized in the pre-World War II days because, not only did they teach the children the language and culture of their forebears, they also provided children who were denied employment in the white community with a tool for obtaining employment in their own ethnic community. East Indian children also received instruction in their first language usually through the home and the temple, and for most Doukhobor children only Russian was spoken at home. Neither the public schools nor the federal schools have seen it as part of their responsibility to help children maintain fluency in their first language or to obtain fluency in their ancestral tongue, but now that UNESCO has spoken out in favour of children beginning their education in their mother tongue,[9] and now that the U.S.A. is moving swiftly towards bilingual-bicultural education for its ethnic minorities, and now that research is testifying to the benefits of bilingualism in children[10] British Columbia cannot ignore the language rights of children much longer. It is surely the responsibility of the school over the years to make children more than they were when they first entered school; this slow suffocation of children's first languages and first cultures cannot do otherwise than make them less than they were.

Churches

It is easy to see the churches only in their role as villains in the suppression of the native Indian languages and cultures through their implementation of Indian Affairs' "English only" policy, and obviously the churches, in their eagerness to make converts, cannot escape a large measure of blame for what occurred. Their actions grew, to some degree, out of ignorance of the interdependence of language, culture and personal dignity, and of the value of bilingualism. The last twenty years has, however, brought an extraordinary increase in knowledge concerning language and language learning, and had the church fathers been acquainted with this knowledge and had they been as ready to learn from the Indians as they were to teach them perhaps more native people today might be bilingual and bicultural, having the best of two worlds instead of existing in a cultural and linguistic limbo. For the methods used in some residential schools at some times to suppress the Indian languages no excuse is acceptable—the mistreatment of any child by any person for any reason should be abhorrent to all.

In another arena, however, the churches showed far more understanding and concern. It was the churches who established kindergartens for Japanese and Chinese-speaking children so that they might learn the English language and Canadian ways before they entered school, and it was the churches who made it possible during World War II for many Japanese teenagers to continue their high school education and to go on to further studies in eastern universities.

Politicians

Finally the question must be asked: did the politicians, the elected representatives of the people speak for the children? Some concerned politicians such as Ernest Winch demanded the vote for Orientals at a time when it was politically unwise to do so; others gave their support to discriminatory legislation; but many remained silent.

The authors of *Admittance Restricted* say, "Society has an obligation to supplement the resources of the family through education and other means so that the lives of children need not be restricted by the facts of their birth; so that all children can acquire the skills necessary to exercise their basic freedoms as citizens; so that having acquired those skills they may make an unhampered contribution to their society."[11] This obligation requires that political decisions must be made if it is to be met, and these decisions will not be made until the silent majority is prepared to accept a greater measure of responsibility for the welfare of all children—society must relinquish the luxury of indifference. A further requirement is that decisions regarding the education of children must be made on the basis of what is educationally sound and not, as has occurred too often in the past, on what is politically expedient. It was, for instance, expedient for politicians to remain silent while Chinese children were discriminated against; but for those children a year out of school or no school at all was educationally unsound. The decision to remove Doukhobor children from their homes and coerce them into an education was another politically expedient decision; it went against the recommendations of those who had studied the community and who rightly felt that time and compromise were better instruments in the long run than force. It was politically expedient for the provincial government to provide no schooling for Japanese-Canadian children during their enforced evacuation; but for the children, had it not been for the dedication of their own school graduates and the help of the churches, those years would have been an educational disaster. Sins of omission can be as harmful as sins of commission: the failure of the provincial and federal governments to come to some agreement regarding financial aid for school districts having a high proportion of non-English-speaking children has put these youngsters at a distinct disadvantage with their Canadian-born English-speaking peers.

Canada has no national policy regarding the education of its children, it has set no minimal standards, it has devised no national programs by which inequalities might be lessened if not eradicated. Canada has no national policy regarding the language rights of children who enter school speaking neither English nor French, not even for its first citizens, the native Indian children. New policies are necessary which put the needs of children ahead of the interests of adults.

> To ignore the highly political nature of children's issues and the repercussions that their resolution would have for existing social and political systems is to deny the dimensions of the struggle ahead. We believe very strongly that what is at stake in our discrimination against children and youth is not only the rights of the young but the human rights of our society.[12]

Notes

INTRODUCTION

1. F.M. Buckland, "Okanagan School," *Seventeenth Report of the Okanagan Historical Society,* 1953.
2. British Columbia, *Sessional Papers,* Public School Reports, 1875-1876, p. 109.
3. British Columbia, *Sessional Papers,* Public School Reports, 1876-1877, p. 24.
4. M. Macfie, *Vancouver Island and British Columbia,* London: Longmans, 1865, pp. 380-381.

CHAPTER ONE: THE NATIVE INDIANS

1. R.C. Mayne, *Four Years in British Columbia and Vancouver Island,* London: John Murray, 1862, pp. 318-319.
2. *Ibid.,* p. 242.
3. Harold Cardinal, *The Unjust Society,* Edmonton: Hurtig, 1969, p. 52.
4. Mayne, *op. cit.,* p. 345.
5. Thomas Crosby, *Among the An-ko-me-nums,* Toronto: William Briggs, 1907, pp. 42-44.
6. J.W.W. Moeran, *McCullagh of Aiyansh,* London: Marshall Bros., 1923, p. 45.
7. Department of Indian Affairs, *Annual Report,* 1876, p. 33.
8. D.I.A., *Annual Report, 1878,* p. 69.
9. D.I.A., *Annual Report, 1883,* p. 112.
10. D.I.A., *Annual Report, 1884,* p. 122.
11. D.I.A., *Annual Report, 1885,* p. 78.
12. D.I.A., *Annual Report, 1887,* p. lxxix.
13. D.I.A., *Annual Report, 1896,* p. 382.
14. D.I.A., *Annual Report, 1898,* p. 345.
15. *Ibid.,* p. 348.
16. D.I.A., *Annual Report, 1899,* p. 397.
17. D.I.A., *Annual Report, 1896,* p. 391.
18. D.I.A., *Annual Report, 1898,* p. 345.
19. *Ibid.,* p. 341.
20. D.I.A., *Annual Report, 1895,* p. xxii.
21. D.I.A., *Annual Report, 1903,* pp. xxviii-xxix.

22. Margaret Butcher, "1916-1919, Correspondence re life in Kitimat," in the Provincial Archives, Victoria.
23. George Manuel and Michael Posluns, *The Fourth World*, Toronto: Collier-Macmillan, 1974, p. 65.
24. *Ibid.*, p. 64.
25. *Ibid.*, p. 67.
26. Interview, July, 1978, with Judge M. Cantryn.
27. Mary Jane Sterling, "Thoughts on Silence," *I Am An Indian*, ed. Kent Gooderham, Toronto: Dent, 1969, p. 37.
28. D.I.A., *Annual Report, 1892*, p. 262.
29. D.I.A., *Annual Report, 1893, p. 133.*
30. D.I.A., *Annual Report, 1894*, p. 166.
31. Jean E. Speare, ed. *The Days of Augusta*, Vancouver: J.J. Douglas, 1973, preface.
32. D.I.A., *Annual Report, 1893*, p. xviii.
33. D.I.A., *Annual Report, 1895*, pp. xxii-xxiii.
34. D.I.A., *Annual Report, 1896*, p. 381.
35. D.I.A., *Annual Report, 1897*, p. 287.
36. D.I.A., *Annual Report, 1898*, p. 345.
37. D.I.A., *Annual Report, 1902*, p. 397.
38. D.I.A., *Annual Report, 1905*, p. 362.
39. George Manuel and Michael Posluns, *op. cit.*, p. 64.
40. Fr. E.C. Bellot, *St. Paul's Annual and Reference Book, 1937*, quoted in Robert Levine and Freda Cooper, "The Suppression of B.C. Languages: Filling in the Gaps in the Documentary Record," *Sound Heritage*, IV, 3 and 4, 1976, p. 71.
41. Robert Levine and Freda Cooper, *op. cit.*, pp. 57-63.
42. Interview, Judge M. Cantryn.
43. H.B. Hawthorn et al., *The Indians of British Columbia*, Toronto: University of Toronto Press, 1958, p. 319.
44. Cardinal, *op. cit.*, p. 53.
45. Interview, July, 1978.
46. Chief Dan George, "My Very Good Dear Friends" in Waubageshig, ed. *The Only Good Indian*, Toronto: New Press, 1970, p. 162.
47. D.I.A., *Annual Report, 1899*, p. xxxi.
48. Hawthorn, *op. cit.*, pp. 319-321.
49. *Ibid.*, pp. 291-311.
50. Canada, Joint Committee of the Senate and the House of Commons on Indian Affairs, *Minutes of Proceedings and Evidence*, Ottawa, 1960, p. 1402.
51. *Ibid.*, p. 702.
52. *Ibid.*, p. 713.
53. *Ibid.*, p. 648.
54. *Ibid.*, p. 604.
55. *Ibid.*, p. 687.
56. H.B. Hawthorn, *A Survey of the Contemporary Indians of Canada*, Ottawa, 1967, pp. 105-138.

57. Arthur Laing, "Indian Education," text of an address by the Minister of Indian Affairs and Northern Development, Vancouver, March 15, 1967.
58. Canada, Education Branch, Department of Indian Affairs and Northern Development, *5,000 Little Indians Went To School,* Ottawa, 1971, pp. 43-45.
59. *Ibid.*, p. 36.
60. *Vancouver Province,* October 26, 1929, p. 3.
61. *Daily Colonist,* October 15, 1950, p. 3.
62. *Daily Colonist*, October 17, 1950, p. 10.
63. Chief Dan George, *op. cit.*, pp. 163-164.
64. National Indian Brotherhood, *Indian Control of Indian Education,* Ottawa: National Indian Brotherhood, 1972, pp. 1-2.
65. *Ibid.*, p. 3.
66. *Ibid.*, pp. 25-26.
67. George Manuel and Michael Poslun, *op. cit.*, p. 191.
68. *Ibid.*, p. 251.
69. W.C. Thomas and R.G. McIntosh, *Return Home, Watch Your Family*, Edmonton: Department of Indian Affairs, 1977, p. 11.
70. *Ibid.*, p. 21.
71. *Ibid.*, Appendix C.
72. June Wyatt, "Self-Determination Through Education: A Canadian Indian Example," *Phi Delta Kappan,* January, 1977, p. 406.
73. June Wyatt, "Native Teacher Education in a Community Setting: The Mt. Currie Program," *Canadian Journal of Education,* 2:3, 1977, p. 14.
74. *Indian Control of Indian Education, op. cit.*, p. 19.
75. *Vancouver Sun*, January 2, 1968.
76. *Vancouver Sun,* August 2, 1968, p. 9.
77. *Vancouver Province*. September 4, 1974.
78. *Vancouver Express,* November 27, 1978, p. 1.
79. Edgar Faure et al., *Learning to Be*, Paris: UNESCO, 1972, p. 220.
80. Canadian Council on Children and Youth, *Admittance Restricted,* Toronto: Canadian Council on Children and Youth, 1978, p. 137.
81. *Indian Control of Indian Education, op. cit.*, p. 28.

CHAPTER TWO: THE CHINESE

1. *Victoria Colonist*, February 14, 1901, p. 8.
2. British Columbia, *Sessional Papers*, 1881, "Petition of the Anti-Chinese Association, April 12, 1880," p. 406.
3. British Columbia, *Sessional Papers*, 1883, "Order in Council: Calling the attention of the Dominion Government to the immense influx of Chinese into the Province, January 18, 1883," p. 345.
4. British Columbia, *Sessional Papers*, Public School Reports, "Report of the Principal of Nanaimo Boys' School, July 4, 1888," p. 199.

5. H.H. Stevens, "The Oriental Problem," (Vancouver, c. 1910), p. 14.
6. *Victoria Colonist*, January 26, 1902, p. 11.
7. *Victoria Colonist*, March 13, 1902, p. 2.
8. *Victoria Colonist*, April 20, 1902, p. 9.
9. *Victoria Colonist*, November 4, 1902, p. 6.
10. *Victoria Colonist*, November 4, 1902, p. 3.
11. *Victoria Colonist*, November 12, 1902, p. 6.
12. *Victoria Colonist*, November 13, 1902, p. 3.
13. *Victoria Colonist*, December 31, 1902, p. 3.
14. *Victoria Colonist*, January 11, 1903, p. 3.
15. *Victoria Colonist*, January 17, 1904, p. 11.
16. *Victoria Colonist*, August 24, 1907, p. 3.
17. *Victoria School Board Minutes*, August 29, 1907.
18. *Vancouver Province*, September 4, 1907, p. 1.
19. *Vancouver Province*, September 13, 1907, p. 1.
20. *Victoria Colonist*, September 12, 1907, p. 2.
21. *Victoria Times*, September 17, 1907, p. 1.
22. *Victoria School Board Minutes*, September 23, 1907.
23. *Victoria Times*, November 14, 1907, p. 5.
24. *Victoria School Board Minutes*, January 8, 1908.
25. *Vancouver Province*, February 11, 1908, p. 1.
26. Vancouver City Schools, *Annual Report for 1908*, p. 8.
27. Vancouver City Schools, *Annual Report for 1909*, p. 8.
28. *Victoria Colonist*, March 28, 1908.
29. *Victoria School Board Minutes*, August 12, 1908.
30. *Victoria Colonist*, August 13, 1908, p. 2.
31. *Victoria Colonist*, September 19, 1908, p. 2.
32. *Victoria Colonist*, October 15, 1908, p. 2.
33. *Victoria Colonist*, December 1, 1908, p. 7.
34. *Vancouver Province*, February 19, 1910, p. 18.
35. *Victoria Times*, October 13, 1921, p. 16.
36. *Victoria Colonist*, August 30, 1922, p. 5.
37. *Victoria Colonist*, October 8, 1922, p. 14.
38. *Victoria Colonist*, January 12, 1922, p. 9.
39. *Victoria Times*, January 12, 1922, p. 18.
40. *Victoria Times*, August 29, 1922, p. 7.
41. *Victoria Times*, October 17, 1922, p. 16.
42. *Victoria Colonist*, September 6, 1922, p. 4.
43. *Victoria Colonist*, September 14, 1922, p. 11.
44. *Victoria Times*, September 6, 1922, p. 2.
45. *Victoria Times*, October 3, 1922, p. 7.
46. *Victoria Colonist*, October 14, 1922, p. 4.
47. *Victoria Times*, November 13, 1922, p. 13.
48. *Victoria Times*, January 29, 1923, pp. 1-2.
49. *Victoria Times*, January 30, 1923, p. 1.

50. *Victoria Times*, March 29, 1923, p. 16.
51. *Victoria Times*, April 5, 1923, p. 20.
52. *Victoria Colonist*, April 8, 1923, p. 4.
53. *Victoria Colonist*, April 6, 1923, p. 4.
54. *Victoria Colonist*, April 6, 1923, p. 4.
55. C.H. Young and H.R.Y. Reid, *The Japanese Canadians*, Toronto: University of Toronto Press, 1938, p. 289.
56. *News Herald*, June 23, 1947, p. 5.
57. H.G. MacGill, "The Oriental Delinquent in the Vancouver Juvenile Court," *Sociology and Social Research*, XXII, 5, May-June, 1938, p. 428.
58. *Ibid.*, p. 438.
59. K. Thiessen, "Subjects—But Not Citizens," *The B.C. Teacher*, XV, 10, June, 1936, p. 13.
60. "Isn't It About Time That We Spoke Up?" *The B.C. Teacher*, XVIII, 2, October, 1938, p. 49.
61. *Victoria Times*, March 18 and 21, 1947.
62. Canada, *House of Commons Debates*, vol. 3, 1947, pp. 2644-47.
63. *Vancouver Province*, March 26, 1960, p. 17.
64. Manpower and Immigration, *1964 and 1974 Immigration Statistics*.
65. Canada, "Federal Government's Response to Book IV of the Report of the Royal Commission on Bilingualism and Biculturalism," document tabled in the House of Commons on October 8, 1971, by the Prime Minister, p. 8584.
66. *Vancouver Province*, May 2, 1977, p. 4.
67. Canada, *House of Commons Debates*, May 12, 1977, p. 5594.
68. Vancouver School Board, *Survey of Pupils in Vancouver Schools for whom English is a Second Language*, Research Report 77-01, Vancouver: Board of School Trustees, 1977, pp. 8-9.
69. Vancouver School Board, *Report of the Task Force on English*, Vancouver: Vancouver School Board, 1975, p. 10.
70. Doug Collins, "Clamp Down, Immigration, Before Things Get Worse," *Vancouver Sun*, May 31, 1975, p. 6.
71. Doug Collins, "Immigration and the Schools—We're the Suckers," *Vancouver Sun*, June 26, 1976, p. 6.
72. Author's unpublished research, December, 1976.

CHAPTER THREE: THE JAPANESE

1. Ken Adachi, *The Enemy That Never Was*, Toronto: McClelland & Stewart, 1976, Tables 1, 2, and 3, pp. 412-413.
2. Mitsui Tadashi, "The Ministry of the United Church of Canada Among Japanese Canadians in British Columbia," M.A. Thesis, Theology, Union College of B.C., 1967, p. 58.
3. British Columbia, Sessional Papers, *Report on the Public Schools of British Columbia, 32nd Annual Report, 1902-1903*, Victoria: King's Printer, 1904, p. C.c.

4. Thomas R.E. MacInnes, *Oriental Occupation of B.C.*, Vancouver: Sun Publishing, 1927, p. 17.
5. "Orientals in City Schools Do Not Exceed 150," *Vancouver Daily Province*, September 13, 1907, p. 1.
6. M.E. Henderson, "The Japanese in B.C.," *The Canadian Magazine*, XXXI, I, May, 1908, p. 11.
7. MacInnes, *op. cit.*, p. 18.
8. H.K. Hutchinson, "Dimensions of Ethnic Education: The Japanese in British Columbia, 1880-1940," M.A. Thesis, University of British Columbia, 1973, p. 78.
9. *The New Canadian*, November 24, 1938.
10. Adachi, *op. cit.*, pp. 101-102.
11. MacInnes, *op. cit.*, p. 34.
12. *Ibid.*, p. 132.
13. *Vancouver Daily Province*, October 4, 1932, p. 1.
14. British Columbia, Legislative Assembly, *Report on Oriental Activities Within the Province*, Victoria: King's Printer, 1927, p. 4.
15. Rigenda Sumida, "The Japanese in British Columbia," M.A. Thesis, Economics, University of British Columbia, 1935, p. 510.
16. *Tairiko Nippo (Continental Daily News)*, February 26, 1925.
17. *Tairiko Nippo*, March 6, 1925.
18. Interview.
19. "Quaint Japanese Pupils Overflow Steveston School," *The Sunday Province*, February 9, 1930, p. 10.
20. Canadian Japanese Association, *A Few Facts About Japanese School Children in Canada*, Vancouver, 1927, p. 4.
21. Letter from George Apps, September 6, 1977.
22. J.H. Putman and G.M. Weir, *Survey of the School System of British Columbia*, Victoria, 1925, pp. 251-252.
23. *Ibid.*, p. 509.
24. *Report on the Public Schools of British Columbia*, 1927, p. M.33.
25. Canadian Japanese Association, *A Few Facts About Japanese School Children in Canada*, pp. 1-2.
26. J.E. Brown, "Japanese School Children," *The B.C. Teacher*, VII, 10, June 1928, pp. 8-11.
27. *Report on the Public Schools of British Columbia, 1941-1942*, p. B.40.
28. Sumida, *op. cit.*, p. 521.
29. Sumida, *op. cit.*, p. 508.
30. Canadian Japanese Association, *Report of the Survey of the Second Generation Japanese in B.C.*, Vancouver, 1935, p. 4.
31. *Ibid.*, p. 19.
32. *Ibid.*, pp. 49-50.
33. *The New Canadian*, April 12, 1940.
34. *The New Canadian*. June 15, 1939.
35. Sumida, *op. cit.*, p. 464.

36. "Big Part In B.C.'s School Life is Played by Japanese Group," *Vancouver Daily Province*, December 27, 1937, p. 16.
37. Putman and Weir, *op. cit.*, p. 38.
38. S.I. Hayakawa, "The Japanese-Canadian: An Experiment in Citizenship," *Dalhousie Review*, XVI, I, April, 1936, p. 17.
39. *Ibid.*, p. 18.
40. The Japanese-Canadian Centennial Project, *A Dream of Riches*, Toronto, 1978.
41. Mavis Yuasa, "We Must Lose to Win," *The B.C. Teacher*, XIX, 6, February, 1940, p. 305.
42. *The New Canadian*, December 29, 1938.
43. J.R. Sanderson, "Dr. Sanderson and Our Japanese Canadians," *The B.C. Teacher*, XVIII, 4, December, 1938, p. 195.
44. "Delta Nippons Escape Levies," *Vancouver Daily Province*, January 13, 1938, p. 12.
45. Halford Wilson, "Brief on the Oriental Situation in British Columbia in the year 1938," Vancouver, 1938, pp. 9-12.
46. *The New Canadian*, February 2, 1940.
47. *The New Canadian*, February 9, 1940.
48. Wilson, *op. cit.*, p. 13.
49. *Annual Report of Vancouver City Schools, 1926*, p. 41.
50. Adachi, *op. cit.*, p. 127.
51. *The New Canadian*, April 15, 1939.
52. *The New Canadian*, April 1, 1939.
53. *The New Canadian*, November 29, 1940.
54. *The New Canadian*, December 18, 1940.
55. *Vancouver Daily Province*, January 14, 1941.
56. *The New Canadian*, April 18, 1941.
57. *The New Canadian*, January 17, 1941.
58. *The New Canadian*, December 6, 1940.
59. *The New Canadian*, June 5, 1940.
60. Joy Kogawa, "What Do I Remember of the Evacuation?" *A Choice of Dreams*, Toronto: McClelland & Stewart, 1974, pp. 54-55.
61. *Vancouver Daily Province*, September 1, 1942.
62. Vancouver School Trustees, *Annual Report*, 1941 and 1942, p. 78.
63. Letter from George Apps, September 6, 1977.
64. *War Time Education of the Japanese in Canada*, n.p. p. 8.
65. Mollie E. Cottingham, "The Japanese Relocation Settlements" in her "History of the West Kootenay District in British Columbia," M.A. Thesis, History, University of British Columbia, 1947, p. 332.
66. *The New Canadian*, July 3, 1943.
67. Canada Department of Labour, *Report on the Administration of Japanese Affairs in Canada, 1942-1944*, Ottawa: August, 1944, p. 15.
68. *The New Canadian*, December 1, 1942.
69. *The New Canadian*, January 23, 1943.
70. *The New Canadian*, April 17, 1943.

71. *The New Canadian*, February 6, 1943.
72. *Vancouver Daily Province*, February 1, 1943.
73. *The New Canadian*, July 10, 1940.
74. *The New Canadian*, August 19, 1942.
75. *The New Canadian*, August 14, 1943.
76. Canada, Department of Labour, *Report of the Royal Commission to Enquire Into the Provisions Made for the Welfare and Maintenance of Persons of the Japanese Race Resident in Settlements in the Province of British Columbia,* Ottawa: January, 1944, p. 10.
77. *Report on the Administration of Japanese Affairs in Canada, 1942-1944,* p. 16.
78. *Vancouver Daily Province*, May 22, 1943, p. 8.
79. *The New Canadian*, May 19, 1943.
80. *The New Canadian*, July 31, 1943.
81. *The New Canadian*, December 4, 1943.
82. Mary Oki, "My World Today," *The New Canadian*, July 1, 1944.
83. "General Policy," *The B.C. Teacher*, XXIV, 5, February, 1945, p. 159.
84. Edith Fowke, "Japanese-Canadians," *The Canadian Forum*, XXV, 300, January, 1946, p. 231.
85. B.K. Sandwell, "A Dubious Future for Japanese Children Who Get Deported," *Saturday Night*, LXI, 42, June 22, 1946, p. 12.
86. *Report on the Public Schools of British Columbia*, 1947-1948, p. JJ81.
87. *The New Canadian*, June 30, 1948.
88. Alan Morley, "Off to Camp in '42," *The Vancouver Sun*, May 31, 1977.
89. *The New Canadian*, December 12, 1959.
90. Adachi, *op. cit.*, p. 366.

CHAPTER FOUR: THE DOUKHOBORS

1. Eli Popoff, "What is a Doukhobor?", *Mir*, II, 3-6, September, 1974, p. 51.
2. British Columbia, *Report of the Royal Commission on Matters Relating to the Sect of Doukhobors in the Province of British Columbia, 1912*, Victoria, 1913, T23.
3. Koozma Tarasoff, *In Search of Brotherhood*, mimeographed Vancouver, 1963, p. 446.
4. *Report of the Royal Commission on Matters Relating to the Sect of Doukhobors, op. cit.*, T23.
5. Tarasoff, *op. cit.*, pp. 402-403.
6. *Report of the Royal Commission on Matters Relating to the Sect of Doukhobors, op. cit.*, T35.
7. *Ibid.*, T44.
8. *Ibid.*, T45.
9. *Ibid.*, T52.
10. *Ibid.*, T65-66.
11. Alexander M. Evalenko, *The Message of the Doukhobors*, New York: International Library Pub. Co., 1913, pp. 48-55.

12. British Columbia, *Sessional Papers*, "Public Schools Report for 1909-1910, No. 39," Victoria, 1911, p. A58.
13. *B.C. Public Service Bulletin*, I, 1, June, 1925, p. 7.
14. *Victoria Times*, February 3, 1923, p. 9.
15. *Victoria Times*, April 2, 1923, p. 18.
16. *Victoria Times*, June 6, 1925, p. 4.
17. *B.C. Public Service Bulletin*, 1925, p. 6.
18. Interview.
19. *Victoria Times*, November 28, 1927, p. 1.
20. *Victoria Times*, April 22, 1926, p. 13.
21. *Vancouver Province*, May 3, 1928, p. 1.
22. *Victoria Times*, August 31, 1929, p. 15.
23. *Victoria Times*, September 4, 1929, p. 12.
24. *Victoria Times*, September 10, 1929, p. 4.
25. R.H.C. Hooper, "Custodial Care of Doukhobor Children in British Columbia, 1929-1933", Diss. University of British Columbia, 1947, pp. 59-64.
26. Interview.
27. Hooper, *op. cit.*, p. 68.
28. Interview.
29. Hooper, *op. cit.*, p. 73.
30. *Ibid.*, p. 96.
31. Interview.
32. Hooper, *op. cit.*, pp. 108-112.
33. Harry B. Hawthorn, ed. *Report of the Doukhobor Research Committee*, Vancouver: University of British Columbia, 1952, p. 120.
34. *Ibid.*, p. 201.
35. *Public Schools Report*. 1932-1933, p. M38.
36. *Public School Report*, 1935-1936, pp. H47-48.
37. Ewart P. Reid, "Doukhobors in Canada," Diss. MacGill University, 1932, pp. 190-191.
38. "The Doukhobor Question and a Suggested Answer," *The B.C. Teacher*, XVIII, 10, June, 1939, p. 509.
39. "Canadianization," *The B.C. Teacher*, XX, 10, June, 1941, pp. 445-446.
40. British Columbia Teachers' Federation, "Brief to the Government of the Province of British Columbia re Teachers in Community Schools," Vancouver, 1945.
41. British Columbia, *Report of the Commission of Enquiry into Educational Finance*, prepared by Maxwell A. Cameron, Victoria, 1945, p. 94.
42. Spiritual Community of Christ, "The Truth About the Doukhobors," Trail, Hall Printing, 1948.
43. Hawthorn, *op. cit.*, p. 132.
44. *Ibid.*, p. 22.
45. *Ibid.*, p. 329.
46. *Ibid.*, pp. 132-133.
47. *Ibid.*, p. 177.

48. *Ibid.*, p. 253.
49. Nelson Allen, "The Canadianization of the Freedomite Children," n.p., pp. 1-21.
50. J.F.K. English, "Statement re: the Work of Mr. John Clarkson," n.p., p. 11.
51. Peter Maloff, "Doukhobors and Canada," Trail: Hall Printing, 1953, p. 1.
52. *Ibid.*, p. 10.
53. "Operation Snatch," n.p. (c. 1955?).
54. *Ibid.*
55. Allen, *op. cit.*, p. 19.
56. Tarasoff, *op. cit.*, p. 838.
57. Silver Donald Cameron, "Children of Protest," *Weekend Magazine*, November 13, 1976, pp. 16-23.
58. Bert Whyte, "Socred Fiasco," *Pacific Tribune*, July 19, 1957, p. 2.
59. Bert Whyte, "Mary Gienger Suicide," *Pacific Tribune*, August 2, 1957, p. 2.
60. "Freedomite Children Flourish under B.C. School System," *B.C. Government News*, VI, 7, August, 1958, p. 6.
61. George Woodcock and Ivan Avakumovic, *The Doukhobors*, Toronto: McClelland & Stewart, 1977, p. 343.
62. Simma Holt, *Terror in the Name of God*, Toronto: McClelland & Stewart, 1964, p. 295.
63. Interview.
64. Sam Fillipoff, "Integration and Assimilation," *Mir*, XVI, May, 1978, p. 36.
65. D.L. Commeree, I.J. Foerster, W.B. Mundy, "Migration of the Sons of Freedom," Diss. University of British Columbia, 1964, part II, p. 17.
66. *Ibid.*, part I, pp. 16-17.
67. Woodcock and Avakumovic, *op. cit.*, p. xvi.

CHAPTER FIVE: THE EAST INDIANS

1. *London Times,* June 23, 1897, p. 9.
2. *Loc. cit.*
3. G.E. Buckle, ed. *The Letters of Queen Victoria,* vol. III, 1896-1901, London: John Murray, 1932, p. 175.
4. *London Times,* June 23, 1897, p. 9.
5. *Loc. cit.*
6. *Ibid.*, p. 11.
6. *Op. cit.*, p. 11.
8. Rudyard Kipling, "The Recessional," *The Five Nations,* London: Methuen, 1903, p. 214.
9. *Vancouver Province,* July 10, 1906, p. 1.
10. *Vancouver Province*, July 21, 1906, p. 8.
11. *Vancouver Province,* July 28, 1906, p. 3.
12. *Vancouver Province,* September 1, 1906, p. 1.
13. *Vancouver Province*, November 24, 1906, p. 1.

14. *Vancouver Province,* September 11, 1907, p. 1.
15. *Vancouver Province,* September 12, 1907, p. 1.
16. William J. Barclay and Saint N. Singh, "Canada's New Immigrants," *The Canadian Magazine,* XXVIII, 4, February, 1907, p. 385.
17. Canada. Royal Commission on Oriental Immigration. *Report by W.L. Mackenzie King, C.M.G., Deputy Minister of Labour, on Mission to England to confer with the British authorities on the subject of immigration to Canada from the Orient and immigration from India in particular.* Ottawa: 1908, p. 7.
18. *Ibid.,* p. 8.
19. *Ibid.,* p. 9.
20. *Ibid.,* p. 10.
21. "The Position of Hindus in Canada," *British Columbia Magazine,* VIII, 9, 1912, p. 665.
22. *Ibid.,* p. 666.
23. Tien-Fang Cheng, *Oriental Immigration in Canada,* Shanghai: Commercial Press, 1931, p. 146.
24. H.H. Stevens, "The Oriental Problem, Dealing with Canada as affected by the Immigration of Japanese, Hindus, and Chinese," n.p., n.d., p. 7.
25. *Ibid.,* p. 8.
26. *Ibid.,* p. 9.
27. *Vancouver Province,* January 13, 1911, p. 1.
28. *Vancouver Sun,* June 5, 1913, p. 6.
29. *Vancouver Sun,* June 16, 1913, p. 1.
30. *Loc. cit.*
31. *Vancouver Sun,* June 17, 1913, p. 6.
32. Quoted in Rajani Kanta Das, *Hindustani Workers on the Pacific Coast,* Berlin: Walter De Gruyter, 1922, p. 70.
33. *Ibid.,* p. 109.
34. British Columbia, Legislative Assembly, *Report on Oriental Activities Within the Province,* Victoria: 1927, p. 7.
35. Ross Tolmie, "The Oriental in British Columbia," B.A. thesis, University of British Columbia, 1929, p. 32.
36. Sadhu Singh Dhami, "Discovering the New World," *Queen's Quarterly, LXXVI,* 1969, p. 200.
37. *Ibid.,* pp. 201-202.
38. *Report on Oriental Activities Within the Province, op. cit.,* p. 21.
39. Freda Walhouse, "The Influence of Minority Ethnic Groups on the Cultural Geography of Vancouver," M.A. thesis, University of British Columbia, 1961, p. 302.
40. Vancouver School Board, *Annual Reports, 1941 and 1942,* p. 78.
41. *The Indo-Canadian,* 3:4, 1967.
42. Norm Buchignani, "A Review of the Historical and Sociological Literature on East Indians in Canada," *Canadian Ethnic Studies,* IX, 1, 1977, p. 94.
43. Lyn Harrington, "The Proud Sikhs of British Columbia," *Saturday Night,* 64, November 20, 1948, pp. 26-27.

44. *Victoria Daily Times,* June 3, 1947, p. 4.
45. *Vancouver Sun,* July 3, 1947, p. 11.
46. Jennifer Munday, "East Indians in British Columbia: A Community in Transition." B.A. Honours essay, Sociology, University of British Columbia, 1953, p. 41.
47. *Ibid.*, pp. 39-40.
48. *Ibid.*, p. 42.
49. *Ibid.*, p. 43.
50. *Ibid.*, p. 55.
51. *Ibid.*, p. 39.
52. J.L. Moody, *An Evaluation of the Khalsa-Diwan-Moberly Educational Program* (*Under the Mango Tree*), Research Report 71-27, Vancouver: Department of Planning and Evaluation, Vancouver Board of School Trustees, 1971, pp. 1-2.
53. *Ibid.*, p. 3.
54. *Ibid.*, p. 30.
55. *Ibid.*, pp. 33-34.
56. Vancouver School Board, *Report of the Task Force on English,* 1975, pp. 18-19; *Survey of Pupils in Vancouver Schools for Whom English is a Second Language*, 1977, pp. 2-4.
57. Mary Ashworth, *Immigrant Children and Canadian Schools,* Toronto: McClelland & Stewart, 1975, pp. 160-161.
58. Michael Ames and Joy Inglis, "Indian Immigrants in Canada," *The Indo-Canadian,* 3-4: 2-6, 1968, p. 3.
59. *Ibid.*, pp. 29 and 36.
60. *Ibid.*, p. 39.
61. *Ibid.*, p. 41.
62. Doreen Indra, "Role of Mass Media in Opinion Formation of Ethnic Communities in Vancouver." Paper presented to the conference on Multiculturalism and Third World Immigrants in Canada," Edmonton, September 4, 1975, p. 15.
63. *Ibid.*, p. 19b.
64. *Ibid.*, p. 20.
65. V.R. D'Oyley, "Schooling and Ethnic Rights," in *Children's Rights: Legal and Educational Issues*, H. Berkeley et al., eds., Toronto: O.I.S.E., 1978, pp. 141-142.
66. Canada. Canadian Consultative Council on Multiculturalism, *First Annual Report*, Ottawa, 1975, p. 48.
67. *Ibid.*, p. 45.
68. Letter from J. Phillipson, Associate Deputy Minister, Ministry of Education, February 2, 1977, to Canadian Council of Christians and Jews, Vancouver.
69. J.W. Berry et al., *Multiculturalism and Ethnic Attitudes in Canada*, Ottawa: Ministry of Supply and Services, 1977, p. 107.
70. *Vancouver Sun,* October 15, 1977.

AFTERWORDS

1. Barbara Ward, *The Home of Man,* Toronto: McClelland & Stewart, 1976, p. 63.
2. B.C. Teachers' Federation, "Crisis Package for Improving Race Relations in B.C. Schools" (mimeographed), Vancouver: B.C. Teachers' Federation, 1978, section C.
3. *Victoria Daily Times,* March 21, 1977, p. 4.
4. *Surrey Leader,* March 10, 1977.
5. *Peninsula Times,* March 2, 1977.
6. *Victoria Daily Colonist,* March 23, 1977, p. 6.
7. *New Westminster Columbian,* May 6, 1977.
8. *Vancouver Sun,* April 21, 1977, p. 4.
9. UNESCO, *The Use of Vernacular Languages in Education,* Monographs on Fundamental Education, 1963.
10. Wallace E. Lambert, "Cognitive and Socio-Cultural Consequences of Bilingualism," *The Canadian Modern Language Review,* XXXIV, 3, February, 1978, pp. 537-547.
11. Canadian Council on Children and Youth, *Admittance Restricted: The Child as Citizen in Canada*, Toronto: Canadian Council on Children and Youth, 1978, p. 10.
12. *Ibid.*, p. 160.

Bibliography

CHAPTER ONE: THE NATIVE INDIANS

Arctander, John M. *The Apostle of Alaska: The Story of William Duncan of Metlakahtla*. New York, 1909.

Begg, Alexander. *History of British Columbia*. Toronto, 1894.

Brookes, I.R. and A.M. Marshall. *Native Education in Canada and the United States: A Bibliography*. Calgary: University of Calgary, 1976.

Butcher, Margaret. "1916-1919, Correspondence re life in Kitimat" in the Provincial Archives, Victoria.

Canada. Department of Citizenship and Immigration. *Indians of British Columbia: An Historical Review*. Ottawa: Indian Affairs Branch, 1960.

Canada. *Annual Reports of the Deputy Superintendent General of Indian Affairs*, 1872-1879, Ottawa.

Canada. Department of Indian Affairs. *Reports, 1880-1937*. Ottawa.

Canada. Department of Indian Affairs and Northern Development. *Indian Education Program*. Ottawa, 1972.

Canada. Education Branch. Department of Indian Affairs and Northern Development. *Indian Education in Canada*. Ottawa, 1973.

Canada. Education Division, Department of Indian Affairs and Northern Development. *The Education of Indian Children in Canada*. (A symposium written by members of Indian Affairs Education Division with comments by Indian people.) Toronto: Ryerson Press, 1965.

Canada. Education Branch. Department of Indian Affairs and Northern Development. *5,000 Little Indians Went to School*. Ottawa: Department of Indian Affairs, 1971.

Canada. Joint Committee of the Senate and the House of Commons on Indian Affairs. *Minutes of Proceedings and Evidence*. Ottawa, 1960.

Canadian Council of Children and Youth. *Admittance Restricted: The Child as Citizen in Canada*. Toronto: Canadian Council of Children and Youth, 1978.

Cardinal, Harold. *The Rebirth of Canada's Indians*. Edmonton: Hurtig, 1977.

Cardinal, Harold. *The Unjust Society*. Edmonton: Hurtig, 1969.

Cronin, Kay. *Cross in the Wilderness*. Vancouver: Mitchell Press, 1960.

Crosby, Thomas. *Up and Down the North Pacific Coast by Canoe and Mission Ship*. Toronto, 1914.

Crosby, Thomas. *Among the An-ko-me-nums*. Toronto: William Briggs, 1907.

Drucker, Philip. *Cultures of the North Pacific Coast*. Scranton, Penn.: Chandler Pub., 1965.

Duff, Wilson. *The Indian History of British Columbia*, vol. 1—"The Impact of the White Man." Victoria: Provincial Museum of British Columbia, 1965.

The Education of Indian Children in Canada. Special edition of *The Canadian Superintendent*. Toronto: Ryerson, 1965.

Fisher, Robin. *Contact and Conflict: Indian-European Relations in British Columbia, 1774-1890*. Vancouver: University of British Columbia Press, 1977.

Gooderham, Kent. *I Am An Indian*. Toronto: Dent, 1969.

Gross, Carl. "Education in British Columbia." Diss., Ohio State University, 1939.

Hawthorn, H.B., C.S. Belshaw, and S.M. Jamieson. *The Indians of British Columbia*. Toronto: University of Toronto Press, 1958.

Hawthorn, H.B. *A Survey of the Contemporary Indians of Canada*. Ottawa: Indian Affairs, 1966.

Kaegi, Gerda. *A Comprehensive View of Indian Education*. Toronto: Canadian Association in Support of Native Peoples, 1974.

Knight, Rolf. *Indians at Work: An Informal History of Native Indian Labour in British Columbia 1858-1930*. Vancouver: New Star Books, 1978.

Laing, Arthur. "Indian Education." Text of an address by the Minister of Indian Affairs and Northern Development, Vancouver, March 15, 1967.

LaRoque, Emma. *Defeathering the Indian*. Agincourt: The Book Society of Canada, 1975.

LaViolette, F.E. *The Struggle for Survival: Indian Cultures and the Protestant Ethic in British Columbia*. Toronto: University of Toronto Press, 1961.

Levine, Robert and Freda Cooper. "The Supression of B.C. Languages: Filling in the Gaps in the Documentary Record." *Sound Heritage*, IV, 3 and 4, 1976, 43-75.

Manuel, G. and M. Posluns. *The Fourth World: An Indian Reality*. Toronto: Collier-Macmillan, 1974.

Mayne, R.C. *Four Years in British Columbia and Vancouver Island*. London: John Murray, 1862.

Moeran, J.W.W. *McCullagh of Aiyansh*. London: Marshall Bros., 1923.

Morice, A.G. *History of the Catholic Church in Western Canada*. Toronto, 1910.

Morley, Alan. *The Roar of the Breakers*. Toronto: Ryerson, 1967.

Moser, Charles. *Reminiscences of the West Coast of Vancouver Island*. Victoria: Acme Press, 1926.

National Indian Brotherhood. *Indian Control of Indian Education*. Ottawa: National Indian Brotherhood, 1972.

Oblate Fathers Indian Welfare Commission. *Residential Education for Indian Acculturation*. Ottawa: Oblate Fathers, 1958.

Parminter, A.V. "The Development of Integrated Schooling for British Columbia Indian Children." Diss., University of British Columbia, 1964.

Patterson, E. Palmer, II. *The Canadian Indian: A History Since 1500*. Toronto: Collier-Macmillan, 1972.

Peake, Frank A. *The Anglican Church in British Columbia*. Vancouver: Mitchell

Press, 1959.
Peterson, L.R. "Indian Education in British Columbia." Diss., University of British Columbia, 1959.
Proceedings of the Conference on the Indian Child and his Education. Vancouver: Extension Department, University of British Columbia, 1967.
Speare, Jean E. ed. *The Days of Augusta*. Vancouver: J.J. Douglas, 1973.
Thomas, W.C. and R.G. McIntosh. *Return Home, Watch Your Family: A Review of the Native Indian Teacher Education Program at the University of British Columbia*. Edmonton: Department of Indian Affairs, August, 1977.
Usher, John. *William Duncan of Metlakatla*. Ottawa: National Museum of Man., 1974.
Waubageshig. ed. *The Only Good Indian*. Toronto: New Press, 1970.
Wellcome, H.S. *The Story of Metlakahtla*. London, 1887.
Willmot, Jill A. ed. *The Indians of British Columbia: A Study-Discussion Text*. Vancouver: Extension Department, University of British Columbia, 1963.
Wyatt, June. "Native Involvement in Curriculum Development: The Native Teacher as Cultural Broker" in *Ethnic Canadians: Culture and Education*, ed. M.L. Kovacs. Regina: Canadian Plains Research Centre, 1978.
Wyatt, June. "Self-Determination Through Education: A Canadian Indian Example." *Phi Delta Kappan*. January, 1977.
Wyatt, June. "Native Teacher Education in a Community Setting: The Mt. Currie Program." *Canadian Journal of Education*, 2:3, 1977.

CHAPTER TWO: THE CHINESE

Angus, H.F. "Underprivileged Canadians," *Queen's Quarterly*, Summer, 1931.
Boggs, T.H. "Oriental Penetration." *International Forum Review*, I, May-June, 1926.
British Columbia. Legislative Assembly. *Report on Oriental Activities Within the Province*. Victoria, 1927.
British Columbia. Legislative Assembly. *Sessional Papers*.
Canada. House of Commons. *Debates*.
Canada. Manpower and Immigration. *Immigration Statistics*.
Canada. *Report of the Royal Commission on Chinese and Japanese Immigration*. Ottawa, 1902.
Canada. Royal Commission on Bilingualism and Biculturalism. *Book IV, The Cultural Contribution of the Other Ethnic Groups*. Ottawa, 1970.
Canada. Special Committee on Orientals in British Columbia. *Report and Recommendations, December, 1940*. Ottawa, 1941.
Gross, Carl H. "Education in British Columbia." Diss., Ohio State University, 1939.
Lavell, M.M.C. "Oriental Missions in British Columbia." Toronto Women's Missionary Society, c. 1909.
Lee, Carol F. "The Road to Enfranchisement: Chinese and Japanese in British Columbia." *B.C. Studies*, 30, 1976, 44-76.

MacGill, Helen G. "The Oriental Delinquent in the Vancouver Juvenile Court." *Sociology and Social Research*, XXII, 5, May-June, 1938, 428-438.
MacGill, Helen G. "Anti-Chinese Immigration Legislation of British Columbia, 1876-1903." Graduating essay, University of British Columbia, 1925.
MacInnes, Tom R.C. *Oriental Occupation of British Columbia*. Vancouver: Sun Publishing, 1927.
Morton, James, *In The Sea of Sterile Mountains*. Vancouver: J.J. Douglas, 1974.
Norris, John. *Strangers Entertained*. Vancouver: Evergreen Press, 1971.
Osterhout, S.S. *Orientals in Canada*. Toronto: Ryerson Press, 1929.
Stevens, H.H. "The Oriental Problem, Dealing with Canada as Affected by the Immigration of Japanese, Hindus, and Chinese." n.p., n.d., (c. 1910).
Vancouver Board of School Trustees. *Annual Reports, 1904-45*.
Vancouver Board of School Trustees. *Report of the Task Force on English*. Vancouver: Vancouver Board of School Trustees, 1975.
Vancouver Board of School Trustees. *Survey of Pupils in Vancouver Schools for Whom English is a Second Language*. Research Report 77-01. Vancouver: Vancouver Board of School Trustees, 1977.
Victoria Board of School Trustees. *Minutes, 1905-16*.
Ward, N.H. and H.A. Hellaby. "Oriental Missions in B.C." London Society for the Propagation of the Gospel in Foreign Parts, 1925.
Ward, W.P. "White Canada Forever: British Columbia's Response to Orientals, 1858-1914." Diss., Queen's University, 1972.
Willmott, W.E. "Approaches to the Study of the Chinese in British Columbia." *B.C. Studies*, 4, Spring, 1970.
Wynne, R.E. "Reactions to the Chinese in the Pacific North West and B.C., 1850-1910." Diss., University of Washington, 1964.
Young, C.H. and H.R.Y. Reid. *The Japanese Canadians*, with a second part on oriental standards of living by W.A. Carrothers. Toronto: University of Toronto Press, 1938.

CHAPTER THREE: THE JAPANESE

Adachi, Ken. *The Enemy That Never Was*. Toronto: McClelland & Stewart, 1976.
Adachi, Ken. *A History of the Japanese-Canadians in British Columbia*. National Japanese-Canadian Association, 1958.
British Columbia. Legislative Assembly. *Report on Oriental Activities Within the Province*. Victoria, 1927.
British Columbia. Sessional Papers.*Reports on the Public Schools of British Columbia*. Victoria.
Broadfoot, Barry. *Years of Sorrow, Years of Shame*. Toronto: Doubleday, 1977.
Brown, J.E. "Japanese School Children." *B.C. Teacher*, 7, No. 10, June 1928, 8-11.
Canada. Department of Labour. *Report of the Department of Labour on the Administration of Japanese Affairs in Canada, 1942-1944*. Ottawa, August, 1944.
Canada. The Royal Commission to Enquire into the Provisions Made for the

Welfare and Maintenance of Persons of the Japanese Race Resident in Settlements in the Province of British Columbia. *Report*. Vancouver, January 14, 1944.

Canadian Japanese Association. *The Japanese Contribution to Canada: A Summary of the Role Played by the Japanese in the Development of the Canadian Commonwealth*. Vancouver, 1940.

Canadian Japanese Association. *Report of the Survey of the Second Generation Japanese in B.C.*, Vancouver, 1935.

Canadian Japanese Association, *A Few Facts About Japanese School Children in Canada*. Vancouver, 1927.

Consulate-General of Japan. *Facts About Japanese in Canada and Other Miscellaneous Information*. Ottawa, 1922.

Cottingham, Mollie E. "The Japanese Relocation Settlements" in her "History of the West Kootenay District in B.C." Diss., University of British Columbia, 1947.

Dahlie, J. "Some Aspects of the Education of Minorities: The Japanese in B.C., Lost Opporunity." *B.C. Studies*, No. 8, Winter, 1970-1971, 3-16.

Daniels, Roger. "The Japanese Experience in North America: An Essay in Comparative Racism." *Canadian Ethnic Studies*, Special Issue, 9, No. 2, 1977, 91-100.

"Dubious Future for Japanese Children Who Get Deported." *Saturday Night*, 61, No. 42, June 11, 1946, 12.

Evenden, L.J. and I.D. Anderson. "The Presence of a Past Community: Tashme, B.C." in *Peoples of the Living Land: Geography of Cultural Diversity in British Columbia*, ed. J.V. Minghi. Vancouver: Tantalus, 1972.

Fowke, Edith and A.G. Watson. "Democracy and the Japanese Canadian." *Canadian Forum*, 25, No. 294, July, 1945, 87-89.

Fowke, Edith. "Japanese Canadians." *Canadian Forum*, 25, No. 300, January, 1946, 231-232.

Gross, Carl H. "Education in British Columbia with Particular Consideration of the Natural and Social Factors." Diss., Ohio State University, 1939.

Hayakawa, S.I. "The Japanese Canadian: An Experiment in Citizenship." *Dalhousie Review*, 16, No. 1, April, 1936, 16-22.

Henderson, Margaret Eadie. "The Japanese in B.C." *The Canadian Magazine*, 31, No. 1, May, 1908, 3-14.

Hutchinson, H.K. "Dimensions of Ethnic Education: The Japanese in British Columbia, 1880-1940." Diss., University of British Columbia, 1973.

Irwin, Jane. "Steveston: The Japanese-Canadian Experience." *Sound Heritage*, 3, No. 3, 1974, 5-16.

Ito, Roy. *The Japanese-Canadians*. Toronto; Van Nostrand Reinhold, 1978.

Japanese Canadian Centennial Project. *A Dream of Riches: The Japanese Canadians 1877-1977*. Toronto, 1978.

Kogawa, Joy. *A Choice of Dreams*. Toronto: McClelland & Stewart, 1974.

La Violette, Forrest E. *The Canadian Japanese and World War II*. Toronto: University of Toronto Press, 1948.

Livesay, Dorothy. *Call My People Home*. Toronto: Ryerson, 1950.

MacInnes, Grace. "Wanted—A Country." *Canadian Forum*, 22, No. 257, June,

1942, 74-76.
MacInnes, Thomas R.E. *Oriental Occupation of B.C.* Vancouver: Sun Publishing, 1927.
Marlatt, Daphne. *Steveston Recollected: A Japanese-Canadian History*. An Aural History. Provincial Archives of British Columbia, 1975.
Marlatt, Daphne and Robert Minden. *Steveston*. Vancouver: Talonbooks, 1974.
Mitsui, Tadashi. "The Ministry of the United Church of Canada Among Japanese Canadians in British Columbia." Diss., Union College of British Columbia, 1967.
Morley, Alan. "Off to Camp in '42." *The Vancouver Sun*. May 31, 1977.
Morris, Philip Avon. "Conditioning Factors Molding Public Opinion in British Columbia Hostile to Japanese Immigration Into Canada." Diss., University of Oregon, 1963.
Norris, John. *Strangers Entertained*. Vancouver: Evergreen Press, 1971.
Oki, Mary. "My World Today." *The New Canadian*, 7, No. 31, July 1, 1944.
Patton, Janice. *The Exodus of the Japanese*. Toronto: McClelland & Stewart, 1973.
Putman, J.H. and G.M. Weir. *Survey of the School System of British Columbia*. Victoria, 1925.
Roucek, J.S. "The Japanese in Canada." *The Study of Current English*, 20, No. 10, October, 1965, through 21, No. 2, February, 1966.
Sanderson, J.R. "Dr. Sanderson and Our Japanese Canadians." *The B.C. Teacher*, XVIII, 4, December, 1938, 195.
Sandwell, B.K. "A Dubious Future for Japanese Children Who Get Deported." *Saturday Night*, 61, No. 42, June 22, 1946.
Shibata, Yuko. *Japanese-Canadians: An Annotated Bibliography*. Vancouver, 1975.
Sugimoto, Howard H. *Japanese Immigration: The Vancouver Riots and Canadian Diplomacy*. Seattle: University of Washington, 1966.
Sumida, Rigenda. "The Japanese in British Columbia." Diss., University of British Columbia, 1935.
Thiessen, Katie. "Subjects—But Not Citizens." *B.C. Teacher*, 15, No. 10, June, 1936, 13-15.
Ujimoto, K. Victor. "Contrasts in the Prewar and Postwar Japanese Community in B.C.: Conflict and Change." *Canadian Review of Sociology and Anthropology*, 13, No. 1, 1978, 80-89.
Vancouver Board of School Trustees. *Annual Reports*.
Ward, W. Peter. "British Columbia and the Japanese Evacuation." *The Canadian Historical Review*, 57, No. 3, September, 1976, 289-308.
Wartime Education of the Japanese in Canada, n.p., 1943.
Wilson, Halford D. "Brief on the Oriental Situation in B.C. in 1938." Submitted by Halford D. Wilson and Harry J. DeGraves, Vancouver, 1938.
Young, Charles H. and Helen R.Y. Reid. *The Japanese Canadians*. Toronto: University of Toronto Press, 1938.
Yuasa, Mavis. "We Must Lose to Win." *The B.C. Teacher*, 19, No. 6, February, 1940, 304-307.

CHAPTER FOUR: THE DOUKHOBORS

Allen, Nelson. "The Canadianization of the Freedomite Children." 21 p. n.p.

Bradley, Kathleen Joyce. "Factionalism in the Doukhobor Movement." Diss., University of Calgary, 1976.

British Columbia. "Doukhobors and Education" in *The B.C. Public Service Bulletin*, I, 1, June, 1915, 5-8.

British Columbia. "Freedomite Children Flourish under B.C. School System" in *B.C. Government News,* VI, 7, August, 1958.

British Columbia. Legislative Assembly, Sessional Papers. *Reports on the Public Schools of British Columbia.*

British Columbia. *Report of the Commission of Inquiry into Educational Finance,* prepared by Maxwell A. Cameron. Victoria: King's Printer, 1945.

British Columbia. *Report of the Royal Commission on Matters Relating to the Sect of Doukhobors in the Province of British Columbia, 1912.* Victoria, 1913.

British Columbia Teachers' Federation. "Brief to the Government of the Province of British Columbia re Teachers in Community Schools." Vancouver, 1945, 3 p.

"Canadianization." *The B.C. Teacher*, XX, 10, June, 1941.

Clarkson, John. "Struggle for Education at New Denver." *Vancouver Sun*, serialized February 2, 3, 4, 5, 1960, as told to Simma Holt.

Commeree, David L., I.J. Foerster and W.B. Mundy. "Migration of the Sons of Freedom." Diss., University of British Columbia, 1964.

Cottingham, Mollie E. "History of the West Kootenay District in British Columbia." Diss., University of British Columbia, 1947.

Dawson, C.A. *Group Settlement: Ethnic Communities in Western Canada.* Toronto: Macmillan, 1936.

"The Doukhobor Question and Suggested Answer." Editorial, *The B.C. Teacher*, XVIII, 10, June, 1939.

Elkington, Joseph. *The Doukhobors: Their History in Russia, Their Migration to Canada.* Philadelphia: Ferris and Leach, 1903.

English, J.F.K. "Statement re: the Work of Mr. John Clarkson." n.p.

Evalenko, Alexander M. *The Message of the Doukhobors.* New York: International Pub. Co., 1913.

Fillipoff, Sam. "Integration and Assimilation." *Mir.* VI, May, 1978.

Gross, Carl H. "Education in British Columbia." Diss. Ohio State University, 1939.

Hawthorn, Harry B. ed. *Report of the Doukhobor Research Committee.* Vancouver: University of British Columbia, 1952.

Holt, Simma. *Terror in the Name of God.* Toronto: McClelland & Stewart, 1964.

Hooper, Ronald H.C. "Custodial Care of Doukhobor Children in British Columbia, 1929-1932." Diss., University of British Columbia, 1947.

Horvath, M. *A Doukhobor Bibliography.* Vancouver: University of British Columbia, 1972.

Johnson, F. Henry. "The Doukhobors of British Columbia: The History of a Sectarian Problem in Education." *Queen's Quarterly*, LXX, 4, Winter, 1964,

528-541.
Katz, Sidney. "The Lost Children of British Columbia." *Macleans*, vol. 70, May 11, 1957, 15-17, 100-108.
Lawrence, Ronald. "New Denver's Happy Children." *The Interior Post*, I, 4, November, 1958, 12-14.
Lyon, John Edward. "A History of Doukhobor Schooling in Saskatchewan and British Columbia, 1899-1939." Diss., University of Calgary, 1973.
Maloff, Peter N. *Doukhobors and Canada: third independent report on the Doukhobor problem*. Trail: Hall Printing, 1953.
Maloff, Peter N. "In Quest of a Solution." n.p. 1957.
Mavor, James. *My Windows on the Streets of the World*, vol. II. London: Dent, 1923.
Maude, Aylmer. *A Peculiar People, The Doukhobors*. New York: Funk and Wagnalls, 1904.
O'Neail, Hazel. *Doukhobor Daze*. Sidney, B.C.: Gray's Publishing, 1962.
"Operation Snatch," 31 p. n.p. (c. 1955?).
Popoff, Eli. *Tanya*. Grand Forks: Mir Publication Society, 1975.
Popoff, Eli. "What is a Doukhobor?" *Mir*, II, 3-6, September, 1974.
Reid, Ewart P. "Doukhobors in Canada." Diss., McGill University, 1932.
Ross, Phyllis Marie. "A Sociological Survey of the Doukhobors." Thesis (B.A.), University of British Columbia, 1925.
Seebaran, Roopchand Boodhram. "The Migration of the Sons of Freedom into the Lower Mainland of British Columbia: the Vancouver experience." Diss., University of British Columbia, 1965.
Sissons, C.B. "What Can We Do With the Doukhobors?" *Canadian Forum*, IV, 46, July, 1924, 298-300.
Snesarev, Vladimir Nicolas (Harry Trevor). "The Doukhobors in British Columbia." University of British Columbia, 1931.
Sorokin, Stefan. "Doukhobor Affairs Inside Out." A letter to Col. J.F. Mead. Union of Christian Communities and Brotherhood of Reformed Doukhobors, 1957.
Spiritual Community of Christ. "The Truth About the Doukhobors: conclusive explanation of the members of the Spiritual Community of Christ—the so-called Sons of Freedom—to the Commissioner of the Royal Commission of Canada." Trail: Hall Printing, 1948.
Stoochnoff, John Philip. *Doukhobors As They Are*. Toronto: Ryerson Press, 1961.
Tarasoff, Koozma. *In Search of Brotherhood*. Mimeographed. Vancouver, 1963.
Union of Spiritual Communities of Christ. *The Doukhobors in Canada*. Grand Forks: U.S.C.C., 1974.
United Church of Canada, Kootenay Presbytery. "A Brief Containing Suggestions for the Solution of the Freedomite Problem." United Church of Canada, 1963.
Whyte, Bert. "Socred Fiasco." *Pacific Tribune*, July 19, 1957.
Whyte, Bert. "Mary Gienger Suicide." *Pacific Tribune*, July 26, 1957.
Woodcock, George and Ivan Avakumovic. *The Doukhobors*. Toronto: McClelland & Stewart, 1977.

Wright, J.F.C. *Slava Bohu*. New York: Farrar and Rinehart, 1940.
Zubek, John and P.A. Solberg. *Doukhobors At War*. Toronto: Ryerson Press, 1952.

CHAPTER FIVE: THE EAST INDIANS

Ames, Michael M. and Joy Inglis, "Conflict and Change in British Columbia Sikh Family Life." *B.C. Studies,* 20, Winter, 1973-1974, 15-49.

Ames, Michael M. and Joy Inglis. "Indian Immigrants in Canada." *The Indo-Canadian*, 3-4: 2-6, 1968.

Berry, J.W., R. Kalin, D.M. Taylor. *Multiculturalism and Ethnic Attitudes in Canada*. Ottawa: Ministry of Supply and Services, 1977.

British Columbia. Legislative Assembly. *Report on Oriental Activities Within the Province*. Victoria, 1927.

B.C. Teachers' Federation. "Crisis Package for Improving Race Relations in B.C. Schools." Mimeographed. Vancouver: B.C. Teachers' Federation, 1978.

Buchignani, Norm. "A Review of the Historical and Sociological Literature on East Indians in Canada." *Canadian Ethnic Studies*, IX, 1, 1977, 86-108.

Canada. Royal Commission on Oriental Immigration. *Report by W.L. Mackenzie King, C.M.G., Deputy Minister of Labour, on mission to England to confer with the British authorities on the subject of immigration to Canada from the Orient and immigration from India in particular*. Ottawa, 1908, 10 p.

Canada. Royal Commission on Bilingualism and Biculturalism. *Book IV, The Cultural Contribution of the Other Ethnic Groups*. Ottawa, 1970.

Canada. Canadian Consultative Council on Multiculturalism. *First Annual Report*. Ottawa, 1975.

Cheng, Tien-Fang. *Oriental Immigration in Canada*. Shanghai: Commercial Press, 1931.

Das, Rajani Kanta. *Hindustani Workers on the Pacific Coast*. Berlin: Walter De Gruyter, 1922.

Dhami, Sadhu Singh. "Discovering the New World." *Queen's Quarterly*, LXXVI, 1969, 200-212.

D'Oyley, Vincent R. "Schooling and Ethnic Rights" in *Children's Rights: Legal and Educational issues*, eds. H. Berkeley et al. Toronto: Ontario Institute for Studies in Education, 1978.

Durward, M.L., J.L. Moody, and E.N. Ellis. *Evaluation of the Punjabi-English Class at Moberly Primary Annex for the 1972-1973 School Year*. Research Report 73-20. Vancouver: Department of Planning and Evaluation, Vancouver Board of School Trustees, 1973.

Ferguson, Ted. *A White Man's Country: An Exercise in Canadian Prejudice*. Toronto: Doubleday, 1975.

Gross, Carl H. "Education in British Columbia with Particular Consideration of the Natural and Social Factors." Diss., Ohio State University, 1939.

Harrington, Lyn. "The Proud Sikhs of British Columbia." *Saturday Night*, 64, November 20, 1948, 26-27.

Indra, Doreen. "Role of Mass Media in Opinion Formation of Ethnic Communities in Vancouver." Paper presented to the conference on "Multiculturalism and Third World Immigrants in Canada." Edmonton, September 4, 1975.

Jain, S.K. *East Indians in Canada*. Research Group for European Migration Problems. The Hague: Mouton, 1971.

Khalsa Diwan Society. "A Report of Correspondence and Documents relating to negotiations between 1939 and 1947, culminating in domiciliary rights being accorded to 210 members of the Indian Community, by the Dominion Government." Vancouver: Khalsa Diwan Society, 1947.

Lal, Brig. "East Indians in British Columbia, 1904-1914: An Historical Study in Growth and Integration." Diss., University of British Columbia, 1976.

Lilley, Doreen A. "East Indian Immigration into Canada, 1880-1920: a bibliography." Mimeographed. Vancouver: University of British Columbia, 1966.

Lockley, Fred. "The Hindu Invasion." *Pacific Monthly*, 1907, 584-595.

Lowes, George H. "The Sikhs of British Columbia." Graduating essay, University of British Columbia, 1952.

MacInnes, Tom R.C. *Oriental Occupation of British Columbia*. Vancouver: Sun Publishing, 1927.

McLaren, E.D. and George C. Pidgeon. "East Indian Immigration." *Westminster Magazine*, I, 8, January, 1912, 23-28.

Mayer, A.C. *A Report on the East Indian Community in Vancouver*. Mimeographed. Vancouver: Institute of Social and Economic Research, University of British Columbia, 1959.

Misrow, Jogesh Chander. *East Indian Immigration on the Pacific Coast*. Stanford, Calif., 1915. (Reprinted San Francisco: R. & E. Research Associates, 1971).

Moody, J.L. *An Evaluation of the Khalsa-Diwan-Moberly Educational Program (Under the Mango Tree)*. Research Report 71-27. Vancouver: Department of Planning and Evaluation, Vancouver Board of School Trustees, 1971.

Moody, J.L. "An Evaluation of the Effects of Bilingual Instruction on the Acquisition of English in Young East Indian Children." Diss., University of British Columbia, 1974.

Moody, J.L. "Evaluation of the Punjabi-English Class at the Moberly Primary Annex for the 1973-1974 School Year." Research Report 74-18. Vancouver: Department of Planning and Evaluation, Vancouver Board of School Trustees, 1974.

Munday, Jennifer. "East Indians in British Columbia: A Community in Transition." B.A. Honours Essay, Sociology, University of British Columbia, 1953.

Muthanna, I.M. *People of India in North America*. Bangalore: Lotus Printers, 1975.

Norris, John. *Strangers Entertained: A History of Ethnic Groups in B.C.* Vancouver: Evergreen Press, 1971.

Osterhout, S.S. *Orientals in Canada*. Toronto: Ryerson, 1929.

Pandia, Muriel. "East Indians in Canada." *The Indo-Canadian*, 3-4: 9-12, 1967.

"The Position of Hindus in Canada," *British Columbia Magazine*, VIII, 9, 1912, 664-668.

Reid, Robie L. "The Inside Story of the Komogatu Maru." *B.C. Historical Quarterly*, 5, 1941, 1-23.

Sandhu, Kernial Singh. "Indian Immigration and Racial Prejudice in British Columbia: Some Preliminary Observations" in *Peoples of the Living Land: Geography of Cultural Diversity in British Columbia*, ed. J.V. Minghi. Vancouver: Tantalus, 1972.

Scanlon, Joseph. *The Sikhs of Vancouver, A Case Study of the Role of the Media in Ethnic Relations*. Carleton University: mimeographed, 1975.

Stevens, H.H. "The Oriental Problem, Dealing with Canada as Affected by the Immigration of Japanese, Hindus, and Chinese." n.p., n.d., c. 1910.

Tolmie, Ross. "The Orientals in British Columbia." B.A. thesis, University of British Columbia, 1929.

Vancouver Board of School Trustees. *Annual Reports.*

Vancouver Board of School Trustees. *Report of the Task Force on English.* Vancouver: Vancouver Board of School Trustees, 1975.

Vancouver Board of School Trustees. *Survey of Pupils in Vancouver Schools for Whom English is a Second Language*. Research Report 77-01. Vancouver: Department of Evaluation and Research, Vancouver Board of School Trustees, May, 1977.

Victoria, Society of Friends. "A summary of the Hindu question and its results in British Columbia." Victoria: Society of Friends, 1911, 11 p.

Walhouse, Freda. "The Influence of Minority Ethnic Groups on the Cultural Geography of Vancouver." Diss., University of British Columbia, 1961.

Williams, J. Barclay and Saint N. Singh. "Canada's New Immigrant." *The Canadian Magazine,* XXVIII, 4, February, 1907, 383-391.

Wilson, J.D. and J. Dahlie. "Negroes, Finns, Sikhs—Education and Community Experience in British Columbia" in *Sounds Canadian: Languages and Cultures in Multi-Ethnic Society*, Paul M. Mingus, ed. Toronto: Peter Martin Associates, 1975.

AFTERWORDS

Ashworth, Mary. *Immigrant Children and Canadian Schools*. Toronto: McClelland & Stewart, 1975.

Ashworth, Mary. "More Than One Language,." *Multiculturalism, Bilingualism, and Canadian Institutions*. Toronto: Guidance Centre, Faculty of Education, University of Toronto, 1979, 80-88.

Berkeley, Heather, C. Gadfield, and W.G. West, eds. *Children's Rights: Legal and Educational Issues*. Toronto: Ontario Institute for Studies in Education, 1978.

Berry, J.W., R. Kalin, and D.M. Taylor. *Multiculturalism and Ethnic Attitudes in Canada*. Ottawa: Minister of Supply and Services, 1977.

B.C. Teachers' Federation. "Crisis Package for Improving Race Relations in B.C. Schools." Mimeographed. Vancouver: B.C. Teachers' Federation, 1978.

Canadian Council on Children and Youth. *Admittance Restricted: The Child as Citizen in Canada*. Toronto: Canadian Council on Children and Youth, 1978.

Cummins, James. "Educational Implications of Mother Tongue Maintenance in Minority-Language Groups." *The Canadian Modern Language Review*, XXXIV, 3, February, 1978, 395-416.

Johnson, F. Henry. *A History of Public Education in British Columbia*. Vancouver: Publications Centre, University of British Columbia, 1964.

Johnson, F. Henry. *The Development of Public and Higher Education in British Columbia, 1849-1975*. Unpublished manuscript, 1975.

Lambert, Wallace E. "Cognitive and Socio-Cultural Consequences of Bilingualism." *The Canadian Modern Language Review*, XXXIV, 3, February, 1978, 537-547.

McGregor, Malcolm F. *The Education and Training of Teachers in British Columbia*. Victoria: Ministry of Education, 1978.

Organization for Economic Co-operation and Development. *Canada*. (Review of national policies for education.) Paris, 1976.

UNESCO. *The Use of Vernacular Languages in Education*. Monographs on Fundamental Education, 1953.

Ward, Barbara. *The Home of Man*. Toronto: McClelland & Stewart, 1976.

Wolfgang, Aaron. *Education of Immigrant Students: Issues and Answers*. Toronto: Ontario Institute for Studies in Education, 1975.